A SLICE OF LIFE

A SLICE OF LIFE

Readings in General Anthropology

EDITED BY

Lionel A. Brown

Grays Harbor College

Rinehart Press / Holt, Rinehart and Winston

SAN FRANCISCO

348892

Library of Congress Cataloging in Publication Data

Brown, Lionel A   comp.
    A slice of life.

    Includes bibliographical references.
    1. Anthropology—Addresses, essays, lectures.
I. Title.
GN29.B76   301.2′08   73-18243
ISBN 0-03-002886-8

© 1974 by Rinehart Press
5643 Paradise Drive
Corte Madera, Calif. 94925

A division of Holt, Rinehart and Winston, Inc.

PRINTED IN THE UNITED STATES OF AMERICA

4 5 6 7   090   9 8 7 6 5 4 3 2 1

CONTENTS

PREFACE

This book is not an introduction to anthropology. It is a carefully selected collection of articles *about* anthropology. The readings are intended for the beginning anthropology major or the undergraduate student taking an anthropology course for interest. The selections included are designed to supplement a text used in an introductory anthropology course. *A Slice of Life* can be used with any text or collection of small books chosen by the instructor as a core for presenting anthropological data and theories. Factual data are held to a minimum; this is consistent with the belief that there is little need in a readings book to duplicate material generally included in a text or a series of lecture sessions.

An important mission of this book is to reach the reader on a comprehensible reading level while maintaining a scholarly attitude toward anthropology. Many articles are from literary sources, and technical essays written by anthropologists for other anthropologists are omitted. Articles are selected with the intention of assisting the reader to see that anthropology is "alive" and concerned with real people, not just with bones, tools, and concepts. The feelings of people are stressed—what it is like to be a Hopi Indian, a Brazilian Indian, an Amishman, an anthropologist in the field.

A Slice of Life is not a collection of articles selected at random; there is a unifying thread of continuity from the first chapter to the last. Each major section is prefaced with introductory remarks that indicate the nature of the selections included within the section. At the end of each section a set of questions and problems is provided for consideration as discussion topics. Although each selection deals with a separate "slice of life," the unifying thread is the continuing thought that all segments of anthropology are strongly related and provide a holistic approach to the study of man. The book provides the reader with a taste of the most exciting of all dramas—the human scene.

I wish to thank all the authors and publishers who allowed their material to be reprinted. I also acknowledge with thanks numerous students in my classes who helped me to recognize the need for the book. Finally, I wish to thank the Rinehart Press staff for their encouragement and assistance during this project.

LIONEL A. BROWN

	Barnouw I	Barnouw II	Hoebel	Beals-Hoijer	Harris	Holmes
1	1	1	1	1	1	1
2	1	1	1	1		1
3		3	3	22	1	2
4	7		5	2	4	3
5	6		4	2	3	3
6	8		6	2	4	3
7	9		7	2	5	3
8	8		6	2	4	3
9	11		11	3	6	3
10	17		9	6	9	4
11	24		9	6	9	4
12	20		10	9	9	5
13	25		10	6	9	5
14	23		9	6	9	4
15	19		10	6	9	4
16		4	31	15	7	6
17		5	31	15	7	6
18		5	31	15	7	6
19	1	1	2	4	8	6
20		23	2	4	8	6
21		23	2	17	23	16
22		1	2	4	8	18
23		25	33	18	8	15
24		25	33	19	18	15
25		19	29	14	22	13
26		18	30	14	22	13
27		20	12	7	8	18
28		16	28	13	10	12
29		16	26	13	10	30
30		8	17	10	11	10
31		26	33	19	19	1
32		26	33	19	19	1
33		26	34	19	19	1
34		3	1	5	1	17
35	14		1	5	9	17
36		3	1	5	1	17
37		27	34	22	5	18
38		27	34	22	5	18
39		27	34	19	5	18

CORRELATIONS TABLE

A Guide to Correlate *A Slice of Life* with Basic Texts

The table opposite contains suggestions for correlating selections in this book with a few widely used textbooks in general anthropology. Selections in *A Slice of Life* are numbered 1 through 39 in the left-hand column, and the remaining columns list textbook chapters that are appropriate to the *Slice of Life* selections. The following texts were used in the concordance:

Victor Barnouw, *An Introduction to Anthropology,* Vols. I and II. Homewood, Ill.: Dorsey Press, Inc., 1971.

E. Adamson Hoebel, *Anthropology: The Study of Man,* 4th ed. New York: McGraw-Hill Book Company, 1972.

Ralph L. Beals and Harry Hoijer, *An Introduction to Anthropology,* 4th ed. New York: Macmillan Publishing Co., Inc., 1971.

Marvin Harris, *Culture, Man, and Nature.* New York: Thomas Y. Crowell Company, 1971.

Lowell D. Holmes, *Anthropology: An Introduction,* 2nd ed. New York: The Ronald Press Company, 1971.

A SLICE OF LIFE

1/ MAN-STUDY: AN OVERVIEW

The purpose of this selection is to guide the reader to an understanding of the nature of anthropology. As with most introductory statements it seems reasonable to expect a tight, coherent definition of the topic under consideration. What is anthropology? It is often defined as the "study of man"; however, this description is too general to be of any real value. The understanding of the *nature* of anthropology is the foundation upon which the rest of the study of man is built. This seemingly easy task of understanding what anthropology is all about is transformed into a formidable one when considering the magnitude of the field. Anthropology is the discipline that integrates man's physical aspects, social framework, cultural endowment, and psychological makeup. Although scholars in many disciplines, such as human biology, sociology, and psychology, study man, these disciplines are, by and large, distinct entities when compared with the holistic approach of anthropology. This holistic approach, looking at all aspects of man as an integrated whole, commands the ability to generalize while dealing with specifics. It is often said that there are so few generalities in anthropology that everyone specializes. If this is so, it is a sad situation. Experts are needed to look at the "big picture" of man. Admittedly, it is easier to analyze a grain of sand than it is to analyze the universe, but we must not forget that parts are only parts and that they interact with each other to make up a whole. That whole in this instance is Man. This is what anthropology is all about!

Another attribute of anthropology is the extensive use of cross-cultural comparative analysis. By covering our world in a geographical sense we are able to analyze human behavior in settings ranging from the smallest and least complex societies to the largest and most complex societies. In doing so, anthropologists are able to recognize similarities and differences in human behavior throughout the world. Recognizing similarities in human behavior helps us to realize that mankind has much in common. By pointing out the differences of human behavior and understanding them within the framework of their own cultural contexts, anthropologists are better able to minimize or eliminate cultural and racial prejudices. Both these efforts help to equip each of us with a tool for success—how to live together as human beings. This is what anthropology is all about!

Perhaps one of the more perplexing problems faced by a beginning anthropology student grows out of the conflict between his growing awareness that specialists are wrapped up in their own interests and his difficulty understanding what these interests have to do with anthropology. Too often the student sees the physical anthropologist looking at bones, the linguist analyzing sound units, the archeologist looking at broken tools, and the cultural anthropologist concerned with the definition of the concept of culture. There they are, but put them all together and the result is the bits and pieces of what makes a human being. This is what anthropology is all about!

From "Anthropology," by George D. Spindler, *Today's Education,* Vol. 52, September, 1963, pp. 28–31. Reprinted by permission of the National Education Association and the author.

1 / Anthropology

GEORGE D. SPINDLER

Anthropology, the study of man, has become increasingly popular within the past few years. Although many people still regard the discipline as a study of old things or exotic customs, the "mystique" often associated with anthropology is rapidly fading and is being replaced by the understanding that anthropology is the science of human behavior. Writers such as George D. Spindler have contributed much to this transition. Spindler's article discusses the general nature of anthropology as a discipline and the specific activities of anthropologists. This selection outlines the framework upon which successive selections in this book may be linked for an orderly understanding of "man-study." The student would do well to reread Spindler's selection at various times during the course of study. We often stray from the path in the woods, but we need to know that one exists and what it looks like. Spindler provides us with a path in the forest of anthropological data.

Anthropology is a complex and diversified subject that goes in a number of directions and utilizes a variety of methods and organizing ideas. I shall attempt to describe it by discussing three questions: What is anthropology? What do anthropologists do? Where is anthropology going today?

What Is Anthropology?

Anthropology is the study of man and his works. This sweeping subject is divided into a number of major subdivisions.

Cultural anthropology is concerned with the differences and similarities in the many ways of dealing with the problems of existence. Its building blocks are ethnographies—detailed descriptions of whole ways of life in particular places and times.

Archeology is the anthropology of extinct cultures—the study of past ways of life as represented by their own actual remains. Archeologists study artifacts (tools, weapons, houses, etc.), and the traces of man's use of the earth's surface (mounds, terraces, irrigation systems, etc.) in order to reconstruct the cultures of past epochs. Archeology joins forces with cultural anthropology and historiography at many points.

Linguistics is the study of man's language—the distribution of different languages grouped into families and stocks, the internal structure of separate languages, and the relationships of language to other parts of culture.

Physical anthropology studies biological man—the characteristics of different human types through time and in space. In its study of human evolution physical anthropology joins with cultural anthropology, for man creates his own environment with culture and thereby directly affects his own evolution. Physical anthropology and archeology also work together closely, for remains are often found with the artifacts that were used when the culture was a whole entity.

Anthropology is comparative. Different ways of life are seen in the perspective of the many dramatic forms human life has assumed on this earth. When an anthropologist describes marriage, government, religion, education, or technology for a particular society, he is describing these forms of behavior in the light of his knowledge of other forms quite different.

Sometimes he makes cross-cultural comparison the major purpose of his work, and he has great collections of comparative data available to help him in this purpose. At other times his work is only comparative by implication, but he collects and analyzes his material quite differently than a psychologist or sociologist ordinarily would because of his cross-cultural, comparative point of view.

Anthropology is holistic. Almost always the anthropologist studies one manifestation of the culture in relation to other dimensions of the whole way of life. He sees the structure of the family, for example, as related to the methods of subsistence the people use to earn a living. He studies religious beliefs and concepts of disease causation and cure in relation to patterns of child rearing, because the former are seen, in part, as projections of the latter.

Anthropology is both scientific and humanistic. Sometimes its methods are objective, precise, and rigorous; sometimes they are empathetic, intuitive, and almost literary in quality. Anthropologists agree that one must live as close as possible to the people one is studying and under the same conditions whenever feasible, in order to understand how they feel, and to see life from their point of view. The basic method of data collection in anthropology is, therefore, what anthropologists call participant-observation.

An anthropologist studying a new culture usually establishes residence with the people for a period of time varying from several months to a year or two and tries to maintain a friendly low-pressure kind of interaction with the people. He tries to observe them unobtrusively in the daily round of work and play so that, insofar as possible, they are un-affected by the fact they are being studied.

Anthropologists are strongly committed to the principle that people do not usually know exactly why they behave as they do. Just as the speaker of a language cannot usually describe the grammatical structure of his native tongue, so too is it rarely possible for a parent to tell the inquirer why children are reared as they are, or why the given and time-honored sequence in an initiation rite is followed to the letter or why a seemingly cumbersome and complex system of kinship terms is in use.

The anthropologist's purpose is to examine behaviors and infer the reasons why these behaviors exist in their particular forms, or for that matter, exist at all. For this purpose, the anthropologist, like other sci-entists, needs theory, for theory provides the logic of inference and, there-fore, guides his interpretation of observed behavior. Theory in modern anthropology is undergoing rapid change at the present time, and many anthropologists are just becoming aware of the need for systematic, rigorous theory.

What Do Anthropologists Do?

In what has been said already, there are some hints as to what anthro-pologists do. They study human behavior and interpret its meaning. They collect genealogies in order to trace relationships among the present mem-bers of the group and their ties with former members. They collect censuses of the population they are studying so that they know its distri-bution, the relationship between population and subsistence, the compo-sition of households and other small social groupings.

Anthropologists transcribe languages, using phonetic systems, or they store them on tape for future analysis in order that their patterns can be analyzed and compared to other languages. They collect personal docu-ments—accounts of dreams, autobiographies, personal experiences—in order to understand the ways in which culturally patterned experience is interpreted by the individual. And they try to be at least marginal partici-pants in all the important events which take place among the people they are studying and to record observations of these events and the reactions of people to them.

Although anthropologists spend a considerable proportion of their pro-fessional lives in the field, the majority have positions in universities or colleges where they teach both undergraduate and graduate students. Their courses bear such titles as Primitive Religion and Philosophy, Social Organization, Culture Change, Personality and Culture, Language and Culture, the Evolution of Man, New World Prehistory. Some courses deal with special fields such as education, law, and medicine, so there are courses called Legal Anthropology, Medical Anthropology, and Anthro-pology of Education.

An increasing number of anthropologists are in demand as consultants, advisers, and analysts for federal agencies that deal with emerging nations and underdeveloped areas of the world. Many anthropologists with positions on university faculties act occasionally as consultants and analysts for industries or governments—both our own and others—and take temporary leaves of absence from their positions for these purposes.

One of the problems of the profession is that there aren't enough anthropologists to meet the demand. There are only about 900 fellows in the American Anthropological Association at present, and this fellowship is not expected to increase rapidly because of the long period of graduate training—from five to seven years—required for the Ph.D.

Where Is Anthropology Going Today?

This last question is one of the most difficult ones to answer, for each part of anthropology is generating new ideas, new methods of study, and building new theory. The whole field is in ferment at present.

Human evolution is one of the perennial problem areas that has received special attention lately. Anthropologists realize that man has always been a creature of culture. Every new tool, no matter how crude or how advanced, directly affects the course of human evolution. In the beginning the use of a simple club reduced selective pressure upon the teeth and jaws, so that those of our remote ancestors who had clubs but smaller jaws and teeth could survive better than similar creatures with bigger jaws but no clubs. And since the hand and the brain are intimately related, selective pressure resulted in larger brains that could guide better tools to man's purposes.

Today evolution continues. Man is fast creating a new physical environment through technology. Smog, pesticides, industrial and household pollutants, radioactive wastes, and fallout are new hazards that have already begun to affect the future course of human evolution. Anthropologists are studying these problems armed with knowledge from biology (the field of genetics is supplying new knowledge about the mechanisms of human heredity), and from their study of how culture adapts to man's needs on the one hand and adapts man to its conditions on the other.

Another trend in anthropology today is the emphasis upon cultural change and cultural stability. The concerns range from questions about the sequence of developments that led to the emergence of great urban centers among the Aztec, Maya, and Inca to the minute details of cultural change within a period of a decade in an American Indian tribe, or in a village in the highlands of New Guinea.

Changes in social groupings, in value systems, in technology, in political leadership, in language, and in personality structure as it adapts to conditions of life brought about by cultural transformation are all being scrutinized with new theories and methods of study. One of the particularly interesting problems is what makes cultural patterns persist in the face of what seems to be overwhelming pressure for change.

Sometimes the answer is quite simple—as in the case of the German villagers who bought tractors but continue to do most of the work in the vineyards by hand. Because the terraced hillside plots are too small to use mechanized equipment, the tractors merely replace the cows (yes, really cows, not oxen) formerly used to haul carts full of workers and equipment up to the vineyards. Sometimes it is very complex, as in the case of some American Indians who continue to use native methods of treating illness despite the availability of modern medicine. The reasons the native practices continue in use are tied in with concepts of disease causation that are a part of a world view vastly different from ours.

Anthropologists are currently giving special attention to many other problem areas, but I shall mention only one. They are developing new methods and techniques of research which will make their studies of behavior more precise.

For example, they are using symbolic logic and formal mathematical models to separate and manipulate the elements of observed behavior. They are applying microanalytic methods of study to the use of space between persons in social interaction with each other (the study of proxemics) and to the gestures and bodily movements that communicate content beyond words and that sometimes contradict words (the study of kinesics). They are carrying out rigorous and detailed analysis of the meaning of utterances (parts of whole expressions) in communication. And they are developing new applications of statistics to test the validity of hypotheses about the relationships between variables. Anthropology, in short, is becoming more scientific.

2 / The Human Animal

WESTON LA BARRE

In this selection Weston La Barre continues the theme set by Spindler's article but zeroes in on the understanding of anthropology as it relates to other disciplines. He stresses the holistic aspect of man's study, with the view that anthropology is concerned with all aspects of man and that anthropology is clearly integrated with other disciplines—social, biological, and physical sciences. La Barre's major point is that man's cultural and physical aspects (mind and body) cannot be properly understood unless they are studied together. Since mind and body interact in the development of each, both should be viewed as an interacting whole —the human animal.

Western culture is a strange paradox. For thousands of years we have proclaimed our primary or even exclusive allegiance to the spiritual world. But somehow, in the meantime, in spite of this protested loyalty—whether backsliding, offhanded, unwitting, absent-minded, or perverse—we have historically created the most unusual and complex material culture the world has ever seen! This result is hardly to be expected from our pretensions and suggests that we have had some confusion about our nature and our motivations, for we have surely shown less confusion about the nature of the physical world. At the same time, we have not been very clear about the nature of the realities we call "spiritual."

A good deal of this confusion comes from the use of traditional concepts, which, when we look at them more critically, we can now see are inadequate. Modern man is coming to realize that there is only one integrated, unified *kind* of world, not two. But this is not all. We are sometimes deeply *motivated* to be confused about our human nature. That is, there are some aspects of man's nature which we have reasons for choosing not to know. In the current and chronic human predicament, man has as many psychological blind spots and wilful misapprehensions about himself as does any patient of a psychiatrist. And for much the same reason: we, like the patient, are afraid of what we are. We wish to maintain other pretenses and to preserve certain delusions about ourselves, not to look at unwelcome facts; and we have our own peculiarly human reasons for all this, as we will see later.

But almost in spite of ourselves the facts about man have been steadily accumulating. Paleontology—the study of ancient life from its fossil remains—has given us a clear picture not only of the biological history behind man but also of the main outlines of his immediate ancestry. Physical anthropology, which used to be a dreary and sterile bone-measuring science, too often used to argue the "superiority" of one race over another, has now become a genuine "human biology." And biology itself, transformed by a century of growing insights into organic evolution, has given us a better sense of man's basic nature and of his place in the larger natural order.

The social sciences have also grown in knowledge. Sociology, soundly based on the essentially social nature of man has learned so much as to be a large group of specialties in itself. Cultural anthropology—the study of the socially inherited behavior patterns of men in different societies—has collected such a mass of information about the various ways in which man can be human that the professional student can barely specialize in one continent alone. Archeology, the main tool in the study of prehistory, now tells us not only the relative sequences of stratification but also, with the carbon 14 technique, even something like absolute dating in time. Comparative linguistics has advanced its claim to being the most exact of the social sciences; and anyone who knows recent work will admit that it has made a good case. Psychology, and especially clinical psychology, has sharpened our understanding of man's behavior; while the more one learns of modern dynamic psychiatry, the more respect for it increases as one of the most subtle, precise, and profound disciplines of the human mind. Indeed—and I think rightly so—few of the newer generation of social anthropologists consider themselves fully equipped to get the best out of field work unless they have some knowledge of clinical psychology and analytic psychiatry. This is only one of the many signs that students of the social sciences are increasingly aware that they have much to learn from one another.

Both in theory and in practice the social sciences are moving steadily in the direction of co-operation and integration. For example, sociologists and anthropologists now borrow each other's insights and techniques with the same abandon as college roommates borrow each other's shirts and neckties. In fact it is hard to tell the difference between them to an interested person, beyond stating weakly, and not at all accurately, that anthropologists study primitive peoples and sociologists civilized ones. Cultural anthropologists are admittedly partly historians, and modern historians are intentionally students of cultural history. Applied anthropology and political science merge skills in administering our Pacific island dependencies. Government cannot get along without the economist. Jurisprudence and the law look into analytic psychiatry for insights, only to discover that the social caseworker has preceded them there. In fact, the modern child-guidance clinic is a team made up of the social worker, the psychiatrist, and the psychologist. The projective techniques of the clinical psychologist are among the best diagnostic tools of modern psychiatry, and of course the field anthropologist has long since borrowed them for research purposes. It is as if we had cut up the subject of man like a meat pie. But as all the specialists start from a common center, when each of them learns more of his own terrain, then all the social scientists begin to realize that the whole is a large circle and not a small triangular wedge—and that there are solid meat, hot potatoes, and gravy in all the slices.

The whole trend of twentieth-century science is plainly toward integration, a fact indicated in the very names of new disciplines: psychosomatic medicine, biochemistry, psychobiology, and the like. The integrative movement in the social sciences derives further significance from this state of affairs. Our knowledge of the parts has now reached a stage when we can begin to seek a "holistic" understanding of larger wholes. Possessing now an anatomy of our various subjects, so to speak, we can begin to see the functioning physiology and relationships of these structures. Science, too, is discovering that there is only "one world."

Probably the best example of this holistic naturalism is found in mathematical physics. By looking at the nature both of stars and of atoms and by an effort of superb intellectual synthesizing, Einstein has sought to encompass them both within one consistent system, expressed in a mere handful of equations. In philosophy—partly derived from modern mathematics but almost equally inspired by the biological concept of the organism—we have Whitehead's impressive and deep-rooted holism, which sees all reality as a system of functional relationships. In psychiatry the commonest criticism of Freud has been that he was far too biological in his psychology. In psychology itself, the older elementistic behaviorism (which, in ignoring consciousness, left out the central fact of psychology) is gone, and modern learning theory is in fact highly concerned with psychic motivation; Gestalt psychology, a sophisticated and contemporary system philosophically, is thoroughly holistic in its very essence. In biology the interest in the ecological approach is giving us a larger sense of the complex relationships of organisms and environments. Perhaps because of the nature of their subject matter, biologists are inescapably driven to a larger organismic view of life; and among biologists, none is more holistic *ab ovo,* so to speak, than Edwin Grant Conklin. W. B. Cannon's pan-systemic physiology and Sir Charles Sherrington's integrative neurology make sense to both psychologists and psychiatrists—and, indeed, the psychosomatic physician applies these same total-organism views to the practice of medicine.

Anthropology, too, is working in this direction. Curiously enough, however, it is one of its greatest scientific successes which has heretofore impeded its progress: the discovery that the physical "racial" differences among men have nothing to do with the specific cultural differences among them. Racial traits are genetically inherited; cultural traits are socially inherited. Since these vary independently, physical anthropologists can study this intricate animal biologically—but they do it mostly without any reference to its most significant and conspicuous animal adaptation, culture! Likewise, some anthropologists (I think mistakenly) believe that their subject matter is solely that *abstraction from human behavior,* culture, and not properly the study of man in all his aspects; and some of them, the "culturologists," have even seriously suggested that we ought to study culture as if human beings had never existed! Nevertheless, as we will see, it is impossible for the biology and the sociology of man to remain forever isolated from each other.

In thus maintaining the unnatural dichotomy between the physical and the "spiritual" attributes of man, anthropology seems largely to have escaped the widespread integrative trend of modern science. It is in an unusual and atypical position in thus housing the ghost of the old body–mind "problem," an animism not yet exorcised from our science. Nevertheless, it is quite plain that physical anthropologists and cultural anthropologists have much of crucial significance to say to each other. Part of the problem is the sheer bulk of the specialized knowledge that keeps them apart. But another part of the problem is that we have been operating with ancient concepts, deeply though often imperceptibly imbedded in our thinking, that we would judge archaic if we were fully aware of them. We still suffer from the old definition of man as half reprobate ape and half apprentice angel, made up partly of opprobrious and regrettable material body and partly of intrinsically perfect "spirit." This definition sees pretty well to it that never the twain shall meet, even conceptually, much less socially.

Many thoughtful anthropologists are beginning to see that it is a mistake to proceed as if the works of the mind had nothing to do with the needs of the body, and as if the structure of man's body had nothing to do with the way his mind works culturally to secure his satisfactions. Anthropologists now see that we have been so successful in establishing the relativity of cultures as to risk throwing out the baby with the bath: the universal similarities of all mankind. Understandably, then, there is now a strong movement back to the search for essential human nature. It is here that the necessary collaboration of the physical and the cultural anthropologist is most significant and fruitful. For man is an animal *with peculiar biological traits as a species* which make him human. Man's *significantly human traits* are possessed indifferently by all the races of men. Of course it remains true that whatever is universally possessed physically by man can never be used to explain cultural variations. But all human beings have a culture of some sort, and cultures are possessed by human beings alone. The possession of cultures uniquely and universally by *Homo sapiens* must therefore be understandable in terms of those biological traits which all groups of mankind jointly share. This does not mean, of course, that any culture can be "reduced" to biology —the more especially since racial differences have nothing to do with cultural differences—but it does mean that the generic fact of culture ultimately rests upon biological traits of the species *Homo sapiens. Man's "human nature" derives from the kind of body he has.* This can be discussed in terms of matter-of-fact, concrete, verifiable, and tough-minded propositions, without special pleading, and without abandoning a consistent naturalism.

Some of these concepts are unfamiliar to most people, and a few of them are a bit technical—but there is hardly any subject matter that is more rewarding to understand than man himself. We have tried to translate the specialists' discoveries into something that makes integrated sense to the thoughtful reader. If he is sometimes surprised about what he discovers concerning this strange and wonderful animal, well, that is the risk that every explorer must take. In any case, this book is an attempt to relate for the intelligent reader what we now know about these matters. It views man, quite simply, as a biological species, with the essential characteristics of his behavior, including social behavior, as growing out of his biological uniqueness. It views man genetically, as the contemporary result of a very long and complex chain of multiple and diverse evolutionary changes. This evolutionary process can be seen as one requiring an enormous and wasteful variety of experiments in order to develop increasingly successful adaptations to the changing environment—the environment in the case of man including his social and political, as well as biological, adaptations. The view of man's animal past, therefore, carries profound implications for *culture as man's ecology,* that is, the adaptations to his peculiar total environment which significantly includes his fellow-man.

3 / Today's Crisis in Anthropology

CLAUDE LEVI-STRAUSS

Read a newspaper or listen to a newscast and you encounter a host of problems, large and small. However, a problem you are not likely to hear on a newscast is the crisis discussed in this article by Levi-Strauss. Having looked at what anthropology is in the first two selections, it appears fruitful to see what the study of man might be like in the future. Levi-Strauss tells the reader what he believes to be the main crisis or turning point in the field of anthropology. Levi-Strauss is primarily concerned with two problems in the field of social or cultural anthropology: that of "vanishing" nonindustrialized peoples, and the alienation of anthropologists among some people. Levi-Strauss concludes that cultural anthropology will not disappear but that it must find a new direction—a new path—to meet this crisis.

The important place social anthropology holds in contemporary thinking may seem paradoxical to many people. It is a science very much in vogue: witness not only the fashion for films and books about travel, but also the interest of the educated public in books on anthropology.

Towards the end of the 19th century people were apt to look to the biologist in their quest for a philosophy of man and the world, and then later to the sociologist, the historian, and even the philosopher.

But for the past several years anthropology has come to play the same role, and today it too is expected to provide us with deep reflections on our world and a philosophy of life and hope.

It is in the United States that this approach to anthropology seems to have begun. As a young nation intent on creating a humanism of its own, America broke with traditional European thinking. It saw no reason why the civilizations of Greece and Rome should be admired to the exclusion of all others merely because in the Old World of the Renaissance, when mankind came to be considered the most proper and necessary study of man, these were the only two civilizations sufficiently known.

Since the 19th century and especially the 20th, practically every human society on our planet has become accessible to study. Why then limit our interests? And indeed, when we contemplate humanity in its entirety we cannot fail to recognize the fact that for 99/100ths of mankind's existence, and over most of the inhabited globe, there have been no customs, no beliefs, no institutions which do not fall within the province of anthropological study.

This was strikingly emphasized during the last war with the struggle waged on a world-wide scale. Even the most obscure and remote corners of our planet were suddenly catapulted into our lives and consciousness and took on three-dimensional reality. These were the lands where the last "savage" peoples on earth had sought safety in isolation—the far north of America, New Guinea, the hinterlands of south-east Asia, and certain islands in the Indonesian archipelago.

Since the war many names, once charged with mystery and romance, have remained on our maps but now they designate landing spots for long-distance jet liners. Under the impact of aviation and with increase in world population our planet has shrunk in size, and improved communications and travel facilities permit us no longer to close our eyes or remain indifferent to other peoples.

Today there is no fraction of the human race, no matter how remote and retarded it may still appear, which is not directly or indirectly in contact with others and whose feelings, ambitions, desires and fears do not affect the security and prosperity and the very existence of those to whom material progress may once have given a feeling of ascendancy.

Even if we wanted to, we could no longer ignore or shrug off with indifference, say, the last head-hunters of New Guinea, for the simple reason that *they* are interested in us. And surprising though it may be, the result of our contacts with them means that both they and we are now part of the same world, and it will not be long before we are all part of the same civilization.

For even societies with the most widely divergent patterns of thought and whose customs and mores took thousands of years to evolve along isolated paths, impregnate one another once contact is established. This occurs in many, devious ways; sometimes we are clearly aware of them, often we are not.

As they spread throughout the world, the civilizations which (rightly or wrongly) felt that they had reached the height of development, such as Christianity, Islamism, Buddhism, and on a different level the technological civilization which is now bringing them together, are all tinged with "primitive" ways of life, "primitive" thinking and "primitive" behaviour which have always been the subject of anthropological research. Without our realizing it the "primitive" ways are transforming these civilizations from within.

For the so-called primitive or archaic peoples do not simply vanish into a vacuum. They dissolve and are incorporated with greater or lesser speed into the civilization surrounding them. At the same time the latter acquires a universal character.

Thus, far from diminishing in importance, primitive peoples concern us more with each passing day. To take only one example, the great civilization the West is justly proud of and which has spread its roots across the inhabited globe, is everywhere emerging as a "hybrid." Many foreign elements, both spiritual and material, are being absorbed into its stream.

As a result, the problems of anthropology have ceased to be a matter for specialists, limited to scholars and explorers, they have become the direct and immediate concern of every one of us.

Where, then, lies the paradox? In reality there are two—insofar as anthropology is chiefly concerned with the study of "primitive" peoples. At the moment when the public has come to recognize its true value, we may well ask whether it has not reached the point where it has nothing more left to study.

For the very transformations which are spurring a growing theoretical interest in "primitives" are in fact bringing about their extinction. This is not really a new phenomenon. As early as 1908, when he inaugurated the chair of Social Anthropology at the University of Liverpool, Sir James Frazer (author of the monumental *Golden Bough*) dramatically called the attention of governments and scholars to this very problem. Yet we can hardly compare the situation half a century ago with the large-scale extinction of "primitive" peoples which we have witnessed since then.

Let me cite a few examples. At the beginning of white settlement in Australia, the Aborigenes numbered 250,000 individuals. Today no more than 40,000 are left.

Official reports describe them herded in reserves or clustered near mining centres where in the place of their traditional wild food gathering parties they are reduced to sneak-scavenging in rubbish heaps outside the mining shacks. Other Aborigenes, who had retreated deep into the forbidding desert, have been uprooted by the installation of atomic explosion bases or rocket launching sites.

Protected by its exceptionally hostile environment, New Guinea, with its several million tribesmen, may well be the last great sanctuary of primitive society on earth. But here too, civilization is making such rapid inroads that the 600,000 inhabitants of the central mountains, who were totally unknown a mere twenty years ago, are now providing labour contingents for the building of roads. And it is no rarity today to see road signs and milestones parachuted into the unexplored jungle!

But with civilization have come strange diseases, against which "primitives" have no natural immunization and which have wrought deadly havoc in their ranks. They are succumbing rapidly to tuberculosis, malaria, trachoma, leprosy, dysentery, gonorrhea, syphilis, and the mysterious disease known as *kuru*. The result of primitive man's contact with civilization, though not actually introduced by it, *kuru* is a genetic deterioration which inevitably ends in death and for which no treatment or remedy is known.

In Brazil, 100 tribes became extinct between 1900 and 1950. The Kaingang, from the State of Sao Paulo, numbering 1,200 in 1912, were no more than 200 in 1916, and today have dwindled to 80.

The Munduruku were 20,000 in 1925—in 1950 they numbered 1,200. Of the 10,000 Nambikwara in 1900, I could trace only a thousand in 1940. The Kayapo of the River Araguaya were 2,500 in 1902 and 10 in 1950. The Timbira 1,000 in 1900 and 40 in 1950.

How can this rapid decimation be explained? Foremost, by the introduction of Western diseases against which the Indian's body had no defence. The tragic fate of the Urubu, an Indian tribe from north-eastern Brazil, is typical of many others. In 1950, only a few years after they were discovered, they contracted the measles. Within a few days, out of the population of 750 there were 160 deaths. An eyewitness has left this stark description:

> We found the first village abandoned. All the inhabitants had fled, convinced that if they ran far away they would escape the sickness which they believed was a spirit attacking the villages.
>
> We discovered them in the forest, halted in their flight. Exhausted and shivering with fever in the rain, nearly all of them had fallen victim to the disease. Intestinal and pulmonary complications had so weakened them that they no longer had strength to seek food.
>
> Even water was lacking, and they were dying as much from hunger and thirst as from the disease. The children were crawling about on the forest floor trying to keep the fires alight in the rain and hoping to keep warm. The men lay burning and paralyzed by fever; the women indifferently thrust away their babes seeking the breast.

But in addition to infectious diseases, vitamin and other nutritional deficiencies are also an important problem. Motor-vascular disorders, eye lesions and dental decay, unknown to primitive man when he lived according to his ancient ways, make their appearance when he is confined to villages and must eat food which does not come from his native forest. Then, even the old and tried traditional remedies, such as charcoal dressings for severe burns, prove useless. And simple diseases to which tribesmen have long been accustomed, become extraordinarily virulent.

The decimation of the Indians is due to other, less direct, causes, such as the collapse of the social structure or pattern of living. The Kaingang of Sao Paulo, already mentioned, lived by a series of strict social rules with which every anthropologist is acquainted. The inhabitants of each village were divided into two groups on the principle that the men from the first group could marry only women from the second group and vice versa.

When their population diminished, the foundations permitting their survival collapsed. Under the rigid system of the Kaingang, it was no longer possible for every man to find a wife and many had no choice but celibacy unless they resigned themselves to mating within their own group—which to them was incest, and even then their marriage had to be childless. In such cases a whole population can disappear within a few years.

Bearing this in mind, need we be surprised that it is more and more difficult not only to study the so-called primitive peoples but even to define them satisfactorily. In recent years a serious attempt has been made to revise existing thinking regarding protective legislation in the countries facing this problem.

Neither language nor culture nor the conviction of belonging to a group are valid as criteria for a definition. As enquiries of the International Labour Organization have emphasized, the notion of *indigenous* people is being superseded by the concept of *indigence*.

But this is only half of the picture. There are other parts of the world where tens and hundreds of millions of people live who were traditionally the subject of anthropology. These populations are increasing rapidly in number in Central America, the Andes, south-east Asia and Africa. But here too, anthropology faces a crisis. Not because the populations are dying out but because of the nature of the people involved.

These peoples are changing and their civilizations are gradually becoming Westernized. Anthropology, however, has never yet included the West within its competence or province. Furthermore, and even more important, there is a growing opposition in these regions to anthropological enquiries. Instances have occurred where regional museums of "Anthropology" have been forced to change their names and can only continue disguised as "Museums of Popular Art and Tradition."

In the young states which have recently obtained independence, economists, psychologists and sociologists are warmly welcomed by universities. The same can hardly be said of the anthropologist.

Thus it would almost seem that anthropology is on the point of falling victim to a dual conspiracy. On the one hand are the peoples who have ceased physically to lend themselves to study by simply vanishing from the face of the earth. On the other are those who, far from dead, are living a great population "explosion," yet are categorically hostile to anthropology for psychological and ethical reasons.

There is no problem about how to meet the first of these crises. Research must be speeded up and we must take advantage of the few years that remain to gather all the information we can on these vanishing islands of humanity. Such information is vital for, unlike the natural sciences, the sciences of man cannot originate their own experimentation.

Every type of society, of belief or institution, every way of life, constitutes a ready-made experiment the preparation of which has taken thousands of years and as such is irreplaceable. When a community disappears, a door closes forever locking away knowledge which is unique.

That is why the anthropologist believes that it is essential, before these societies are lost and their social customs destroyed, to create sharper observation techniques, rather like the astronomer who has brought electronic amplifiers into play to capture the weakening signals of light from distant stars racing away from us.

The second crisis in anthropology is much less serious in the absolute since there is no threat of extinction to the civilizations concerned. But it is much more difficult to deal with out of hand. I wonder whether it would help matters if we tried to dispel the distrust of the people who were formerly the anthropologist's field work by proposing that our research should henceforth no longer be "one way only." Might not anthropology find its place again if, in exchange for our continued freedom to investigate, we invited African or Melanesian anthropologists to come and study us in the same way that up to now only we have studied them?

Such an exchange would be very desirable for it would enrich the science of anthropology by widening its horizons, and set us on the road to further progress. But let us have no illusions—this would not resolve the problem, for it does not take into consideration the deep motives underlying the former colonized peoples' negative attitude to anthropology. They are afraid that under the cloak of an anthropological interpretation of history what they consider to be intolerable inequality will be justified as the desirable *diversity* of mankind.

If I may be permitted a formula which, coming from an anthropologist, can have no derogatory connotation even as pure scientific observation, I would say that Westerners will never (except in make-believe) be able to act the role of "savages" opposite those whom they once dominated. For when we Westerners cast them in this role they existed for us only as *objects*—whether for scientific study or political and economic domination. Whereas we, who in their eyes are responsible for their past fate, now appear to them inevitably as directing forces and therefore it is much harder for them to look at us with an attitude of detached appraisal.

By a curious paradox, it was undoubtedly a feeling of sympathy that prompted many anthropologists to adopt the idea of pluralism (this asserts the diversity of human cultures and concomitantly denies that certain civilizations can be classified as "superior" and others as "inferior." Yet these very anthropologists—and indeed all anthropology—are now accused of denying this inferiority merely to conceal it, and hence of contributing more or less directly to its continued existence.

If therefore, anthropology is to survive in the modern world, there can be no disguising that it must be at the price of much deeper changes than a mere enlarging of the circle (very restricted it is true up to now) by the rather childish formula of offering to lend our toys to the newcomers provided they let us go on playing with theirs.

Anthropology must transform its very nature and must admit that, logically and morally, it is almost impossible to continue to view societies as *scientific objects,* which the scientist may even wish to preserve, but which are now *collective subjects* and claim the right to change as they please.

The modification of anthropology's subject matter also implies modifications in its aims and methods. And these fortunately appear quite feasible, for our branch of science has never defined its purposes in the absolute but rather as a relationship between the observer and his subject. And it has always agreed to change whenever this relationship has been modified.

Doubtless, the property of anthropology has always been to investigate on the spot of "from within." But only because it was impossible to investigate at a distance or "from without." In the field of the social sciences, the great revolution of our times is that whole civilizations have become conscious of their existence, and having acquired the necessary means to do so through literacy, have embarked on the study of their own past and traditions and every unique aspect of their culture which has survived to the present day.

Thus, if Africa, for instance, is escaping from anthropology, it will not so easily escape from science. In place of the anthropologist—that is the outside analyst, working from the outside—study of the continent will be in the hands of African scientists, or foreigners who will use the same methods as their African colleagues.

They will no longer be anthropologists but linguists, philologists, historians of facts and ideas. Anthropology will gladly accept this transition to richer, more subtle methods than its own, confident that it has fulfilled its mission by keeping alive so much of the great riches of humanity on behalf of scientific knowledge, so long as it was the only branch of science able to do so.

As to the future of anthropology itself, it seems to lie now at the far extreme and the near extreme of its traditional positions. At the far extreme, in the geographical sense first, since we must go further and further afield to reach the last of the so-called primitive populations, and they are getting fewer and fewer; but in the far extreme in its logical meaning too, since we are now interested in the essentials.

On the near extreme, in the sense that the collapse of the material foundations of the last primitive civilizations has made their intimate experiences one of our last fields of investigation in place of the weapons, tools and household objects that have disappeared. But also because as Western civilization becomes more complex with each passing day and spreads across the whole of the earth, it is already beginning to show signs of the sharp differences which anthropology has made it its business to study but which it could formerly do only by comparing dissimilar and widely separated cultures.

Here, no doubt, lies the permanent function of anthropology. For if there exists, as anthropologists have always affirmed, a certain "optimum diversity" which they see as a permanent condition of human development, then we may be sure that divergencies between societies and groups within societies will disappear only to spring up again in other forms.

Who knows if the conflict between the old and new generations, which so many countries are now experiencing, may not be the ransom that must be paid for the growing homogenization of our social and material culture? Such phenomena seem to me pathological but anthropology has always been characterized by its ability to explain and justify forms of human behavior which men found strange and could not understand.

In this way anthropology at every phase has helped to enlarge the currently held and always too constricting view of humanity. To picture the disappearance of anthropology, one would have to conjure up a civilization where all men—no matter what corner of the globe they inhabited, and whatever their way of life, their education, their professional activities, their age, beliefs, sympathies and aversions—were, to the very roots of their consciousness, totally intelligible to all other men.

Whether one deplores it, approves it, or merely states it as a fact, technical progress and the development of communications hardly seem to be leading us to this end. And as long as the ways of thinking or of acting of some men perplex other men, there will be scope for meditation on these differences; and this, in a constantly renewing form, will be the abiding province of anthropology.

Part 1 / QUESTIONS AND PROBLEMS FOR DISCUSSION

1. Define anthropology in terms appropriate to you and list the activities of four specialists in anthropology.
2. Explain how the activities of different types of anthropologists are interrelated.
3. Discuss one of the special qualities of anthropology that sets the discipline apart from other social sciences.
4. What is the importance of La Barre's "body–mind" concept as it relates to the proper understanding of man?
5. Levi-Strauss states that the so-called primitive peoples are merging swiftly with other civilizations. In your own view, do you see this as a crisis in anthropology? Why?

2/ MAN BECOMES MAN: BUT HOW?

About 2 million years ago a barrel-chested, semiupright fellow in Africa awoke to a brilliant sunrise and began his daily search for food. At that time he had no name, but now his fossilized remains are immortalized with the label *Australopithecus* (southern ape-man). The physical remains of this nameless fellow and the way in which he spent his day reveal a great deal about early man and how he has used his physical and mental abilities in varied times and places to create an existence for himself and his kind of being. Of the many individuals that have lived and died, only a small percentage have done so in situations that favor fossilization; and only a small fraction of these have been eroded from the earth's bowels to be analyzed by paleoanthropologists. Because the fossil evidence of man's past is incomplete, only glimpses of man's development can be described with reasonable certainty. Yet these glimpses—these slices of life from man's past—can be assembled within a scientific framework to provide continuity throughout the story of man's evolutionary development. Equipped with fossil remains, the tools by which time is measured, and knowledge of evolutionary processes, the anthropologist has the task of reconstructing the biological and cultural aspects of man's past.

One of the most basic decisions in the field of anthropology is the distinction between the biological and cultural levels of man's aspects. Although this distinction tends to produce separate bodies of knowledge, students of anthropology are trained to realize that there is no clear-cut distinction between the two levels, and that only by applying their efforts simultaneously to both biological and cultural factors can the study of man have real meaning. Physical anthropology has many subdivisions: anthropometry is concerned with the measurement of living human beings; the study of race—what races are and how they are formed—is an aspect of physical anthropology well known to the public; a third division, the evolutionary development of man, has also captured the public's interest. In these and other divisions of physical anthropology we attempt to understand man in terms of the interaction of biological and cultural factors.

There is no question that man has a past. Now more than ever man needs to understand his past so that he may understand himself. The articles included in this section tell us how man became man. Emphasis is placed upon the development of early man and upon the more recent diversification of human forms commonly referred to as "races."

4 / The Long Journey of the Primates

JOHN NAPIER

Tracing the long journey of primates through time is a formidable task, especially in view of the scarcity of early primate fossil remains. However, the large and growing body of facts allows for increasingly sufficient evidence for the evolution of modern man from early primate forms. Establishing the long record of primate evolution is similar to putting together a puzzle when you are given only one piece at a time. But soon the gaps are filled in and a convincing picture takes form. In this selection John Napier relates the story of primate evolution by comparing the structural and functional attributes of modern man to those of nonman (nonhuman primates). Several important questions are answered. What did early primates look like? When and how did the human line diverge from the ape line? When did man become man? Napier's long journey spans a time from about 70 million years ago to about 400,000 years ago. At the latter date Homo sapiens *come upon the scene.* Homo sapiens *is not modern man—but that is another story.*

The story of man and his ancestors is like a play in which the key character does not appear until the last scene. Yet by the time he finally makes his entrance the audience has already got a very good idea, from what has gone before, of the sort of person he is going to turn out to be.

To say man is the "key" actor in the drama of primate evolution, of course, is to take a very biased view. There is no doubt that if this article were being written by a giraffe, for example, man might find himself allotted a very minor and probably most obnoxious part in the evolutionary saga of the primates. It is natural that man should be self-centred in his approach to primate evolution but that does not mean that he is not capable of thinking in any other way.

Many of my zoological colleagues, for instance, are principally interested in analysing the background of the non-human primates, the lemurs, monkeys or apes. But I am an anthropologist, which means that man is the central theme of my research so it is not surprising that I am primarily interested in the appearance of those structural and functional features by which we characterize man today. This being so we must clarify our ideas and decide just what we should be looking for in the primate fossil record.

First of all we must examine the nature of our criteria and select those characters that are unique to modern man and can truly be called his "hallmarks." There are quite a number of characters that we might choose but, bearing in mind that our source material is limited to fossil bones and teeth, the range is naturally rather restricted. The possession of speech and language is the most outstanding human hallmark of all but unfortunately it leaves no trace in ancient bones.

One can make all sorts of inferences that speech evolved at such-and-such a time but there is no scrap of direct evidence to support such an assertion. The ability to speak lies, first of all, in the shape and musculature of the mouth, tongue, soft palate, pharynx and larynx; and secondly, in the centres of the cortex, or outer shell, of the brain which govern the muscular control of the various "soft" parts mentioned above. Although many ingenious suggestions have been put forward none as far as we know can help us to recognize the capacity for speech from a study of bones.

There are numerous cultural phenomena which we would regard as significant hallmarks but, again, we cannot use them because they leave no physical evidence behind. Behaviour itself does not fossilize but the extra-corporeal accessories of behaviour *do*.

Evidence of a hunting economy can be determined from the living sites (or living "floors" as they are called) of early man; in the same way tool-making behavior can be identified. Much as a modern picnic site can reveal to an intelligent inquirer all he needs to know about the habits and social status of the picnickers, so living floors of early man with their hearths, their animal remains, their wall-paintings, their burials and so on can be read and interpreted by archaeologists.

Unfortunately the background to man that we are committed to investigate extends many millions of years further back in time when no living floors and no artifacts existed. Apart from the evidence of stone or bone tools as supplements to our understanding of human dexterity we shall not be leaning very heavily on the evidence of "fossil behaviour." What, then, are to be our criteria?

When we think about man and compare him with non-man one of the first things that strikes us is that he stands upright and walks on two legs. But this is not nearly a precise enough definition to exclude the many non-human primates who are also capable of upright bipedalism. Nor does it exclude, for example, the bears. For a more exact criterion we must draw upon our knowledge of the biomechanics of human walking.

Human walking is a highly complex affair. This is not the place to stuff you with technical details like a Strasbourg goose with rich food, but to ask you to accept the simplified—but nonetheless valid—conclusion that modern man shows a unique method of walking which we call *striding*.

Striding involves the muscles and the joints of the vertebral column, the pelvis, the leg and the foot in a complicated and precisely integrated series of manoeuvres. An alternative term for striding is heel-toe walking. We are now in a position to formulate our first hallmark: *man stands upright and when walking habitually uses a bipedal, striding gait.*

The second characteristic that strikes us is the dexterity of the human hand, which is infinitely capable, exquisitely delicate but, at the same time, alarmingly powerful—powerful enough to cleave a brick in half with a karate chop, or to tear a city telephone directory into two equal parts.

The essential component of the human hand is its *opposable thumb,* which provides the means for grasping objects with strength (the power grip) or with delicacy (the precision grip). The opposable thumb is therefore an obvious hallmark, but unfortunately it is not unique to man; all living Old World monkeys and apes possess opposable thumbs.

Once again we must draw upon our knowledge of the functional anatomy of man's hand to set us on the right track. Man's precision grip is much more sophisticated than any monkey's or ape's; when he places his forefinger and thumb together in a precision grip he is employing the two most acutely sensitive areas in his whole body. The sensory input from these small areas provides the neurological basis for the sort of skill that a watchmaker, a plastic surgeon or an assembler of micro-circuits possesses.

Sometime ago, in order to provide a means of quantifying the precision grip of primates, I introduced a simple ratio called the *opposability index* to express the relative lengths of the forefinger and thumb. The opposability index of men is 65. The score for a chimpanzee is 43 and for a baboon, which approaches nearest to man in this respect, it is 57. So now we are in a position to formulate the second hallmark: *man possesses an opposable thumb whose length is approximately 65 per cent the length of his forefinger.*

The third feature that strikes us about man is that his brain is large and rounded; but of course brains do not fossilize and so we can only make deductions about the brain from the study of its container—the brain-box. Unfortunately, apart from overall shape and size, there is no means of determining the nature of the brain by a simple examination of fossil skulls.

What is more, size itself is a somewhat misleading indicator because it is naturally variable within a species; for example among modern human populations the brain volume ranges from 950 to 2000 cubic centimetres. The average volume is about 1400 cc. Brain size is related to body size— bigger animals have bigger brains—and, in some way that we don't fully understand, to intelligence.

Nevertheless, brain size is a valuable guide to the palaeontologist who is attempting to follow the track of man through time. From the earliest pre-human stages to the final flowering of the human family expressed in the species *Homo sapiens,* a steady trend towards enlargement is seen. Here, then, is the basis of our third hallmark, which can be expressed thus: *man, relative to his body size, has a large, rounded brain that may exceed 1400 cc in volume.*

Finally, we notice that man possesses small, even teeth arranged in an elegant parabolic form in his upper and lower jaw. The human teeth, like those of all living primates, are of four types: incisors, canines, premolars and molars. Together in both jaws they total 32, a number characteristic of all Old World monkeys and apes but not New World monkeys or prosimians.

Unlike the apes, man's teeth are all more or less the same vertical length; the canines, which form massive elongated and projecting teeth in the apes, are small, short and discrete in man. Human molars bear low, rounded cusps in contrast to the sharp, prominent cusps of apes and monkeys. The human third molar in both jaws is often small and is frequently absent, whereas in apes the third molar is often the largest of the series.

There are many other differences but these few should be adequate for the purpose of defining the fourth hallmark as follows: *man's teeth are small and are arranged in the jaws in a parabolic curve, the third molar being the smallest of the series and the canines non-projecting*

With these hallmarks in mind we ought to be able to pick up the trail of man during our journey through the past. The trip will be rather like travelling by train between two cities a thousand miles apart. Most railway systems are very complicated affairs with numerous junctions, switching points, branch lines and dead-end terminals, so we have to constantly be on our guard that we do not become shunted along long-forgotten tracks that simply finish up at the end of nowhere at a pair of rusty buffers.

There is a very real danger of this happening because evolution frequently involves a form of mimicry as a result of which similar characters crop up in unrelated or distantly related forms. We have already seen for example that walking on two legs is not uniquely the possession of man. This form of mimicry is more properly termed *parallelism* and the theory behind it is that, given a similar set of environmental opportunities, animals with a common ancestry will tend to evolve in a similar way.

The best example of parallelism in primate evolution is that the monkeys of the New World and the Old World, which are related through a common ancestor living 40 million or so years ago, share so many physical characters that it is hard for the average person to tell them apart even seeing them side by side in a zoo.

Man has a double ecological heritage. His earliest ancestors were tree-living creatures well adapted to moving, feeding, mating and sleeping high above the ground in tropical forests. His later forebears were ground-livers spending their lives among tropical woodlands and grasslands in competition with the myriads of ground-based mammals, including the large, predatory, carnivores.

His two phases are complementary; without an arboreal background he could never have succeeded on the ground. He possesses neither the fleetness of the impala nor the killer power of the leopards, cheetahs and lions; but he has, through his arboreal background, acquired talents which were of infinitely greater value.

He could run on the ground *and* he could climb trees; he could evade dangers by subtle manoeuvres undreamed of by the instinct-dominated predators and with his emancipated hands he could use weapons and tools to protect himself and to obtain food. Hands were far more efficient than the hooves of his ungulate competitors. Paradoxical as it may seem, man's success as a ground-living primate was entirely due to his arboreal heritage.

The earliest ancestors of the primates were among the first mammals to make their appearance. At this stage, some 70 million years ago, primates-to-be were small, long-nosed, ground-living animals rooting among the leaves of the forest floor for their insect food, and distinguishable only by obscure characters of the teeth and skull from the other long-nosed insectivorous creatures.

With hindsight, some authorities feel they can recognize these primates-to-be even though they possessed none of the *arboreal characters* by which we now recognize the order. They may well be right, but to those of us interested in living primates (including man) the order, effectively, came into being when the primates started to live in trees.

Plesiadapis is a most unprimate-like primate and is totally deficient in arboreal adaptations, while *Smilodectes* and *Notharctus,* which appeared a few million years later, were already advanced tree-climbers.

Arboreal characters can be briefly summarized as follows:

• Mobility of the hands and feet and particularly of the thumb and big toe which are well separated from the other digits and, in some primates, capable of being opposed.

• Replacement of sharp claws by flattened nails, associated with the development of sensitive pads on the tips of the digits.

• A shortening of the snout associated with a reduction in the apparatus and the functions of smell.

• Convergence of the eyes towards the front of the face associated with the development of stereoscopic vision.

• A large brain relative to body size.

• An upright posture which may be confined to the upper part of the body in some but applies throughout in others.

The lemur-like Eocene family the Adapidas (including the genera *Notharctus* and *Smilodectes*) possesses most of these arboreal adaptations: nails had replaced claws and sensory pads were developing on the finger tips, the eyes were converging and the snout was shortening, the brain was relatively large, and the locomotion pattern involved an upright posture of the upper part of the body while in the lower part the hips and knees were acutely flexed.

This last feature, alone, merits our particular interest because the upright posture is one of the hallmarks we are committed to trace. Later forms such as *Necrolemur,* an early European tarsier-like primate, and *Hemiacodon,* a North American form, show a similar postural pattern.

The next recognizable stage in the fossil record is seen during the geological epoch known as the Oligocene; at present the ancestor-descendant linkages between the Oligocene and Eocene primates have not been proved. Most of our information about the Oligocene primates comes from a region of Egypt called the Fayum, now desert but once covered with dense tropical forest.

Between 25 and 35 million years ago the Fayum was the home of an extraordinary variety of ape- and monkey-like creatures. Some, like *Parapithecus,* were probably destined to become true monkeys; some, like *Aeolopithecus,* to become "half-apes" like the gibbons, and some, like *Aegyptopithecus,* to become true apes like the chimpanzee and the gorilla.

It has even been suggested very tentatively that one of these creatures, called *Propliopithecus,* represents the earliest known member of the human lineage. Both *Propliopithecus* and *Aegyptopithecus,* of which only teeth or jaws are known, show some of the characters which anticipate the human condition. *Aegyptopithecus,* while possessing some human-like dental characters, also has features which are strongly reminiscent of later apes.

This raises an important point: the relationship of man and apes. Nearly everyone would agree that their relationship in terms of anatomical structure and physiological and biochemical functions is extremely close. The principal issue is how close? When did the ape line and the human line diverge?

There are at least four schools of thought which we can call the "late-late," the "late," the "early" and the "early-early." Personally, I favour the late school but there is something to be said for the early school, which would hold that the human lineage dates back to *Propliopithecus,* some 30 million years ago.

The late school favours the early Miocene species from Kenya, East Africa, called *Proconsul africanus* (or something very like it) as a likely candidate. We know a little bit about the gait, the skull and the teeth of *P. africanus.* The gait was quadrupedal and therefore provides no particular hint of future bipedalism; the hands are rather human-like in proportion but the evidence of an advanced type of precision grip is absent; the opposability index has been estimated at 56. The brain is still rather primitive but was quite large in terms of body size, and the teeth—like those of *Aegyptopithecus*—are ape-like rather than man-like, but not so completely specialized that one could not envisage an evolutionary reversal to a human-like form.

During Miocene times volcanic activity, rift-valley formation and mountain-building were in full swing. One of two consequences of this orogeny and the coincidental cooling of the earth's surface, which had been steadily proceeding throughout the Tertiary era, was the spread of grasslands at the expense of forests. Grasslands (or savannas) offered new evolutionary opportunities to a variety of mammals, including the expanding population of primates in the rapidly shrinking forest zones.

A few primate stocks, including the ancestors of man and the ancestors of the modern baboons, evidently reacted to the challenge of the changing environment. In this way new horizons were opened up for our remote human ancestors, and for the evolution of the critical hallmarks of mankind.

The earliest human ancestor as we see it at present was a creature called *Ramapithecus* known from north-west India and East Africa. Our material evidence for the potential humanity of *Ramapithecus* is slight and consists only of jaws and teeth but is, nevertheless, very revealing.

Ramapithecus has a distinctly man-like tooth form lacking all the ape-like characters seen in *Aegyptopithecus zeuxis* and *Proconsul africanus*. The dental arcade is rounded, the canines are small and the molar teeth do not increase in size from front to back as in the apes. *Ramapithecus* lived between 12 and 14 million years ago but of course his ancestors may have evolved several million years before this date.

The next recognizable stage in the human lineage started, apparently, at least 4 to 5 million years ago. There is fragmentary evidence that pre-human creatures belonging to the genus *Australopithecus* existed in two areas of East Africa, called Kanapoi and Lothagam. We pick up the trail of these near-men two million years later in the area of Lake Rudolf, again in South Africa, and in Tanzania at Olduvai Gorge; in all these regions they are most prolific. The early (Lothagam and Kanapoi) australopithecines do not tell us very much, but the later forms in East and South Africa show many of the characteristics of the gait, brain size and tooth form that we are searching for.

Australopithecines are generally regarded as near-men. Technically, under the curious rules of current anthropology, they do not qualify for the accolade of human beings, but at Olduvai Gorge 1.75 million years ago some of us accept the fact that the zoological genus *Homo* (man) first made his appearance. His way of life appears to have been that of a scavenger, a hunter of small game, and a tool-maker.

Homo habilis, as this early man is called, was a bipedal walker and probably a "strider"; his brain was still small by modern standards but bigger than his predecessors', and his teeth showed a slight advance on the teeth of the australopithecines. His hands were of a human type but lacked the refinements of precision grip possessed by modern man.

Homo habilis was succeeded in the fossil record by *Homo erectus,* known from South-East Asia (Java), Asia (China), Europe (West Germany) and both North and East Africa. Early *Homo erectus* (from Java) had a bigger brain than *Homo habilis* (*H. habilis,* 656 cc; *H. erectus* 935 cc) and the later manifestations of this species, from Peking for example, showed a maximum brain size of 1225 cc.

In spite of this large brain volume, *Homo erectus* possesses a skull of primitive and easily recognizable shape. His gait is assumed to have been both bipedal and striding. The form of his hands is unknown, so the only guide to the extent of his dexterity are the tools that he made. These fall broadly into the class of "power tools," stone artifacts of simple construction designed for relatively crude purposes such as killing and skinning animals, cutting wood and pounding vegetable products. It has been shown by experiment that these could have been constructed and used in the absence of an advanced form of precision grip.

Perhaps it was an increase in brain size that stimulated the evolutionary improvement of the hand, but perhaps it was the other way about. Anyhow it seems highly probable that the complexity of the brain, the precision capabilities of the hand and the evolution of "precision tools" were closely interlinked.

Exactly where and when *Homo erectus* passed the baton in the human relay race to *Homo sapiens* is not known. It may have happened in different parts of the world, at different times, and in different ways. There is no saying which geographic population of early men did it first.

With the evolution of *Homo sapiens,* which is dated somewhere between 250,000 and 400,000 years ago, our railway journey is almost at an end and we are entering the suburbs of the metropolis. Most of us can begin to put on our overcoats and lift our cases down from the rack. The engine-driver has read the signals correctly, the signalman has done his job and our work is virtually over—over for some, but not for all. The complexities of the suburban system are still to be negotiated, and for certain experts this part of the trip is a matter of deep concern.

They are the specialists in the growth of agriculture, of citizenship, of social and political systems, of the spread of populations and the intermingling of genes, processes which are leading us slowly but inexorably towards the eventual unification of mankind in a single biological and cultural entity. Only when the train comes to a final stop at the terminus—at some future date—will these people reach for their overcoats and suitcases and dismount.

Reprinted from Paul L. DeVore, Editor, *The Origin of Man* (transcript of a symposium sponsored by the Wenner-Gren Foundation for Anthropological Research, April 2–4, 1967). Reprinted by permission of the publisher.

5 / An Ape's-Eye View of Human Evolution

SHERWOOD WASHBURN

Man has long observed nonhuman primate behavior. Now it is time for the ape to analyze man's behavior. In this selection Sherwood Washburn turns the table in a speculative analysis of man's evolution as viewed from the treetop level of the ape. Washburn considers, for example, population density of human and nonhuman primates as it relates to the division of labor to obtain an adequate diet. Also of prime interest is the topic of tool use in relation to human and nonhuman primate behavior. This comparative method is used to determine the major differences and similarities in man and other primate behavior in an attempt to uncover what kinds of forces have been operative in human development since the divergence of the human line from the nonhuman primate line.

I have taken for the text of my sermon: "We apes did not live by teeth alone." Some years ago, Hallowell suggested that when we talk about the creatures that preceded man, we should talk in terms of proto-culture and reserve the term "culture" for *Homo sapiens.* If we look at the sequence of the past two million years, there are, perhaps, three major stages. There is a period of *Australopithecus,* both *africanus* and *robustus;* then, of *Homo erectus;* and finally, that of *Homo sapiens.* And I suggest that the rules for interpreting behavior in each of these stages are very different. Hence, we do not want to confuse the rules for interpreting the behavior of *Homo sapiens* with those of the two earlier stages or of the Pongidae that went before that. And I suggest further that the relation of the brain to the behavior of these creatures is specific and definable, and I think we should be very much concerned with what lies behind the word "learning." It is a very general category and should be broken down into a series of specific things that apply very differently in the different stages of hominid and human behavior.

Now, if we look at man from an ape's point of view—and this is easy for somebody coming from Berkeley—we notice first that we are ourselves only slightly modified apes. We have the long arms, the chromosomes, and the biochemistry of apes, which should make it easy for us to see things through an ape's eyes. However, more seriously, I think the most recent studies of the behavior of contemporary monkeys and apes gives us a base line for our human problems that is quite different from the base line that we had just a few years ago. From an ape's point of view, some of the problems that we worry about aren't problems at all; while certain matters that we hardly consider pose serious problems to our hypothetical ape.

For example, if we look at the behavior of all the non-human primates, we find that these creatures are incredibly restricted in the area that they occupy. Only the gorilla and the baboon have ranges as great as fifteen square miles; while in the majority of the non-human primates, an animal spends virtually its entire life within two or three square miles—a tiny area. Here, then, are creatures with excellent vision who climb into trees and survey distant territories that somehow never become a matter of curiosity or importance to them and, consequently, never come into their experience. So one of the great problems of human history is to decide when the human way of considering territory and range diverged from the way of all non-human primates. We think it's such a simple thing to walk ten miles in a straight line, and we would be surprised to find a tribe that didn't know 300–400 square miles. But this is wholly unique if we look at it from the point of view of the non-human primates. And this is what I mean when I say that from an ape's-eye view, certain problems emerge that are hardly mentioned in the literature at present.

How, then, could we decide when our ancestors stopped viewing a tiny range as normal and began to act as we do? Obviously, this answer can only come from archaeology, and I would like to suggest that archaeologists consider the notion of range as something of major importance to be investigated. The things which, so to speak, put the bite on the ape's view of range would be those matters that made it important to expand. For example, any substantial amount of hunting in an area of only two or three square miles would simply drive the game out of the area. Any large amount of hunting implies following wounded animals and, hence, moving over relatively large areas. So I think that as soon as we find that hunting is definitely a part of the record, we have to assume that the creatures involved were occupying much larger ranges than is the case with monkeys and apes. The materials used in tools may also be used to make an estimate, however crude, of the long-past ranges. If we can show that a kind of stone found in an archaeological site has its nearest source ten or fifteen miles away, then it is clear just from this that these animals occupied a larger range than contemporary non-human primates.

Another kind of problem that has come up repeatedly in our discussions is the question as to whether we should be surprised to find two or three species coexisting in one locality. In this case, if we take the ape's point of view, we find that nothing could be of less concern to an ape than whether or not there are half a dozen species in his locality. When I was working with Dr. Schultz in Borneo some years ago, we found ten species of primates of several different genera living in one small area. We collected nine of them but didn't collect any *Homo;* although collecting *Homo* is an old custom in that area of North Borneo. The notion that it is so complicated to have two or three kinds of *Homo* or two or three kinds of primates in the same place comes from looking backward from the present rather than considering the situation of the majority of monkeys and apes. If one goes into any part of the Old World tropical rain forest, one finds a great variety of monkeys and apes together. And I am sure that this must have been equally true in the past, when these forests were much more extensive.

The point has been brought out in discussion here that it would take a lot of ecological separation to permit the coexistence of the large *Australopithecus robustus* and the smaller *africanus.* Yet this is in total contradiction to everything we know about non-human primates. It doesn't take much ecological separation to have in one small area in Uganda three kinds of *Cercopithecus* monkeys, two kinds of *Colobus* monkeys, one kind of mangabey, and two kinds of apes. There is not much separation in such a case, and it seems to be sufficient that the different species can rely on different parts of the habitat in times of crisis. And this, I repeat, is a perfectly normal situation among the non-human primates.

What, then, is remarkable about man in these regards? Well, first, that he occupies a huge range—even the most minimal human behavior requires a great deal of space. And, second, man is unusual among the primates in that, as I interpret the record, there was only one kind of man after the Middle Pleistocene. And the reason for this is his culture. He was an efficient hunter, too tough to have any competition from other members of his species. He was making fire and complicated stone tools and was killing large animals. There is a calculus we can apply to this. The more our ancestors became like us in the sense of efficient toolmaking, fighting, hunting, making fires, and so on, the less likely it became that there would be two species of man living at the same time. It is not especially surprising that there should have been, say, two species at the *Australopithecus* level of time. The remarkable thing is that from *Homo erectus* on there is only one species. I think that this is a measure of the effectiveness of human culture. If we look at the ground-living baboons and the cats, who are very effective in their own way, we find that it takes at least a dozen species of these creatures to occupy the area that one species of Middle Pleistocene man occupied. Therefore, the lack of speciation is a measure of the effectiveness of culture.

Let's see what the ape would think about population density. All through the anthropological literature one finds the idea that as man became more and more effective, his population density increased. Of course, this is completely contrary to the ape's view of human evolution. If we look at the distribution of small monkeys or of baboons in Africa or in Southeast Asia today, we see that their density runs a hundred times as high as that of men living under hunting conditions. DeVore says the density of baboons in the Amboseli Reserve is on the order of twenty-five per square mile. Or let's take just ten per square mile, which would be the distribution in Nairobi Park. Estimates on hunting peoples are on the order of one per ten square miles—one percent of the distribution of baboons! Now, baboons aren't very successful if we compare them numerically to other non-human primates. *Cercopithecus aethiops,* the vervets that Struhsaker has been studying, go well over one hundred per square mile. And in one place, he estimates four hundred per square mile as the distribution of one species of monkey, and there are several other species in the same area.

It is only in exceedingly recent times that the population density of human beings has approached that of the non-human primates, largely since the beginning of agriculture. The reason for this is that man's ecological niche, so to speak, was his effectiveness over a great many climatic situations. He was effective from South Africa to China to Europe, and there is no species of non-human primates that even approaches this kind of range. But in any one part of this range, he was less well adapted than the local primates in that particular area. As Dr. Dobzhansky pointed out, the ability to adapt to a wide variety of situations is a characteristic of man, but this doesn't necessarily imply great adaptation to a local situation.

For example, a great deal is written about man's adaptation to the savannah. I would like to point out that if we take baboon adaptation to the savannah or that of the *entellus* monkey to ground-living in India as a standard, man is extraordinarily poorly adapted to the savannah. The animals can do without water for a very long time. When a troop of baboons comes in from a really hot day on the plains, what do they do? A few of them drink, but not very many; it just isn't very important to them. Man cannot eat most of the things on the savannah, so he needs the aid of cultural benefits to provide both food and water—something the baboons do not need at all. Man is remarkable, then, in the variety of habitats that he can occupy through cultural means—even far back in his evolution—but not in terms either of population density or special adaptation.

A point that DeVore and I have mentioned several times that seems worth stressing in this regard is the matter of a home base, a place that animals can return to. The non-human primates have no such place. They come back to different places after being out on the plains all day, and this means that the troop must always stay together. If animals are isolated, they have no place to go and become subject to predation. So one problem for archaeology that is exceedingly important is to decide whether early sites represent places where the animals were staying for considerable periods of time or simply occupied occasionally for a night.

To return to the point with which I began, let's take a look now at the question of learning, taken this time from an ape's point of view. As men, we learn so easily the things that we are interested in that we totally underestimate the great problem of origin. We drop questions of origin out of our pursuits and forget that it is not so much a question of learning skills or language in a limited sense but, rather, how we got the structure which enables us to learn language or tool skills that should really be the focus of our attention. There is a biology, then, that goes along with the evolution of culture up until very recent times, and one cannot consider the evolution of man's tools and behavior without considering the evolution of the biology. If you look at the general record, you find something on the order of two million years, according to the potassium–argon dates, where you find the use of only very crude pebble tools. This is incredibly slow evolution, if we think of it in relation to the Middle Pleistocene. Then, in turn, if we think of the rate of tool evolution in the next few hundred thousand years—Acheulian and the like—it is also incredibly slow by comparison with the rate for *Homo sapiens*. We are so accustomed to thinking of agriculture, the industrial revolution, and other things that operate solely at the cultural level in very short time spans that we underestimate the problem of the genetic development of a behavioral basis for learning over long-term human evolution.

Let's consider tool-use for a moment, since it is the easiest of these problems. George Schaller has shown that orangs tear off limbs and throw them, at least in the direction of George Schaller. This matter of tearing off limbs and shaking them appears to be widely-distributed behavior among the monkeys and apes, as Wallace thought a long time ago. According to Jane Goodall's excellent accounts, chimps show a wide range of tool-using activities—sticks to get at termites, sticks of a different size to get at fire ants, leaves to clean the body or to get water, and rocks for throwing or, according to observations in West Africa, for breaking palm nuts. Here, then, is a wide variety of use of objects by a pongid, a use that is very different from that of any animals other than primates. Jane Lancaster first pointed out to me that the tool-use of most non-primates is something very specific, such as the use of stones by sea otters or the use of a thorn by a particular kind of bird. This is one kind of behavior that is lodged in experience and in the central nervous system of the animal; while the chimp uses a variety of objects for a number of different objectives.

I think that we will discover that the behavior of the gorilla is far more like that of the chimpanzee than appears from present accounts. I am not criticizing George Schaller's excellent monograph, but the problem here is the length of the study and the conditions under which the study was made. Schaller was with the gorillas for less than 500 hours, and by this time in her study Goodall hadn't seen termiting, drinking, hunting, or many of the other things in her study that we consider the most important. This is my point here concerning primate studies, and it is very discouraging—

as when Irv DeVore pointed out that after 1,400 hours of observing baboons, we were completely wrong as regards their predation. This means that to get really accurate studies, they have to be long enough so that relatively infrequent kinds of behavior are well represented in the studies. And this requires about 2,000 hours, or about two or three years of work. Anyway, one reason I feel that the gorilla is going to be found to be really like the chimpanzee and should be classified in the same genus is, among many other comparisons, that the throwing behavior of gorillas in the zoos is exactly the same as that of chimps. This is not a general comparison but involves the precise way in which the gorilla holds things and the way he swings in throwing. And it's hard for me to believe that this behavior in all its details, so similar to that of the chimpanzee, occurs in the zoo but never in natural conditions.

If we return now to the general topic of the origin of tool-use in terms of human evolution, I'd like to stress two major different kinds of origin that have been brought out in papers by Hall, one of the top men in this field. One is the, so to speak, economic origin that we have already talked about here, and the other is the possible origin of tools in agonistic display. The chimpanzee throws rocks at creatures it is displaying against or pulls branches off trees and swings them, without hitting anything in either case. The gorillas do the same thing, so here are two species that use objects in agonistic display in such a way that they might eventually discover the effectiveness of hitting their target; even though this wouldn't represent an immediate economic return. I have always wondered how effective throwing and use of the club began. And I can imagine that if an animal was accustomed to relying on good big canine teeth for fighting and hunting, we would be very unhappy to substitute for those canines a club that was never used to hit the thing the animal was swatting at. In these apes, then, we have two different roots towards the development of tools, economic and agonistic. Again, there is no suggestion that these animals are close ancestors of ours. Whatever kind of phylogeny one wants to make of man, there are millions of years between anything like a human ancestor and the contemporary apes. There must have been millions of apes over millions of years using tools for economic and display purposes and, consequently, countless chances for the discovery of the potential effectiveness of these tools.

Tool origin seems to have taken a very long time, and if we look at the relation of tools to the brain, I think we can see why this is the case. I don't know why it should be so, but in anthropology we have stressed the cortex almost exclusively. I suppose this is because the cortex is particularly well-developed in man, but the cerebellum, which is concerned more with skill functions, is just as large as the cortex is. Our cerebellum is approximately three times the size of that of the great ape with large areas devoted to the thumb and the hand. And I think we should see in this difference in size and distribution the conclusion that the parts of the brain that are involved with skills must be greatly developed before tool-use will be effective. It is easy for us to learn manual skills, because our brains have evolved in accordance with these skills. But from an ape's point of view, the things that man does without effort—the detailed use of the fingers, and so on—are impossible and even inconceivable.

Another thing coming out of the work of Goodall and others that is contrary to what we usually think and say is the fact that the improvement of tools comes as early as does their use. The chimpanzee selecting something to termite with pulls off the side branches, tears off the leaves, and makes it the proper length. In other words, if the creature is intelligent enough to use tools in the first place, it doesn't just use whatever is lying around but selects something appropriate and then improves it. So, we can be pretty sure that improvement accompanied use way back before the introduction of any kind of stone tools or anything like the Oldowan Culture.

Now, I'd like to suggest that if something like tool-use is, so to speak, built into the brain, we have a variety of ways of comparing differences in the brain and differences in behavior and should be able to tighten down on this problem. The first index of whether something like manual skill is built into the brain can be found in the play of juveniles. Much of the social play of the non-human primates—rough chasing around and the like is comparable to social play in young human beings. But there is a class of object-play, in which the young human takes tremendous pleasure in fooling around with objects, that has no counterpart in non-human primates. It's true that if you put a monkey or ape in a cage furnished with nothing but one or two objects, I suspect that out of total boredom it will investigate the objects and push them around slightly. But this is very different from what young humans do with objects. One of the friends that met me at the airport had brought along a two-year-old, and I watched this kid fooling around. A stranger went over to a candy machine, stuck in some money, pushed a button, and got some candy. The kid immediately went over to the candy machine and pushed every point on it, obviously hoping to get a comparable reward. The non-human primates don't see this sort of combination and don't act this way at all. So, since manual dexterity is built into the brain and the biology of our species, it comes out in play in a very important way. And we can use the study of play to help us understand the background of contemporary human behavior.

In the language session, the same kind of thing was pointed out. Earl Count reminded us that the human infant, so to speak, plays with language in a way that non-human primates never do, and I believe this is entirely correct. Anyone who has watched and heard the behavior of children before speech realizes that they must have a built-in structure that leads to a quantity of babbling noises, which then can begin to form along the lines of the exceedingly simple rules outlined for us by Dr. Slobin. This is something else that simply never happens in the behavior of the other primates.

Another way of getting at these things is in terms of the ease of teaching animals. If an animal is biologically so constructed that something is easy for it to do, then we find that it's not very hard to teach it to do that sort of thing. And I think that it would be instructive to some people who talk a lot about learning to use tools to take a tame monkey and suffer through the problems of trying to teach the creature to do anything that we would regard as minimal effective use of tools. A couple of students were working on this last summer at Berkeley, and I must say that my admiration went out to the monkey for devising so many methods of obtaining the defined objectives without using the tools it was given. Unfortunately, the first tools given it were made of wood, and the monkey preferred the taste of the tools to that of the grapes that were supposed to be his reward. Seriously though, ease of learning—something that Dave Hamburg and I have discussed many times—is something built into an organism and represents things that have been favored by natural selection over the last many thousands of years. So, taken in this light, the pattern of ease of learning is a way that we can interpret the human long-past in detail—and I stress "in detail" as a perfectly feasible objective in this approach.

Again, I would like to draw a parallel with language and the point that Jane Lancaster made in the language session. You can't teach the non-human primates to name in any human sense, and the reason for this is that they do not have the structures in the central nervous system that are necessary for naming. They can learn that a certain color or shape will bring a reward, but they simply cannot learn naming. In terms of the origin of language, then, it is tremendously important to discover the beginnings of the ability to name and the factors that selected for a structural basis for naming during evolution. My own belief—and I think that Mrs. Lancaster would agree with this—is that the situation which originally led to naming was the making of tools. There may have been a couple of million years of making stone tools, far more complicated ones than any the chimpanzee makes, before the ability for naming was established.

In summary, I think that there are a number of tremendous problems that emerge almost for the first time when we look at human affairs from the standpoint of our knowledge of contemporary monkeys and apes. By reversing the usual perspective, we begin to wonder why language and manual skills and a broad concept of territory did not evolve in a very large number of primates over millions of years. I have used the word "tool," at least in speaking of Acheulian times and onwards, almost symbolically as something that stands for a very wide range of human abilities. And I think that if we look at the important things that humans can do and non-human primates can't do, we see that it amounts to much more than just language and tool skills. We can control our emotions, cooperate, learn, and plan to a degree that would be incomprehensible to any non-human primate. All these things depend on the human brain and are the structural results of human evolution, particularly during the past five or six hundred thousand years. And for this reason, behavioral genetics holds an important key to understanding human evolution. Huxley has said that man is closer to the apes than they are to the monkeys, but if we look at the major behavioral differences I have stressed, I think we'll find that man is truly very different from either.

6 / Emerging Man in Africa

RONALD SINGER

In this selection Singer brings to life the sequential story of man's evolutionary development in Africa. The continent of Africa, often referred to as the "cradle of mankind," reluctantly unfolds its past of more than 1 million years of hominid evolution. Singer traces the steps from early australopithecines to modern man by raising questions and attempting to answer them as they relate to the explanation of the ecological processes —the interaction of emerging man to his total environment. Of particular interest in Singer's article is the description of the way of life of early australopithecines as it relates to the need for development of the tool-making process. A few of the evolutionary steps outlined by Singer would be modified if the article were rewritten today, but the passage of time does not supersede Singer's lucid handling of the story of how man emerged in Africa.

The varied and generous African environment provided the lost paradise where the Hominidae separated from the Pongidae, and, during the course of ten million years, radiating forms moved along a number of evolutionary avenues. Many of these avenues led into a cul-de-sac, but some broadened into the human pathway.

The most significant phase in the study of human origins in the first half of the twentieth century was initiated in 1924 when Raymond A. Dart, then the Professor of Anatomy at the University of the Witwatersrand, recognized the importance of a fossil baboon skull brought to him by a student, Miss Josephine Salmons. The skull derived from a quarry being mined at Taung in Bechuanaland, whence shortly after parcels of pink, bone-bearing breccia—calcified sediment or debris cemented in blocks— were dispatched to Dart. Included therein was the endocranial cast or mold of the interior of the skull, as well as parts of the broken skull into which it fitted. He immediately observed with great excitement that the mold was three times the size of a baboon brain and larger than that of any adult chimpanzee. These remains represented the now-famous juvenile *Australopithecus* ("southern ape") *africanus,* which Dart described in 1925 when he indicated the unique presence of hominid characteristics in an otherwise pongid skull. In the face of an effusive series of critical and unbelieving blasts from experts outside Africa, Dart, with his Australian tenacity, persisted in his initial conclusion. Only eleven years later Dart's insight was irrevocably supported by Robert Broom's recovery of the brain cast and skull of *Plesianthropus* (now *Australopithecus*) *transvaalensis,* fondly termed "Mrs. Ples." Subsequent discoveries stimulated research and discussion throughout the anthropological world—some seeking to disprove, others trying to support the descriptions of the many australopithecine fossils found in South Africa.

Thus it was under a cloud that *Australopithecus,* the first of the primitive hominids, was born. Since 1925 skeletal remains of about 100 individuals have been recovered in the Transvaal at Sterkfontein, Kromdraai, Swartkrans, and Makapan Limeworks. Out of this series have crystallized two genera, *Australopithecus* and *Paranthropus* (which some scientists believe should be merged into the former), two species, and four subspecies.

The most spectacular of these Transvaal sites are the caves at Sterkfontein and in the Makapan Valley. In caverns, water-eroded or dissolved out of massive hills of dolomite and travertine, the fossilized remains of hundreds of mammals (antelopes, carnivores, rodents, baboons, australopithecines, and many others) are now found cemented by lime into the floors, which have been disturbed by roof falls and by miners' blasting operations. The success of the miners has resulted in innumerable headaches for the paleontologist and geologist.

When scientists were first brought to the Makapan Limeworks caves they found large ramifying blast holes in the side of the hill. Study and analysis later revealed the likely sequence of events prior to economic excavations. At some depth below the surface, probably more than a million years ago, a large cavern was formed by water action on the limestone. Subsequently, through formation and enlargement of cracks in the roof, a large block of dolomite crashed to the floor, partly sealing off the lower part of the cavern and creating another cavern above it. After a further period of time, water action caused much of the roof to collapse onto the floor of the upper cavern, so that the "cave" now had a large communication with the exterior. Naturally, while all of this was going on, percolating water also produced channels deeper down so that lower caverns, which could later communicate with the upper ones, were also being created.

When the sediments were being washed into the cave, large amounts of animal bones were also being deposited on the sloping floor at various places. The four primary questions that arise are:

Were all the bones, which include a small percentage of australopithecine remains, brought in by different carnivores using the cave as a lair during a long period of time?

Alternatively, are the fossil remains a midden resulting from australopithecine occupation?

Did australopithecines alternate with carnivores in occupying this vast, ramifying cave?

Is this a midden of a more human animal whose victims included the australopithecines?

Carnivores and rodents have undoubtedly played a part in the cave story, but as yet it cannot be decisively determined, in the absence of any lithic industry at the Makapan Limeworks caves, whether or not the australopithecines occupied them or were only part of the remains of predatory activities of carnivores or some, as yet undiscovered, more advanced hominid form. At Swartkrans there is suggestion of the latter animal in the few fragmentary remains of *Telanthropus,* which may ultimately prove to represent a pithecanthropine. Professor Dart has continuously maintained that the majority of the bony remains were tools of the australopithecines. However, I am not convinced that any of these bones were *fashioned,* or manufactured, into tools, although it is obvious that any sharp or blunt bony object may have been *utilized* as a tool. In the light of the fact that in South Africa the australopithecine remains have been recovered exclusively from cave deposits, it has been assumed that the ape men were cave dwellers. But if one considers their remains merely as a small part of, and scattered among, the large assemblage of fossilized fauna, then their cave-dwelling nature is purely an assumption, not a conclusion. Actually, the great depth of the caverns, the ape men's lack of knowledge of fire, and the geological evidence of the presence of substantial amounts of subterranean water during the main period of bone deposition work against such an assumption. Furthermore, elsewhere, australopithecine remains have been recovered from open-site deposits, namely Olduvai Gorge, Laetolil, Lake Chad, Jordan Valley, and Java. That such primitive hunters and gatherers of food would have dwelt in caves seems to be an unproved and unlikely behavioral pattern.

One aspect of the possible habits of australopithecines requires comment. At this very early stage of human history it is probable that the man-apes were living either in troops like modern baboons or in family units like modern gorillas. They lived in an environment dominated by giant mammals, such as now-extinct forms of elephant, hyena, wild pig and wart hog, saber-tooth tiger, rhino, lion, baboon—animals that are best avoided in open combat. So far as the man-apes were concerned, despite powerful, large jaws, their canines lacked a "ripping" quality, and gripping hands were the substitutes for claws. Here, then, was the challenge that required astuteness, experience, and the ability to improvise in a difficult situation. Brute strength or speedy legs did not constitute a sufficient defense mechanism, but sharp wits were required as well as the ability to throw stones, wield sticks, and grapple efficiently. The latter may have involved the creation of the idea of teamwork: while one individual held away an animal's savage jaws, another would respond to the call of alarm and move in with a rock, stave, or heavy bone and bludgeon the beast to death. Survival of the relatively defenseless australopithecines may have depended on the development of an efficient communicating system. Consequently, the dangerous environment, interacting with an innate mechanism and ability to adapt rapidly, created the humanizing tendencies. The freed hands and the enlarging brain were the major devices required to open the evolutionary doors to technological skill and social success. The australopithecine remains represent about 100 individuals, which in general were small animals. The *Australopithecus* female, slender and broad-hipped, weighed roughly 60 pounds, the *Paranthropus* probably half as much again. They were essentially bipedal, and had skulls with a combination of characteristics specific to both pongids and hominids. The hominid jaws, teeth, palatal contour, and jawbone are set against a small pongid cranium resting on a projecting, heavy-jowled face. The pelvis and vertebral column are much more like those of a true man than of any ape.

The Transvaal fossils are real "links" and they demonstrate that the anatomical requirements for the erect posture were present before the brain expanded. It would appear that the concomitant attributes of freed upper limbs, such as the manufacture of tools, the development of a technical tradition, and various "superior" sociological adaptations, were advances associated with an enlarging brain. At the Sterkfontein site there are two distinct phases. The earlier contains abundant *Australopithecus* remains (more than 100 specimens) and this extensive deposit has revealed not a trace of stone artifacts or even foreign stone. Overlying this is a more recent breccia with very scanty *Australopithecus* fossils, but here there are complex stone artifacts, which are less sophisticated than the hand ax culture associated with pithecanthropine remains in North Africa (Ternifine and Sidi Abderahman).

The *Australopithecus* remains at Makapan Limeworks are not associated with any stone tools, so that, in general, it can be stated that about 95 per cent of the remains of this genus are clearly not found with stone implements, while about 5 per cent, at only one site, are associated with an early Chelles-Acheul industry. If the australopithecines manufactured stone implements, and there is no way yet of establishing this, then by definition, they were "human," or true men. However, if the australopithecines were not tool-makers, as would seem possible, then there was present at that time a more advanced form whose victims were these ape men and who were the successful competitors for that particular environment. In the evolutionary sense it appears that the presently known australopithecines were "too late" to be the direct ancestors of true man, but they were very close to those ancestors and may constitute an experimental cul-de-sac that radiated from the true hominid ancestral stock.

Geological and faunal evidence available at the South African sites indicates that the earlier Sterkfontein deposit is the oldest (Lower Pleistocene), followed by the Makapan Limeworks, and then the later phase of Sterk-fontein. Only *Australopithecus* has been recovered from these sites. This sequence is followed by the deposit at Swartkrans and then that at Krom-draai, and these two sites are typified by the occurrence of *Paranthropus*. The pithecanthropine *Telanthropus,* as well as stone tools, make their appearance at the time of the later deposition at Sterkfontein. It is of con-sequence to recognize that when *Paranthropus* arrived on the evolutionary scene, toolmaking was already an established industry.

Corroborative evidence of the wide distribution of the ape men in Africa was recently uncovered by Mary Leakey in the vast bone repository in the Olduvai Gorge of Tanganyika, where a systematic fossil hunt has been pursued for about 30 years. This australopithecine skull was dubbed "nutcracker man" by Louis Leakey, because of the large, squarish teeth in the upper jaw, and he referred the material to a new genus, *Zinjanthro-pus,* but it is highly likely that instead it is another species of *Paranthropus.* On the same level (in Bed I) as "Zinj" were also the remains of many mammals and a large number of stone artifacts. In respect to the latter, the questions once again arise: was "Zinj" the manufacturer or was he the victim of those stone bludgeons, manufactured by a more advanced con-temporaneous form? In other words was he the killer or the kill? The latter is suggested by such indirect evidence as: (a) the nature of the as-sociated remains does not differ particularly from the thousands of fossil remains, many similarly grouped, found elsewhere at Olduvai; (b) some of the remains of "Zinj," adult and juvenile, are found scattered in the same area; and (c) a similar scanty distribution of man-ape fragments relative to extensive faunal remains is seen elsewhere, where no stone artifacts have been recovered.

Late in 1960, a large fragment of the lower jaw and two bones (pa-rietals) of a skull of juvenile age (possibly of one individual) were re-covered in Bed I, some feet lower than the "Zinj level" and a short distance away. Some teeth, two clavicles, a portion of a foot, six finger bones, and two ribs were also found. Although Dr. Leakey refers to this site as a "pre-*Zinjanthropus* level," it is not clear what the time lapse between the two levels really was. However, it is probable that it was short. A satisfac-tory reconstruction of the parietal bones is doubtful, and at this early stage of their study it seems that the jaw and cranial bones belonged to a young australopithecine, possibly a species of *Australopithecus.* The juvenile pa-rietal bones are cracked but the fracture is typical of the result of gen-eralized pressure of the tons of soil and rock resting on it rather than the dramatic "murder" first attributed to it in the newspapers. In any event, "murder" is a term applicable only in relation to laws of human society.

The remarkable little australopithecines were not confined only to the Transvaal and Tanganyika. It should be mentioned that as early as 1939 the latter area provided evidence of the presence of these ape men when some australopithecine-like teeth were discovered by Kohl-Larsen on the

Serengeti Plains, not too distant from Olduvai. In faraway Java an australo-pithecine jaw was recovered just before the Second World War, and during 1961 remains of man-apes were reported both from Lake Chad in North Africa and from northern Israel. Thus we are getting a clearer impression of the widespread nature of the australopithecines, indicating probable migrations over thousands of years extending through the terminal Pliocene and early Pleistocene, which resulted in adaptation to new environments, for better or for worse. We cannot yet assess when and why man-apes ultimately became extinct.

What of the earliest recognized true man in Africa? From the Olduvai Gorge came news in late 1960 of the discovery of "Chellean Man," named because of associations with relatively advanced implements. He could be considered on the same relative evolutionary footing as *Pithecanthropus* from Java and China, the earliest toolmakers who knew the use of fire. Chellean Man could be considered as an African variant of the genus, with more massive bony supraorbital projections and a number of other minor variations. In North Africa at Ternifine, in Algeria, three human lower jaws were found with many faunal remains and Chelles-Achel implements. It is considered that these jaws (unhappily placed in a new genus, *Atlanthropus*) also belong to the African *Pithecanthropus* complex. The pithecanthropines, with their distinct hominid posture and with only a few ape-like features, constitute essentially a stage of mankind that is ancestral to the later forms, Neanderthal Man and modern *Homo sapiens*. Early pithecanthropines probably overlapped in time and territory with the australopithecines, and may have survived to less than 400,000 years ago.

Although the term Neanderthal Man should be strictly reserved for those stocky, cold-adapted men who occupied the continent of Europe during, at least, the first cold phase of the last glaciation, about 100,000 years ago, one is tempted to interpret similar morphological types living contemporaneously in Africa and Asia as racial variants of the Neander-thals. The immediate post-pithecanthropine phase is at present represented in Africa by two skulls, one from Broken Hill in Northern Rhodesia (Rhodesian Man) and the other 2,000 miles to the south, from Hopefield in South Africa (Saldanha Man). About thirty years ago the fragmentary remains of another beetle-browed individual were discovered approximately 1,000 miles north of Broken Hill near the shores of Lake Eyasi on the Serengeti Plains, not far distant from the Olduvai Gorge. The badly pre-served remains were tentatively reconstructed and named *Africanthropus*. Incorrectly placed in a new genus, the *Africanthropus* probably represents a form of *Homo* that is closely related to the Broken Hill and to the Saldanha skulls.

The Broken Hill skull was discovered in the lowest part of what had been a subterranean cave that was blasted open by miners in 1921. As in the case of the Limeworks caves, the skull, fossilized faunal remains, and artifacts accumulated at the bottom of a sloping floor. The skull is massive, with thick, projecting brow ridges, surmounted by a flat, sloping forehead. It is so gross-looking that for many years some scientists preferred to consider it as a pathological anomaly—an acromegalic. However, this doubt was dispelled when, in 1953, the author and a field assistant recovered fragments of a skull at Hopefield that, when reconstructed, was indisputably akin to Rhodesian Man. The new discovery was named Saldanha Man because of the proximity of Hopefield to the historically known Saldanha Bay. The site is on a farm called "Elandsfontein," and consists of a large eroded area (about 2.5 miles by 1.5 miles in size) in the bushy Sandveld. During the ten years of field work I carried out with teams of students and colleagues, more than 20,000 fossils and about 6,000 stone artifacts have been recovered from the surface of the fossiliferous floors that lie between the 40-foot-high sand dunes of Elandsfontein farm.

This remarkable, fossil-strewn site must be seen to be believed. Almost every foot of the surface between the dunes reveals a recognizable fossilized bone as well as hundreds of minute chips of fragmented bone. From this site more than 35 mammalian genera and many more species have already been diagnosed. These animals represent a mixture of the grassland and bushveld faunas, a situation seen today around the Etosha Pan in South West Africa, where arid conditions have forced these two different types of fauna to congregate around the only constant drinking place in a vast region. The Hopefield fauna, 20 per cent of which are extinct forms, occupied the site during the period extending from the tail end of the Middle Pleistocene to the early part of the Upper Pleistocene of southern Africa—that is, about 200,000 to about 100,000 years ago. The breakdown of the faunal forms, coupled with pollen analysis, leads to a picture of the landscape at that time—open savanna country merging with distant scrub and bushveld, and forested regions scattered toward the mountains on the horizon.

About 15 miles from Hopefield is another fossil site at Langebaanweg. Here, too, commercial interests have unearthed a wealth of fossils—the upper layers overlap the Hopefield period, while the lower, phosphate-bearing strata are yielding fossils of a Lower and Middle Pleistocene epoch: three-toed zebrines, archaic elephants, and short-necked giraffids. Sea invasion of the extensive site (about six square miles) is indicated by the presence of numerous sharks' teeth scattered among some of the mammalian remains. If a hominid should be discovered here, it may well prove to be another "key" form in the intricate evolutionary mosaic.

Thus Saldanha and Rhodesian Man, who, although found 2,000 miles apart, are alike as brother and sister (in the evolutionary sense), represent the African variation of the Neanderthal equivalent of Europe and of Asia. Interestingly, the African and Asian forms are more like each other than either is to the European form. We can picture that distant period as having three major racial variants of mankind on three major continents, which, though separated by distance, came into contact with each other by intercontinental migrations, sharing their cultures and mixing their stocks so as to blend the later, more modern forms of mankind.

7 / The Real Adam

ROBERT T. ANDERSON

*When did man become man? At what time? At what place? Where in
the evolutionary scheme of things can we say, "Here is the first man"?
Too often students and laymen expect to find the answers to these questions when there are no answers. At this point frustration and misunderstanding may set in. But they shouldn't; the simple truth is that there was
no first man, no missing link; there are several "first men" and several
"missing links." In this selection Robert T. Anderson, in a brilliant yet
simple manner, tells us why there can never be agreement on the question of who the first man was.*

I remember having seen a television program in which the entertain-
ment focused upon three individuals, each of whom claimed to be a certain
person, someone such as Mr. John Doe, the first man to climb Mt. Some-
thing-or-other. A panel of judges was allowed to ask questions, but eventually each judge had to state his conclusion as to which of the three
truly was the person they all claimed to be, and which were the im-
posters. After a suitable pause for a commercial, the climax came when
the moderator requested, "Will the real John Doe please stand up?" With
that, the audience learned who actually was the man they all claimed to
be. My remembrance of this program quickened as I was thinking about
the question of who the first real man might have been. We have a number
of candidates with a claim to being the true Adam, and of the evidence
we have, we need to be able to ask, "Will the real Adam please stand up?"

Anthropologists speak of *Australopithecus* as unquestionably a true
man (hominid), and most agree that when we get more information on
Ramapithecus we will find that he too is a man rather than an ape. I am
going to suggest that neither of these was the real Adam, but in order to
argue this point, I need first to draw attention to an unexamined assumption which tends to distort this kind of inquiry.

As concerns the first appearance of man, we tend unconsciously to think
in terms of the biblical tradition of an instantaneous creation. We tend to

assume, even when we think in evolutionary terms, that one day (or in one millennium or one epoch), man more or less suddenly appeared. Yet it is clear that the appearance of man was a gradual event stretched over a very long period of time measured in millions of years. Because the evolutionary process is so drawn out, it is impossible to say when one species of animal has given place to another. Speaking in terms of grades tends to obscure this fact, since grades constitute artificial, more or less arbitrary breaks in what in fact was an endless sequence of successive generations, each very much like its predecessor. Even with grades, however, it can be difficult to say when advanced apes have been replaced by primitive men.

Ramapithecus and *Australopithecus* are termed hominids because they had some of the characteristics of modern man, and in particular because they had upright posture and the ability to use tools. I do not object to calling them hominids on those grounds. Let us say they were hominids. But then to be a hominid need mean no more than that you are a bipedal, tool-using primate. It describes you and me. But it also describes Pliocene and Pleistocene primates whose small brains and primordial cultures make them seem far more akin to progressive apes than to *Homo sapiens.*

Call these earlier creatures hominids if you will, but let it be clearly understood that man as we know him today did not appear until much later. Who was Adam? If Adam was capable of family loyalty, if Adam had a soul, if he could speak, then Adam was *Homo erectus* and lived at least 300,000 years ago. But if in addition to these gifts, Adam had a sensitivity which made him care tenderly for his less fortunate kinsmen and worry about their souls when they died, then Adam was Neanderthal man of roughly 125,000 years ago. Or, if Adam had all of these abilities, but surpassed them in the poetic synthesis made possible only by art, music, and dance, and if Adam had a brain shaped for the first time just like ours, then Adam was *Homo sapiens* of as early as perhaps 40,000 years ago. Finally, if Adam was the first man to evolve a way of life that survived into historic and modern times as hunting and gathering peoples who laid the groundwork for the rise of civilization, then he was Mesolithic man of no more than some 20,000 years ago.

Who was Adam? He never existed. At no one point did the ape suddenly become a man. Over several million years, man's humanity grew. It is growing still, and our understanding of this gradual process is distorted if we attempt to interpret it in terms of prescientific concepts.

From "More Complete View of Man's Ancestors," *Science News*, Vol. 99, No. 9, 1971, p. 141. Reprinted by permission of The Institution for the Popularization of Science.

8 / More Complete View of Man's Ancestors

SCIENCE NEWS

As additional fossil remains of human lineage are found and dated, the jigsaw puzzle of man's development becomes more complete. This article considers the position of early fossil finds from the Lake Rudolf area in Kenya, Africa. One current theory on evolution contends that modern man evolved, within the past 2 million years, from Australopithecus, *a form having physical traits of both man and ape. Fossil remains from around Lake Rudolf suggest that the man–ape line can be pushed back about 5.5 million years. Two interpretations are likely. First, if the Lake Rudolf fossils are indeed* Australopithecus, *this strengthens the case for placing* Australopithecus *in an ancestral line leading to* Homo habilis. *Second, if the Lake Rudolf fossils are actually* Homo habilis, *this suggests that both* Australopithecus *and* Homo habilis *existed at about the same time, and that* Australopithecus *could be excluded from man's ancestry. Although detailed studies on these Lake Rudolf fossils will take some time to conclude, the reader can easily see in this selection how the sudden discovery of additional fossil remains contributes toward a more complete view of man's past.*

Man and ape share a common ancestry. That idea is no longer questioned. But our picture of the nature of a common ancestor, the point in evolution where the hominid line diverged from the pongid or ape line, and of the course of evolution of man-like life forms is cloudy.

New discoveries, however, have consistently pushed back scientific estimates of when man's ancestors originated. Almost 50 years ago, the skull of an infant primate was discovered in South Africa and given the name *Australopithecus.* The skull was found in deposits of ages of less than a million years. Since then, numerous other *Australopithecus* specimens have been unearthed. Somewhat later, Dr. Louis S. B. Leakey discovered in Olduvai Gorge in Tanzania a specimen that some experts classify as *Australopithecus,* and others maintain is instead a *Paranthropus,* another form of early hominid, that was 1.75 million years old. He originally called it *Zinjanthropus,* or nut-cracker man. An arm bone fragment from Kanapoi near the southern end of Lake Rudolf in northern Kenya dated in 1967 at 2.5 million years old has recently been found to be actually more than 4 million years in age.

But there is still a large gap between these forms and the man–ape *Ramapithecus,* the oldest form that most authorities admit to the hominid line. *Ramapithecus* is 14 million years old.

On a 1967 expedition to the Lake Rudolf region, a team led by Prof. Bryan Patterson, Agassiz Professor of Vertebrate Paleontology at Harvard University, discovered a jawbone fragment from the oldest specimen of the *Australopithecus* line yet recovered. After careful analysis of the specimen and dating of the sediments at Lothagam Hill where it was found, the scientists announced last week that the jaw fragment is about 5.5 million years old.

This age, though significantly older than previous finds, "is not unexpected now" says Dr. T. Dale Stewart, a physical anthropologist at the Smithsonian Institution. Scientists have steadily been pushing back the ages of *Australopithecus* ever since the first specimen was discovered.

The specimen, found by Arnold D. Lewis, head of the preparation laboratory of Harvard's Museum of Comparative Zoology, which sponsored the expedition, is part of the right half of a lower jaw. Prof. Patterson believes that the jaw represents a species close to *Australopithecus africanus,* of which numerous specimens are known from areas in South Africa.

The bone belonged to a being that, says Prof. Patterson, "we would recognize as closely related to ourselves if we were to see it alive today." The age of locations where *A. africanus* has been found is not precisely known, but it now appears that they were older than the Olduvai succession. If so, the researchers say, *A. africanus* could have been an ancestor of the form that appears at the base of that succession, *Homo habilis.* The other hominid of that period, *Paranthropus* (late Pliocene–early Pleistocene), had a different gait from the lineage that ultimately led to modern man and is now known to have had a long history independent of the *Australopithecus* line. The new specimen, says Dr. Patterson, appears to be distinct from *Paranthropus,* suggesting that the two lineages may have diverged in the early Pliocene, which began 13 million years ago.

Prof. Patterson tentatively identifies the jawbone fragment as a female's, as the jaw appears slightly smaller than in other *Australopithecus* finds. The fragment's single tooth is well worn, indicating, he says, a mature individual and an abrasive diet. The creature was probably omnivorous.

The find is the oldest member of the hominoid family yet found in deposits of Pliocene–Pleistocene age. It was the Pleistocene epoch that saw the advances and retreats of the glacial ice sheets. The immediately preceding epoch, the Pliocene, began about 12 million years ago. It is now evident, the paleontologists say, that the human lineage was evolving throughout this stretch of time and that the beginnings of the hominid line occurred still earlier.

The Lake Rudolf area, says Dr. Stewart, is the only place in Africa where such accurate dating is possible, because of volcanic deposits that permit potassium–argon dating. The area also yields many mammalian fossils, particularly elephants, which were evolving rapidly at that time and provide relatively accurate age indications.

From "Adaptation and Race," by Jean Hiernaux, *The Advancement of Science,* Vol. 23, April, 1967, pp. 658–662. Reprinted by permission of the British Association for the Advancement of Science.

9 | Adaptation and Race

JEAN HIERNAUX

Previous selections have dealt with the problems of how man became man. In this selection by Jean Hiernaux, we turn to a consideration of the reasons some groups of modern man differ from other groups. It is a simple matter to observe that all individuals are not alike in appearance and that groups also differ in appearance. Too often these differences are merely referred to as racial differences without understanding what a race is and how racial groups are formed. Hiernaux looks at the misunderstood problem of race by providing a definition of race, describing the processes of adaptation, and relating adaptation to race formation. He skillfully uses examples of the evolutionary processes of mutation, hybridization, and genetic drift to explain race formation (past and present) as a result of man's ability to adapt to local environmental situations. Hiernaux's concept of race as a genetic population is consistent with the current use of the understanding of the dynamics leading to human diversity.

Before developing the theme of this paper, it is necessary to define what is meant by the terms "Race" and "Adaptation."

The adjective "racial" refers to the hereditary patrimony. Two groups will be said to differ racially in skin color, for instance, if they differ in their collective hereditary patrimony, or "gene pool," for this feature. "Racial" is thus synonymous with "genetical" when the latter adjective is applied to groups of people. "Genetical" should be used in preference to "racial" because it is unequivocal.

An observed difference between two groups may be a matter of a difference between the gene pools, or of different environments influencing the expression of identical gene pools, or the combined effect of differences in environment and in gene pool. For, in most features, the individual's heredity determines only a range of possible values, within which his real value depends on his environment. Skin color, for instance, is influenced by sun-tanning, and weight by diet. It is of great theoretical and practical importance to distinguish how much in a difference is genetical, and how much is expressional.

In the matters that concern us now, we look to groups of people as to gene pools. We must therefore define them in genetical terms. The unit of study is called the breeding or mendelian population, or, in short, the population. This unit denotes a group of people who share in a common gene pool because they intermarry without internal geographical, social or other barriers while an effective barrier—usually a relative one —separates them from other populations.

Many anthropologists are interested also in larger units, called races. It has however been questioned whether human diversity can objectively be cut into such large discrete units, and an increasing number of biological anthropologists are convinced that the arbitrary element in any subdivision of mankind into races is such that the procedure entails more confusion than simplification. As a matter of fact, classificatory schemes of mankind currently proposed number nearly as many as the classifiers themselves; they differ greatly in the number and their method of delimitation of races. A group of 22 biological anthropologists from all over the world, assembled in 1964 by UNESCO in order to give their views on the biological aspects of the race question, stated that "many anthropologists, while stressing the importance of human variation, believe that the scientific interest of these classifications is limited, and even that they carry the risk of inviting abusive generalizations." This risk is evident. For instance, you may find an African population more similar to an Asian one in its ABO blood group frequencies, and to a European one in its fingerprints frequencies, than to another African population near to it by its total gene pool. What is observed in a population is valid only for that population. Extrapolation is not permissible in anthropology because each population is unique in its combinations of gene frequencies.

Turning now to the term "adaptation"—this will be understood here as a modification leading to a better performance in a specific environment. In this sense, it does not include those modifications of behavior which are aimed at avoiding a stress, for instance a lowered muscular activity in the heat. How important such behavioral responses are compared with adaptation as defined above will not be discussed here. In many situations, man has evolved the capacity to achieve adaptation through nonbiological, or cultural, changes. He can resist cold, for instance, by clothes and house-heating. Biological adaptation, usually interwoven with cultural adaptation, presents as several different categories. The adult retains a limited plasticity which allows him, for example, to increase his performance during a period of hard work in a hot environment, a phenomenon usually called acclimatization. It is reversible, though its effects may be of long duration. Plasticity is much more pronounced during development, and may then affect morphology as well as function. In some situations, environment induces deviations in the morphological development which are adaptive to it, and which are irreversible once growth has stopped. Such an adaptation through developmental plasticity, like acclimatization, is not transmitted by heredity.

There is only one way by which an adaptation can become fixed in the gene pool of a population: it is through selection. In this case, "performance" in the stated definition of adaptation means survival. Suppose that, for a given hereditary trait, a population possesses two genes, A and B, in its gene pool. Since genes go by pairs, an individual may be AA, AB, or BB. If the AA adults contribute more to the next generation than the AB's and BB's (by having more children, dying less often before reproducing, or by both mechanisms), gene A will increase in frequency from one generation to the next until the frequency of B is reduced to nil. If AA is advantageous only in certain environments, while other environments favor BB, the absence of gene B in the former environments, and of A in the latter ones, are cases of genetic adaptation. Such an extreme contrast of 0 and 100 per cent gene frequencies is probably very rare amongst human populations, if it even exists. On the contrary, what seems quite common is the case in which genotype AB is favored, in some environments at least, compared with both AA and BB, by a value depending on a variable of the environment. In this situation, selection leads to an equilibrium between the frequencies of A and B, the level of which depends on the intensity of the selective agent. The result is called "balanced polymorphism," and the process responsible for it is called "heterosis." The best known example of it in man, and the only one that seems really elucidated today, concerns the chemical composition of the hemoglobin, the red pigment of the blood. Some populations possess two variants of hemoglobin, each determined by a single gene: the so-called "normal" hemoglobin A, and the sicklemic hemoglobin S. SS individuals usually die before reaching puberty, and therefore leave no progeny, while the AS's display a higher genetic fitness than AA's by being more resistant to malignant malaria, a great killer of children in a large part of the world. In a malarious population in which these genes are present, the frequencies of A and S genes tend to an equilibrium which represents an adaptation to the severity of malaria.

Since we are dealing with the theme "Adaptation and Race," and the concept of race having been reduced to that of gene pool, the question is: "How much of the differences in gene pool between human populations represents genetic adaptation?"

For evaluating the extent of genetic adaptation, we must first consider the other factors making for differences between gene pools, and weigh their possible importance in the genesis of current human diversity. They are: mutations, hybridization, and random fluctuation or genetic drift.

Mutations, which produce new genes, are rare phenomena, and are incapable of generating notable frequencies of the mutant genes unless they are backed by adaptive selection, the mechanism of which has been just described, or unless genetic drift or related mechanisms happen to multiply the mutants. It is important to note that mutations might provide different materials for building equivalent balanced polymorphisms in different parts of the world. For example, the A–S hemoglobin polymorphism is present in malarious areas of Africa, Arabia, India, and Southern Europe. An A–E hemoglobin polymorphism is present in malarious southeastern Asia and maybe represents an adaptive equivalent of the A–S polymorphism, in an area where the hazards of mutations created gene E but no gene S as mutants from gene A. A more complex A–S–C hemoglobin polymorphism is found in a western African area, with an extension through the Sahara up to North Africa and Sicily. It is not clear whether E and C compete or respond to different environmental stresses (even for S, it now appears that resistance to malaria is not the whole story; resistance to leprosy has also been evidenced). Still other genetic polymorphic systems, like thalassemia and an inherited enzyme (glucose-6-phosphate dehydrogenase) deficiency are also suspected as responding to malaria. In some populations, they coexist with the A–S polymorphism; how they interact with it is still unclear. As all this shows, the effect of genetical adaptation depends not only on the nature and intensity of the environmental stress, but also on the genes present in the gene pool. It is the very rarity of mutations that makes them play a role —an indirect one—in the diversity of human populations.

Hybridization of a population means immigration of genes from a different mendelian population. This process shifts the gene frequencies of the first population in the direction of those of the second, by an amount proportional to the relative influx of genes. Hybridization unceasingly changes the pattern of differences between the world's populations, but its levelling effect excludes it as a source of the human diversity.

Random fluctuations in gene frequencies, or genetic drift, increase with a decrease in population size. The theory of probability shows indeed that large populations are likely to keep stable in their gene frequencies, while restricted ones tend to show fluctuating frequencies, a tendency possibly leading to the loss or fixation of genes. Until the discovery and diffusion of means of food production (agriculture and stock raising), a recent event indeed when compared with the duration of man's evolution, mankind was composed of small bands of hunter–gatherers, disposing each of a large territory. In those circumstances genetic drift surely met favorable opportunities of acting all over the world. Two kinds of events are capable of producing sudden changes in gene frequencies, which are similar to the generation-to-generation genetic drift by the fact that they are nondirectional and only statistically predictable. In the first one, a small group of individuals leaves a large population and founds a new one. The resulting "founder effect" had many opportunities to operate in the past. Most African tribes, for instance, claim to have originated by such a process. The second kind of event is a sharp reduction in the number of a population by war, epidemics, or natural cataclysms, all events which repeatedly struck mankind.

Genetic drift is much more powerful on these traits which are determined by one gene, like blood groups and hemoglobin types, than on traits whose hereditary component consists in a number of independent genes acting additively, like body size, proportions, and most descriptive traits. These multifactorial traits, however, show no less diversity between human populations than monofactorial traits. This suggests that adaptation is a paramount factor in the genesis of the genetic diversity between human populations.

This conclusion has been reached by exclusion of other factors as main sources of diversity. To demonstrate cases of selective adaptation is by no means easy in the human species. Man is unique in his cultural capacity for modifying his environment, and in the extent and frequency with which his populations migrate or change the size of their territory. An observed polymorphism may very well reflect an adaptation to an environment quite different from the one in which the population now lives: gene frequencies can change but slowly; the population may be a relatively recent newcomer in its current environment, or it may have modified its environment recently by cultural means (think of the effects of eradicating malaria on the hemoglobin polymorphism). Thanks to a technological innovation giving it advantage over the surrounding ones, a population may have enormously spread its size and territory over a variety of environments and replaced local populations which were better adapted biologically to their milieu. Given mankind's history, even a moderate association between a gene frequency and an environmental variable, like the one between S hemoglobin gene and malaria, looks highly suggestive of genetic adaptation.

The search for such associations between a gene frequency and a quantified aspect of the environment is actively pursued by a number of anthropologists. It is impeded by the fact that few aspects of the environment are properly quantified on a world scale yet. The best known attributes of the milieu are climatic variables, yet it seems probable that blood hereditary characteristics, which constitute today the vast majority of known monofactorial traits, are sensitive mainly to pathological factors, the intensity of which remains to be scientifically established in large parts of the world. Moreover, some data suggest that infectious agents themselves change their properties as a genetic adaptation to the human host, at the rapid rate permitted by their short life cycle. It might therefore be that selective pressure from pathology is highly variable in time on some systems. In the field of monofactorial traits, the evidence for adaptation as the main source of human diversity still rests more on theoretical grounds than on factual verification.

Demonstrating genetical adaptation is still more difficult in the case of multifactorial traits, like stature, weight, and bodily proportions. Most, if not all of them present an "expressional" component in their diversity, the isolation of which is no easy task. For instance, body weight, a feature partly determined by heredity, manifests a statistical tendency to be lower in human populations living in the tropics. There are theoretical reasons to believe that a low weight is physiologically advantageous in a hot climate, and some experimental verification of this advantage has been made. On the other hand, we know that nutrition is poorer, as an average, in the tropical zone than in the temperate one, and that diet directly affects weight. How much is genetical and how much is expressional in the association of mean weight with latitude? Two African populations of different origin living side by side in Rwanda for several centuries and eating similar diets today show largely different weight to stature ratios. A genetical component is here evidenced in the difference, but we do not precisely know in which climate the two groups have lived in the past; this prevents us from testing any hypothesis identifying a specific climatic variable to which genetical adaptation would have occurred. Research into the association of several anthropometrical variables with climate in sub-Saharan Africa is now in progress. It has revealed many significant associations, many of which convincingly involve some genetical adaptation. Weight shows a significant correlation with several climatic variables, but human plasticity for it is so marked that one can but hesitate to identify those variables as selective agents on the basis of such evidence. At the same time, we must keep in mind that climate is only one aspect of the environment. A poor diet lowers mean weight by influencing the expression of the population's hereditary patrimony for weight. On the other hand, a low weight is advantageous for somebody doomed to a low caloric intake. Selection favoring genetically light people is therefore conceivable; it would produce a genetical adaptation adding its effects to the expressional influence of poor nutrition in lowering mean weight. If one remembers that climate strongly influences diet in simple farming communities, one sees how complex is the interpretation of the observed relations between climate and weight. It will need a multidisciplinary and international effort, like the one currently planned by the International Biological Programme, for us to advance beyond our limited understanding of the question.

Another example. There is a tendency in related mammals to show larger protruding organs in hot climates. A similar tendency has been found in man for the relative length of the lower limbs. The physiological advantage of such an association has been elucidated. Bodily proportions are, for a large part, determined by heredity. We are therefore strongly tempted to interpret the relation between climate and the trunk to lower limb ratio in terms of genetical adaptation. Rightly so indeed: European children born in the tropics do not develop the long legs usual in Africans. Part of the association might however be due to developmental plasticity: mice reared in the heat develop a longer tail.

However large our ignorance, the more we know, the more important appears the role played by genetical adaptation in those differences between human populations which strike the eye, and are usually referred to as "racial" differences, as well as in less visible ones. Differences in skin color and in nose shape, for instance, appear to result mainly from genetical adaptation.

How deep is genetical adaptation of human populations? In other words, what is the price of biological adaptation to an environment in terms of capacity to success in another one? History and biology give us ample evidence for answering this question. We know of many historical cases of successful transplantation of a population into a strikingly different environment. A widespread distribution of an initially restricted group is repeatedly recorded by historians, prehistorians or human palaeontologists. The works of environmental physiologists show that all human populations are alike in their modes of reaction when faced with a given climatic stress; the differences in efficiency in their reaction once they are acclimatized are slight, if they appear at all. Contrasting with most animal species whose subdivisions tend to adapt strictly to specific environments, man is characterized by a general adaptability. The 22 UNESCO experts referred to above were unanimous in stating that "general adaptability to the most diverse environments is in man more pronounced than his adaptations to specific environments." How man did escape partitioning and local specialization is clear: by the extent of his migrations and interbreeding.

The roots of this distinction of man lie in the unique nature of his progress. To give the word again to the 1964 UNESCO statement: "For long millennia, progress made by man, in any field, seems to have been increasingly, if not exclusively, based on culture and to transmission of cultural achievements, and not on the transmission of genetic endowment." Biological success of a population, which means its increase in number, is achieved in man essentially through cultural advance, most often of a technological nature. Cultural advantage is also the mover to faraway implantation and possible replacement of a population genetically better adapted to the local conditions but less advanced by some aspects of its culture. Culture again provides man with more and more efficient nonbiological means of coping with the departure from optimal genetical equilibrium which migration in a fresh environment may involve. Success in this cultural adaptation lightens or possibly annuls the selective pressure for genetical adjustment.

If we now consider man's place in nature, what made him so successful on earth is his genetic capacity for culture. This major distinction is so essential for his survival in any environment that, at the light of current knowledge at least, all populations seem to be equal in this respect. Adaptation to local environment was and still is a paramount factor in the genesis of genetical or "racial" differences between human populations, but these differences are minor and unessential compared with man's general physiological adaptability and his general capacity to find non-biological means of coping with the variations of his environment, including the new biological challenges which cultural evolution itself unceasingly generates.

Part 2 / QUESTIONS AND PROBLEMS FOR DISCUSSION

1. List and discuss the evolutionary significance of the anatomical and physiological similarities of man and apes.
2. In Anderson's selection he raises the question: "Who was Adam?" What is the major point that Anderson is attempting to resolve by asking this question?
3. Describe, as fully as you are able, the activities of a typical day in the life of *Australopithecus*.
4. Why are the traits of sickle-cell anemia and malaria found in similar geographical areas?
5. Discuss why man's capacity for culture is such an important factor in the analysis of his successful adaptation to changing environmental conditions.

3/ LIFE IN A HANDFUL OF DIRT

An archeologist in the field holds up a handful of dirt and looks at it. The dirt appears to have little or no significance, yet there is life in it. The life of the past is often without features, without memorable events to make it vibrant. It is the task of the archeologist to bring forgotten life-styles into the proper perspective of the present. Archeologists uncover and study material remains of the past peoples, whether it be only a few hundred or several thousand years ago. There is general agreement among archeologists that the main thrust of their activities is threefold: to reconstruct cultural history, to record the nature of past ways of life, and to study the processes of cultural change. These objectives are, by and large, ones that most persons in the larger field of anthropology strive for; the net result is the study of how people live. Archeology is often referred to as the "ethnology of the past"; the major distinction is that ethnology deals with living peoples. Archeology is often called "pre-history," the study of man prior to written historical accounts. And as we look back on the previous selections dealing with man's evolutionary past, it is difficult to make a distinction between what is commonly thought of as "archeology" and what is called "paleoanthropology," the study of early fossil man. The previous selections on physical anthropology told how man became man. Attention in this section is focused on the development of man's cultural heritage. The selections that follow demonstrate the growth of man's life-style in the Old World; the New World; and the "world down under," Australia.

10 / Art Galleries in Prehistory

JOHN PFEIFFER

*One of the more eloquent writers of prehistoric man and his cultural
traditions is John Pfeiffer. This excerpt from one of his recent books
transports the reader to France and Spain so that he may experience a
part of prehistoric man's early achievements in painting. Pfeiffer's descriptive accounts of these artworks sets the scene for discussion as to
whether the animal paintings in these caves were an end in themselves or
whether they were used as imitative magical attempts to produce successful
hunts. Most historians agree that the early cave paintings represent both
hunting magic and a desire for artistic expression. Both interpretations go
hand in hand with the quest to understand late Paleolithic man's intellectual achievements.*

The world's first great art "movement" lasted more than 20,000 years,
from Aurignacian to Magdalenian times. Some of its most spectacular
products are found in underground galleries, away from natural light in
the passages and chambers and niches of limestone caves, and indicate
in a most vivid fashion how completely hunting dominated the attention
and imagination of prehistoric man. He rarely drew people, and never
anything that would be recognized as a landscape (although there are a
wide variety of signs which have no obvious meaning). His overwhelming
concern was with game animals seen as individuals, clearly defined and
detached, and isolated from their natural settings.

It is difficult to conceive of a reason why most of this art should have
been produced in parts of the Old World which are still centers of artistic
endeavor in modern times. But such happens to be the case; the great
majority of art caves are located in France and Spain. (According to a
recent count, France has sixty-five sites and Spain thirty.) About half of
all known sites are concentrated in three regions: along a ninety-mile stretch
of the northern coast of Spain, in the French Pyrenees fifty miles south
of Toulouse, and in the countryside around Les Eyzies.

The Les Eyzies region includes the largest cluster of art sites as well as the most striking of the lot, the famous Lascaux cave located in the woods on a plateau above the valley of the Vézère. Four boys and a dog discovered it during a walk early one September afternoon in 1940, the dog disappearing down a hole half-concealed by roots and moss and the boys scrambling after. (Boys are officially credited with the discovery of about a dozen art caves, but the unofficial count would be considerably higher, since archaeologists often receive sole credit for caves they originally learned about from boys in the neighborhood.)

What they were the first to see by the wavering light of a homemade oil lamp thousands of visitors, tourists as well as archaeologists and artists, have seen many times since. There is no prelude to the splendor of this gallery. The entrance leads down a short flight of stairs directly into the main hall, into a world of huge horned animals painted red and black. In a way, the first moment is the high point of the visit. You stand silent in the dark and lights are turned on and images appear as if projected on a screen, in a kind of three-dimensional panorama since the wall curves in front of you and around at the sides. For that moment, almost before the eye has a chance to look and before the ideas and questions start flowing, you take it all in at once.

Then the experience breaks into parts. The animals become individuals in a frieze along the upper wall of the hall, along an overhanging ledge formed by the scooping-out action of an ancient river. Four bulls in black outline with black curving horns dominate the assemblage; one of them, the largest cave painting yet discovered, measures eighteen feet long. Two of the bulls face one another, and five red stags fill the space between them. The frieze also includes six black horses, a large red horse, three cows, a so-called "unicorn" (actually a two-horned creature resembling no known species), and a number of other animals which are difficult to distinguish because they are partly covered by more recently painted figures.

Below the frieze two dark holes mark passages which branch off from the main hall and lead to places underground which have not yet been thoroughly explored. The left-hand passage slopes downhill far into the rock. It contains more than forty pictures, among them a group of six large horses and three cows covering part of the wall and the entire ceiling near the entrance, a menacing black bull with head and horns lowered, and a brown horse falling over backward at the end of the passage, that is, the end of the easily navigable part of the passage. From here on it narrows to a twisting tunnel which runs still deeper into as-yet-uninvestigated parts of the cave.

The other passage is even more intriguing. A small chamber, which looks like a rather uninteresting dead end until one comes closer, lies off to the side. One must step carefully at this point because there is a pit here under a domed ceiling covered with a tangle of engraved lines and crisscross patterns and unidentifiable remnants of some red and black paintings. The edge of the hole is worn smooth as if many persons had lowered themselves to the bottom in times past, perhaps by rope. (A fragment of three-ply rope has been found in the cave.)

Today an iron ladder extends into the pit. It leads to a ledge and a work unique in the records of cave art—a buffalo disemboweled by a spear through its hindquarters, a stick-figure man with a bird's head falling backward directly in front of the buffalo, a pole with a bird on it below the man, and to the left behind the man a two-horned rhinoceros. The most remote part of the cave lies more than two hundred feet past the pit (known as the Shaft of the Dead Man) and the enigmatic scene. The way in becomes lower and lower until one must crawl through, winding past little alcoves containing engravings of lions and other animals. It crosses a shallow pit and ends at a cleft blocked with clay.

Lascaux has been closed to the public ever since 1963, and most prehistorians believe it should never have been opened in the first place. The more popular a cave, the faster its art deteriorates, mainly because exhaled carbon dioxide reacts with limestone and accelerates the erosion of rock surfaces and the formation of calcium films that obscure paintings. This happened at Lascaux; in addition, colonies of green algae began spreading over the walls. There has been some talk about a grand reopening now that *le mal vert* has apparently been conquered, perhaps with a built-in glass tunnel which would help protect the art from the effects of exhaled air. But the risk of further deterioration is still great, and the cave will probably remain closed indefinitely.

Two major art caves are located some fifteen miles downriver from Lascaux in Les Eyzies: Font-de-Gaume and Les Combarelles. Font-de-Gaume has about two hundred paintings and engravings, many of which have also deteriorated, but after several visits one learns to follow the sweep of the visible lines, imagine the missing lines and re-create paintings which in their original condition may have surpassed those of Lascaux. Les Combarelles consists of a long narrow passage containing more than 300 engravings, many of which cannot be seen unless they are lighted from the side and at just the right angles. The region includes many other sites—the Cap Blanc shelter with a frieze of six sculptured horses; Bernifal and its engraved mammoths, one of them hidden in a narrow fissure; and the Cougnac cave, supposedly found by divining-rod methods, which includes a large elk in black outline and, drawn inside the elk just above its foreleg, a human figure with three spears or darts stuck in it.

There is also the little cave of Commarque, at the foot of a cliff under a ruined medieval castle. Commarque is noted for a magnificent horse's head which has been engraved at about eye level in a narrow side gallery and may be extremely difficult to find. One cannot see the engraving, which is about two feet long, unless the light of his lamp strikes the limestone surface at just the right angle. Some people have searched for several hours without finding it, while others find it after only a few minutes. (I explored the cave with three other searchers, and it took us about forty-five minutes to locate the engraving.)

The art of prehistoric man has inspired some strange and wonderful responses in us, his latter-day descendants. In the beginning, perhaps inevitably, the main response was violent disbelief and ridicule; as usual, the main reason was the traditional tendency to underrate people who lived so long ago. The tendency is understandable. After all, it seems reasonable to suppose that the lower their status, the higher our own would appear by comparison. But it does not work out that way, because modern man is so close to them that efforts to belittle the past always belittle the present as well.

11 / Where Did the First Americans Come From?

JUAN COMAS

Out of the depths of the Pacific and Atlantic oceans we are haunted
by the esoteric past of the lost continents of Mu and Atlantis. Also lurking
in the shadows are lost tribes of the Phoenicians, Israelites, and other
peoples long gone. All are patiently waiting to be claimed as the "first
Americans." In the following article Juan Comas briefly considers such
myths and legends dealing with massive transoceanic migrations before
settling down to the serious task of analyzing the scientific basis as to how
America was populated. Comas surveys the major stages in the develop-
ment of New World prehistory. He begins with the early hunting–gathering
stage introduced about 40,000 years ago from eastern Siberia, continues
with the early agricultural stage as evidenced in the southwestern United
States and in Mexico, takes note of the civilizations that developed in
meso-America and in Peru, and considers the native American populations
from the sixteenth century to the present. Comas's brief survey is a read-
able account of the questions we must ask ourselves about the biological
and cultural features of the "first Americans."

Where did the first inhabitants of America come from? At what time
in history did their immigration to the American continent begin? These
are the first questions we must ask ourselves before seeking to determine
the biological and cultural traits of the first settlers in America.

I have used the terms "immigration" and "settlers" on purpose, thereby
explicitly rejecting the belief commonly held at the end of the last century
and in the first decades of the present century, according to which the
New World saw man evolve independently from earlier forms as in the
Old World, and hence that early forms of man existed in the Americas
many hundreds of thousands of years ago.

This is the theory held by the so-called "autochthonists," who based
their beliefs on the discovery of bone remains on the American continent
attributed—erroneously—to hominids less evolved than *Homo sapiens*

and unearthed in geological strata judged to be—also erroneously—much older than has since proved the case.

Going counter to this belief is the fact that only the less evolved primates, that is, lemuroid fossils corresponding to the Eocene period at the beginning of the Tertiary Era (some 55 million years ago) have ever been found in America. As to the present-day living species, the New World comprises only the simpler types of simians, known scientifically as platyrrhines, but there is no trace of the higher types of primates, called catarrhines, which include apes and the anthropoids.

As for the ancestors of *Homo sapiens,* such as the pre-hominids and hominids, they are completely unknown to the Americas though they have been found in Africa, Asia and Europe. All of the prehistoric bone remains found on the American continent indisputably belong to modern man and hence are much more recent than any of the more primitive forms such as *Homo erectus* or Neanderthal Man discovered elsewhere.

Many suppositions have been advanced over the years (and passionately argued) to explain where the first settlers in America came from. The list includes the Phoenicians, Hebrews, Etruscans, Egyptians, Sumerians and Aryans, but no scientifically valid proof for any of these suppositions has been forthcoming, nor, for that matter, for the existence of the imaginary, fabulous Atlantis as the birthplace of the first Americans.

Certain writers in the 19th century and even in the present century took it for granted that all the Indians of America stemmed from a common biological stock. This gave rise to the common saying that: "all Indians are alike in colour and other features. When you've seen an Indian from one region you have seen them all."

This was based on the idea that all the migrants to the New World were Mongols of Asian origin who had crossed the Bering Straits at different epochs going back no earlier than 20,000 to 25,000 years ago. According to this hypothesis, the physical and cultural differences observed among the Indians of the Americas can be explained in two ways: partly by the different degrees of biological evolution of the migratory groups that crossed north-east Asia in the course of thousands of years; partly by the differing environments of the various regions of America the settlers established themselves in.

Other scientists, however, are of the opinion that from remote antiquity there coexisted on American soil human groups of different physical characteristics and of different origins. All the scientists who support this "multi-racial" thesis nonetheless unanimously agree that the Mongoloid element that crossed the Bering Straits from Siberia at different periods of migration by far dominates all other groups.

According to Paul Rivet, former director of the Paris Musée de l'Homme, the populations of pre-Columbian America are the result of migrations to the continent of four racial groups: Mongols and Eskimos via the Bering Straits, Australoids and Malayan–Polynesians across the Pacific. Rivet based his conclusions not only on the findings of physical anthropology by studying data on physical and other characteristics of Indian groups from southern South America and those of Indians from certain areas in Brazil, Baja California and Ecuador, but also on cultural and linguistic analogies with population groups in Oceania.

A. Mendes Corrêa, of Portugal, advanced the theory that an Australo-Tasmanian human element populated America not by sailing across the Pacific but by marching across Antarctica, island-hopping across the string of archipelagos between Tasmania and Tierra del Fuego at the southern tip of South America!

Mendes Corrêa has indeed demonstrated that between 15,000 and 6,000 B.C., Antarctica was free of glacial ice and actually had a temperate climate at the time. Obviously, no archaeological proof exists to confirm this Antarctic migration hypothesis, and it will be extremely difficult, not to say impossible, to uncover any evidence with the permanent ice cap now covering all of the Antarctic continent.

According to Jose Imbelloni of Argentina, one cannot truly understand the racial and cultural history of early America without taking into account the contribution of the peoples of south-east Asia. Imbelloni concludes that seven distinct racial groups migrated to America: Tasmanoids, Australoids, Melanesianoids, proto-Indonesians, Indonesians, Mongoloids and Eskimos. In his works he describes and delineates a total of 11 types of Amerindians.

More recently (1951) Joseph Birdsell of the U.S.A. sharply criticized the contradictory views concerning the population of the Americas put forward by various multi-racial exponents such as G. Taylor, R. B. Dixon, H. S. Gladwin, E. A. Hooton, E. W. Count, F. Weidenreich and J. Imbelloni. He advanced his own hypothesis that America had been settled by a mixture of two racial groups, Mongols and "Amurians" or archaic Caucasoids who had also reached the New World via north-east Asia.

As proof of this dual origin, Birdsell claims to have found "Amurian" traits in contemporary American Indians, among the Cahuillas of the interior of Lower California and among the Yuki and Pomo of the northern Californian coast. But if the Indians of North and South America were indeed the result of the mixture of only the two Mongoloid and Amurian strains, there ought to be a much greater similarity in blood groups than has actually been observed, particularly as regards the A-B-O and M-N groups.

There have been repeated efforts to establish similarities and indeed possible contacts between the "redskins" of the Atlantic seaboard of the United States and the prehistoric Caucasoid man of the Cro-Magnon type who peopled western Europe at the beginning of the Upper Paleolithic or Old Stone Age. Such claims cannot be dismissed since they do contain an element of possibility but no proof of any kind has yet been forthcoming.

From the above we can summarize our conclusions concerning the first inhabitants of the American continent as follows:

1. No authochtonous human population ever existed in America.

2. Never was there nor is there now any biologically homogeneous Amerindian type.

3. The overwhelming population migration consisted of Mongoloids.

4. There is still doubt and debate as to what and how many other human types also populated America, the most widely accepted hypotheses being 2 (Birdsell), 4 (Rivet) and 7 (Imbelloni).

The advocates of each of these hypotheses naturally explain the physical and other differences between the various types of Amerindians in different ways, and no definite conclusion can, of course, be reached until more extensive data are obtained. However, the large number of archaeological explorations carried out in recent years in various parts of the Americas has unearthed a rich store of stone implements and other objects as well as, to a lesser extent, fossilized human remains which, with our modern dating techniques including carbon-14 now permit us to establish with relative certainty when man first appeared in America and a chronological time-table of his presence there.

Thus we now know that man was present in the United States, for example, as early as 38,000 B.C. at a site found at Lewisville, Texas. Other prehistoric sites have been clocked at 27,650 B.C. (Santa Rosa, California); 19,500 B.C. (La Jolla, California); 8,505 B.C. (Gypsum Cave, Nevada); 7,883 B.C. (Plainview Site, Texas); and 6,274 B.C. (Allen Site, Nebraska). In each case we must allow a few hundred years or more plus or minus as is customary for C-14 readings. The people who lived in this area between 40,000 years ago and 8,000 years ago were all hunter–gatherers.

The oldest human settlement in Mexico has been found to be Tlapacoya in Mexico State, where a disc-shaped file and an obsidian knife have been unearthed dating back to 20,200 B.C. (plus or minus 2,600 years) and 21,150 B.C. (1,950 years) respectively. Later prehistoric sites are also known, of course, which show that they too belonged to hunter–gatherers.

Here are a few examples of datings from South America (plus or minus years are omitted): crude stone tool industries in Venezuela (14,375 B.C. and 12,275 B.C.); cultural remains in Lagoa Santa, Brazil (8,024 B.C.); pre-ceramic lithic culture in Lauricocha, Peru (7,566 B.C.); Inithuasi Grotto at San Luis, Argentina, with a pre-ceramic lithic industry (6,068 B.C.); a cultural complex on the high terraces of the Gallegos River in southern Patagonia dating from between 10,000 and 7,000 B.C.; excavations in Chile (9,380 B.C.) and elsewhere in southern Patagonia (8,760 to 6,700 B.C.).

From the above examples a very interesting observation can be made, namely, that as we proceed southward the datings of the hunting and gathering cultures are less ancient. Is this a confirmation of the thesis that the settlers of America came exclusively by way of the Bering Straits and that South America was therefore peopled many millennia later than North

America? I believe it is still too early to say and we must wait for further research and investigations.

It is generally agreed, for the moment, that the oldest date of 38,000 to 40,000 years ago corresponds to the beginnings of the warming up period of the last Ice Age in North America (known as the Wisconsin glaciation) when it was possible to cross from eastern Siberia to Alaska and thereby reach the more temperate regions of southern North America.

Culturally, the first hunter–gatherers evolved until they became sedentary groups after learning to cultivate plants and domesticate animals. This was a slow and gradual process, but we have evidence of prehistoric sites where hunter–gatherer tribes were simultaneously engaged in the cultivation of squash, chile beans and later, maize.

Such agricultural sites have been found at Tamaulipas, Mexico, dating back to between 7,500 and 5,500 B.C., at Sierra Madre, Mexico (4,500–2,500 B.C. and 5,000–3,000 B.C.). In the Tehuaca area of the State of Puebla in Mexico several prehistoric sites have been unearthed offering definite proof of the existence of agriculture between 6,000 and 5,500 B.C.

In New Mexico (USA) agricultural levels have been found at a site known as Bat Cave, dating back to about 3,300 B.C. while in the Peruvian Andes agricultural complexes dating between 4,700 and 3,000 B.C. have been found at Huaca Prieta, Nazoa, Paracas, Chilica, and other sites.

The evolution from the hunter–gatherer stage to agriculture occurred in America independently of the same development in the Old World. Research in plant genetics, ecology and ethno-history as well as chronological datings have effectively demonstrated this, thus refuting the thesis that agriculture was introduced into America from Asia.

The initial phases of an agricultural economy are known to have occurred in different parts of America, first with seasonal sedentary settlements and then year-round permanent agricultural sites. Central America and the Peruvian–Bolivian area are at least two of the centres on the continent which originated the cultivation of certain species of plants. Graded terraces and *Chinampas* (incorrectly called "floating gardens") are two typical techniques used here in early intensive agriculture.

From this point we see the beginning of a new process of development, the so-called "high cultures" based on what Gordon Childe has termed the "urban revolution," depending on extensive cultivation of maize, yucca, potato, beans and squash as well as the manufacture of ceramics, the use of polished stone implements and the beginning of the textile industry, etc.

In Meso-America (Mexico, Guatemala, parts of Honduras and El Salvador) the high cultures began around 1,500 B.C. in the highlands. This was the case with the Toltec, the Aztec and Zapotec civilizations which ended with the arrival of the Spaniards in the 16th century. The Olmec, Maya and Totonec civilizations emerged in the lowlands a little later than 1,500 B.C.

In the Peru–Bolivia area, both along the coast (Huaca Prieta, Cupisnique, Paracas, Mochica, Nazoa, Pachacamac, Chuncay and Inca civilizations) and in the Andean uplands (Chavin, Cajamarca, Huaylas, Huilca, Qalassaya, Tiahuanaco and Inca civilizations) the high cultures began to develop about 1,600 B.C. until their decline at the end of the 15th century A.D.

Alongside these great civilizations there also existed much less advanced cultural groups, hampered no doubt by the rigours of their surroundings and habitat. Notable amongst these were the populations living in the great river valleys of the Amazon, Orinoco and Paraná as well as their many tributaries.

From the 16th century, with the conquest, colonization and acculturation stemming from the arrival of European immigrants, the original Indian population of America underwent the following three major modifications:

1. The Indians have dwindled to the point of extinction, as in Uruguay, Cuba, Haiti, Dominican Republic and Puerto Rico; or a reduced number are confined to reservations, as in the United States.

2. The Indian population still exists but has little contact with the rest of the country, living within its own self-sufficient economy, virtually untouched by the process of acculturation. Such populations are found in the Amazon and Orinoco river basins, eastern Peru, Bolivia, Ecuador, etc.

3. Large-scale intermingling of races has taken place to the extent that the majority of the inhabitants are biologically and culturally mixed, though small pockets of Indian populations, where less intermingling and acculturation have taken place, continue to exist, as in Mexico, Guatemala, the Andean plateau regions of Ecuador, Peru and Bolivia.

12 / Investigating the Origins of Mesopotamian Civilization

FRANK HOLE

This selection considers the Neolithic period in the Near East (8000–3000 B.C.). Frank Hole examines an ecological approach to the growth of the world's first civilization, the Sumerian civilization in Mesopotamia. The ecological framework Hole uses assumes that physical environment, technology, religion, and other cultural aspects cannot be considered apart from the total picture. The approach simply investigates the history of cultural change within an ecological system. The study of ecosystems is not unique to Hole, but this selection represents a tight, coherent application of the concept as it is applied to early Near East agricultural traditions. Although Hole's article is primarily a consideration of early Sumerian civilization, the reader should be aware that Hole is discussing criteria that are frequently used in describing the nature of early civilization throughout the world.

In Southwest Asia, between 8000 and 3000 B.C., human society developed from self-sufficient bands of nomadic hunters to economically and politically integrated city dwellers who specialized in a variety of occupations. A central archeological problem is to try to discover the factors that triggered these fundamental changes in man's way of life. For want of evidence and for want of a satisfactory model of the conditions existing during the period in question, searching for origins and attempting to discover the course of events that led to civilization is difficult. Prehistorians deal with nameless cultures, trusting to reconstructions from physical remains for their picture of life in ancient times. They must work directly with geographic, technological, and demographic factors and only indirectly infer ideologies and philosophical concepts. Archeologists are thus limited in what they can hope to learn by the nature of their data and the tools they have for interpreting them. Within these limits, however, it is possible to construct some plausible theories about the origins of civilization and to test them through controlled programs of excavation and analysis. In this article I define the problem under consideration in ecological terms, review the current evidence, and suggest topics for further study.

Mesopotamian (Sumerian) civilization began a few centuries before 3000 B.C. and was characterized by temples, urban centers, writing, trade, militarism, craft specialization, markets, and art. Inferred characteristics are a class-stratified society and well-defined mechanisms for regulation of production and distribution of resources. To be sure, Sumerian civilization must have had many other important but intangible characteristics, but most of these cannot be inferred from archeological data.

The early Mesopotamian civilizations were restricted to southern Mesopotamia, the alluvial plain that stretches south from Baghdad to the Persian Gulf. Remains of immediately antecedent cultures have been excavated in the same area, and still older cultures have been excavated in the surrounding Zagros mountain valleys of Iraq and Iran and on the steppes at the verge of plain and mountain in Khuzistan, southwest Iran.

Intensive agriculture is a precondition for civilization. The Sumerian societies for which we have some historical records were sustained by cultivation of irrigated barley and wheat, supplemented by crops of dates, and the production of sheep, goats, cattle, pigs, and fish. In 8000 B.C. people were just beginning to plant cereals, raise animals, and live in permanent villages; their societies were small, self-sufficient, egalitarian groups with little differentiation of occupation or status. These people had fewer of the artifacts and qualities of civilization than the Sumerian city dwellers had 5000 years later. In this article I use 8000 B.C. as a convenient base line and attempt to assess some 5000 years of culture history.

Theories of Development

Recognizing the obvious changes in society that occurred during the 5000 years, archeologists and others have proposed causal factors such as characteristics of geography to account for them. The most detailed examination of the relationship between geographic features and social forms has been made by Huntington, but other scholars working with data from Southwest Asia have had more influence on archeologists. For example, in attempting to explain the origins of agriculture, Childe proposed climatic change, specifically desiccation, as the initiating event and set off a chain of thought that is still favored by some authors. Childe argued that "incipient desiccation . . . would provide a stimulus towards the adoption of a food-producing economy. . . ." Animals and men would gather in oases that were becoming isolated in the midst of deserts. Such circumstances might promote the sort of symbiosis between man and beast implied in the word *domestication*. Although Childe's theory is attractive, there is no conclusive evidence that the climate in Southwest Asia changed enough during the period in question to have affected the beginnings of agriculture and animal husbandry.

It was once fashionable to think of culture as inevitably rising or progressing, and this trend was thought to be analogous to biological evolution. Except in a most general way, however, modern prehistorians do not think of universal stages of cultural development. Rather than focusing on evolutionary stages, many scholars have examined the role of particular social and economic activities in triggering the emergence of complex forms of society. For instance, Marxists have explained the form of society (government, broadly speaking) on the basis of modes of production. Marxist evolutionists even today explain the development of social classes and political states in similar terms. They argue that, as people gained control over the production of food, the concept of private property crept in, and later the mass of people were exploited by the propertied few. "The creation of a state was necessary simply to prevent society from dissolving into anarchy due to the antagonisms that had arisen." Information on the emergence of Sumerian civilization that might support this idea, however, is lacking.

Another attempt to correlate technological systems and social advances was made by Karl Wittfogel in *Oriental Despotism*. He contended that, where people had to depend on irrigation, they inevitably led themselves into an escalating dependence on an organizational hierarchy which coordinated and directed the irrigation activities. "The effective management of these works involves an organizational web which covers either the whole, or at least the dynamic core, of the country's population. In consequence, those who control this network are uniquely prepared to wield supreme political power." Although Wittfogel's analysis seems valid in many instances, archeological investigation in both Mesopotamia and the Western Hemisphere leads to the conclusion that there was no large-scale irrigation at the time of the emergence of the first urban civilization.

An Ecological Approach

Single factors such as technology are unquestionably important, but they can be understood only within the cultural, social, and geographic context. A more comprehensive view that takes into account the interrelation of many factors is called human ecology. In a consideration of cultural development, the relevant concept in human ecology is adaptation, hence the approach is to try to discover how particular factors influence the overall adaptation of a society. By means of the general approach, human ecology attempts to understand what happened in the histories of particular cultures. It does not address itself to making general statements about cultural progress or evolution.

In an ecological approach, a human society is treated as one element in a complex system of geography, climate, and living organisms peculiar to an area. To ensure survival, various aspects of a human society must be complementary and the society itself must be successfully integrated with the remainder of the cultural and physical ecosystem of which it is a part. From the ecological view, such factors as technology, religion, or climate cannot be considered apart from the total system. Nevertheless, some parts of the system may be considered more fundamental in the sense that they strongly influence the form of the other parts. Anthropologists, through their study of modern societies, and archeologists, through inference, find that such factors as geographical features, the distribution of natural resources, climate, the kinds of crops and animals raised, and the relations with neighboring peoples strongly influence the forms that a society may take. These factors comprise the major elements of the ecosystem, and societies must adapt themselves to them.

Archeological Evidence

For the period 8000 to 3000 B.C., archeological data are scattered and skimpy. This naturally limits the generality of any interpretations that can be made and restricts the degree to which we can test various theories. Ideally we would wish to work with hundreds of instances representing the range of environmental and cultural variation; instead, for the whole of Southwest Asia we can count fewer than 100 excavated and reported sites for the entire range of time with which we are dealing. Of course the number of unexcavated or unreported sites about which we know something is far greater, but we cannot but be aware of how little we know and how much there is to find out.

In all of Southwest Asia only about 15 villages that date to 8000 B.C. have been excavated, and only two of these, Zawi Chemi and the Bus Mordeh levels at Ali Kosh, give good evidence of the use of domesticated plants or animals. In short, data for the time of our base line are woefully inadequate. We have much fuller information about the villages of 5000 B.C., but, unfortunately, for periods subsequent to 5000 B.C. the *kind* of data we have changes drastically. Thus, although there is historical continuity in the series of known sites, there is discontinuity in some of the data themselves because few archeologists have worked sites spanning the whole period from 8000 to 3000 B.C. Most of the sites dating to about 3000 B.C. were excavated by "historic" archaeologists who struck levels that old only incidentally as they plumbed the depths of the cities they were digging. These scholars depended far less on artifacts than on history for their interpretations. The earliest sites were dug by prehistorians who based their inferences on results generated by an array of scientific experts. In order to understand the origins of civilizations, we thus need to bridge two quite different "archeological cultures." Archeologists and their various colleagues working in the early villages painstakingly teased out grains of charred seeds, measured metapodials and teeth of early races of sheep or cattle, and analyzed the chemical and mineral constituents of obsidian and copper; their counterparts working in the historic sites busied themselves with the floor plans of temples, the funerary pottery in the graves, the esthetics of an art style, and the translation of cuneiform impressions in clay.

Bearing in mind the reservations I have already expressed, we can begin to try to pick a coherent path through 5000 years of history. In dealing with Mesopotamia, it is usual to regard the presence of towns, temples, and cities as indicative of civilization. If we do so, we can divide our history into two parts, beginning with small food-producing villages and following with more complex societies that include towns and cities. In the ensuing discussion I assess the available evidence and, for both forms of community, outline the characteristics and indicate how the community developed.

Food-Producing Villages

Small food-producing villages have had a long history, but here we are chiefly interested in those that existed between 8000 and 5000 B.C. None of these communities is known thoroughly, and the following descriptions are based on data from several excavated sites and from surface surveys. The fullest data come from the phases represented in Ali Kosh and Tepe Sabz, in southwest Iran, and from Jarmo, Sarab, and Guran in the Zagros mountains. Additional data derive from extensive surveys in Khuzistan and the valleys of the Zagros.

During this period villages are small and scattered, typically less than 1 hectare in size and housing perhaps 100 to 300 people. They are situated on the best agricultural land in regions where farming is possible without irrigation. From a handful of sites known to be about 10,000 years old, the number of settlements had increased by 5000 B.C., when many villages were within sight of one another and almost every village was within an easy day's walk of the next. There is no evidence of great migrations or any serious pressure of population during this time. By 4000 B.C. some villages occupy areas as large as 2 hectares.

The increase in population appears to have been a direct consequence of improved agricultural techniques. In 8000 B.C., only primitive, low-yield races of emmer wheat and two-row barley were grown; sheep and goats were both in the early stages of domestication. By 5000 B.C. a modern complex of hybrid cereals and domesticated sheep, goats, cattle, and pigs were being exploited, and irrigation was practiced in marginal agricultural areas such as Deh Luran. The effects of developed agriculture are soon apparent, for, by 4000 B.C., settlement of new areas by prehistoric pioneers can be shown clearly in such places as the Diyala region to the east of Baghdad. The age of the earliest settlements in southern Mesopotamia proper is unknown, but it would be surprising if groups of hunters and fishers had not lived along the rivers or swamps prior to the introduction of agriculture. The oldest settlement, Eridu, has been dated to about 5300 B.C., but there are no contemporary sites. In fact, there are few villages known in southern Mesopotamia that antedate 4000 B.C.

Towns and Cities

The millennium between 4000 and 3000 B.C. saw the rapid growth of towns and cities. Villages were also abundant, but some evidence suggests that they were less numerous than in earlier periods. . . . The trends I describe here pertain almost exclusively to southern Mesopotamia; in the north and in the valleys of the Zagros, the pattern remained one of small villages and—emerging later than their counterparts in the south—townships.

From southern Mesopotamia, archeological data for the period before 3000 B.C. are skimpy. Deep soundings at the bases of such sites as Eridu, Ur, Uqair, Tello, Uruk, and Susa and test excavations at Ubaid, Ras al-Amiya, and Hajji Mohammad are about all we have. Only at Ras al-Amiya is there direct evidence of agriculture, although at Eridu a layer of fish bones on the altar of temple VII suggests the importance of the sea and of fishing. Archeological evidence from several of the remaining sites consists either of temple architecture or pottery, the latter serving more to indicate the age of a site than the social or cultural patterns of its inhabitants. Some temple plans are known, but published data on domestic architecture are few, and the sizes of the communities can be inferred only roughly.

There are extensive enough excavations at sites like Uruk, Khafajah, Kish, Ur, and Nippur to indicate the scale of urbanism and many of its more spectacular architectural and artistic features for the period after 3000 B.C. The largest Early Dynastic site was evidently Uruk, where 445 hectares are enclosed by the city wall; contemporary Khafajah and Ur comprise 40 and 60 hectares, respectively. By contrast, the Ubaid portion of Uqair had about 7 hectares.

Historical Reconstructions

Pictographic writing began by about 3400 B.C., but it is difficult to interpret, and in any case early writing tells little about society; it is confined to bookkeeping. Nevertheless, by depending on myths, epics, and tales written some 1000 years later, scholars have attempted historical reconstructions of the emerging urban societies.

The oldest texts that characterize the Sumerian community are no earlier than 2500 B.C. and were written at a time when the "Temple-city" had already become the characteristic feature of the Mesopotamian landscape. In the view of many authors, the city was an estate belonging to gods of nature and maintained on their behalf by completely dependent and relatively impotent mortals. Controversy centers around the degree to which the temple controlled the economy. The extreme view is that it controlled everything while the more popular moderate view is that it controlled only part of the economy. In the Early Dynastic period, it seems clear, some, if not all, people were responsible to a temple which in turn directed most of the production and redistribution of goods and services. For practical purposes there was no distinction between the economic and the religious roles of the temples, but their administrators may not have had much political influence. Some temples listed large staffs of attendants, craftsmen, laborers, and food producers, but the precise relationship of these people to the temple is by no means clear. Moreover, such staffs would have been associated with the largest temples and not with the host of lesser temples and shrines that seem to have been present in the larger cities. Political control was vested variously in the *en* (lord), *lugal* (great man, or king), or *ensi* (governor-priest), depending on the historical period, the city referred to, and the translator of the text. In early times religious and secular titles seem not to have been held by the same person. Jacobsen describes, for pre-Early Dynastic times, a "primitive democracy" with the leader appointed by and responsible to an assembly of citizens. . . .

Environment and Subsistence

By combining the geographic, economic, and historical data, we can construct some plausible theories about the course of development and the situations that triggered it. The remarkable thing, from an ecological view, is the change in relations between men and products, and then between men and their fellows during the 5000 years. If we return for a moment to the pre-agricultural ways of life, we find small bands of hunters exploiting the seasonally available resources of a large territory by wandering from one place to another. Each community was self-sufficient, and each man had approximately the same access to the resources as his fellows. The earliest villagers seem to have maintained this pattern, although, as agriculture and stock breeding became more developed and important economically, the villagers tended more and more to stay put. People settled down where they could raise large amounts of grain, store it for the future, and exchange it for products they did not produce. In return for dependability of food supply, people gave up some of their dietary variety and most of their mobility. From a pattern of exploiting a broad spectrum of the environment, there developed a pattern of exploiting a relatively narrow spectrum.

As long as people stayed where they could find sufficiently varied resources through hunting and gathering, they could be self-sufficient. When people settled in villages away from the mountains, out of the zone of rainfall agriculture, they were no longer independent in the sense that they personally had access to the varied resources they desired or needed. Psychologically and sociologically this marked a turning point in man's relations with his environment and his fellows. Southern Mesopotamia is a land with few resources, yet in many ways this was an advantage for the development of a society. In a land without timber, stone, or metals, trade was necessary, but the role of trade in the emergence of civilization should not be overemphasized. Date palms and bundles of reeds served adequately instead of timber for most construction, and baked clay tools took the place of their stone or metal counterparts in other areas. On the other hand, travel by boat is ancient, and extensive land and sea trade is attested in early documents. It was easy to move goods in Mesopotamia.

In order to live as well as the farmers in Deh Luran did, the Sumerians had to cooperate through trade, barter, or other means with their fellow settlers. We should remember that the barren vista of modern Mesopotamia on a dusty day does not reveal the full range of geographic variation or agricultural potential of the area. Swamps and rivers provided fish and fowl and, together with canals, water for irrigation and navigation. With sufficient water, dates and other fruits and vegetables could be grown. The unequal distribution of subsistence resources encouraged the beginnings of occupational specialization among the various kinds of food producers, and this trend was further emphasized after craftsmen started to follow their trades on a full-time basis.

Economics and Management

Because of the geographic distribution of resources and the sedentary and occupationally specialized population, a social organization that could control production and redistribution was needed. Clearly, any reconstruction of the mechanics of redistribution in emerging Mesopotamian civilization is subject to the severe limitations of the evidence. If we recognize this, however, we may then seek in contemporary societies analogs that may help us imagine appropriate redistributional structures. In modern economies, money markets act as the agency of redistribution, but in virtually all "primitive" societies where surpluses or tradeable goods are produced, a center of redistribution of another kind grows. The "center" can be a person (for example, the chief); an institution, like a temple and the religious context it symbolizes; or a place, like a city with some form of free markets. Jacobsen suggests that in Sumeria temples served as warehouses, where food was stored until times of famine. . . .

In Mesopotamia, most of the surplus labor or food went directly or indirectly into building and maintaining temples. One would also have expected the chief to use a good bit of the surplus to support himself and his family, to pay the wages of craftsmen, and to buy the raw materials that were turned into artifacts, such as jewelry and clothing, that served to distinguish his rank. Others in the lord's biological or official family would also have profited from his control of the resources and ultimately have become recognized as a social class entitled to special prerogatives. This social stratification would have been associated with a similarly burgeoning system of occupational differentiation.

In an emerging system where both technology and governmental forms are relatively simple but susceptible of improvement, there is a maximum opportunity for feedback. That is, if a certain level of production will support a certain degree of social stratification, efficient management by the social elite may result in more productivity. It is interesting to speculate on how much the construction of enormous irrigation systems during later Mesopotamian history may have depended on the rising aspirations of the ruling elite.

Although the need for management of production might in itself have been sufficient cause for a developing social stratification, other factors were probably contributory. Turning now to law and politics, I should point out that, with the establishment of irrigation and the concentration of population in urban centers, man's basic attitudes toward the land must have changed. The construction of irrigation systems, even if primitive, makes the land more valuable to the builders, and this, if it did nothing else, would lead to some notions of property rights and inheritance that had not been necessary when abundant land was available for the taking. An irrigation system also implies that some men may have more direct control over the supply of water than others. This could have led to an increase in the power of individuals who controlled the supply of water, and it certainly must have led to disputes over the allocation of water. It seems inevitable that a working system of adjudicating claims over land would then have been necessary, and the task may have fallen to the chiefs (lords).

The presence of "neighbors" also has ecological implications; it is worth recalling that property invites thievery. Adams argues that the "growth of the Mesopotamian city was closely related to the rising tempo of warfare," and Service points out that the integration of societies under war leaders is common, and clearly an adaptation to social–environmental conditions. Several Early Dynastic II cities had defensive walls, attesting to conflict between cities and perhaps between settled farmers and nomadic herders, but the historical evidence for warfare begins only about 2500 B.C.

If we consider both the agricultural system and the wealth, we see conditions that enhanced opportunities for leadership and, ultimately, for direction and control. With these situations, the emerging systems of rank and status are understandable without our resorting to notions of "genius," "challenge and response," or immigration by more advanced peoples.

Religion

The role of religion in integrating emerging Mesopotamian society is frequently mentioned. By 3000 B.C. texts and temples themselves attest to the central place of religion in Sumerian life; theoretically, at least, cities were simply estates of the gods, worked on their behalf by mortals. How closely theory corresponds to fact is a question that cannot be answered. Although we cannot date their beginnings precisely, we know that temple centers were well established by 5000 B.C., and that towns and temples frequently go together. Whether towns developed where people congregated because of religious activities or whether temples grew in the market centers where the people were cannot be decided without more data. . . .

In regard to this limited view of the role of religion, it is well to recall that major settlements had several temples. At Khafajah, for example, perhaps as early as 4000 B.C. there were three temples, and a fourth was added later. Our image of the Sumerian temple is nevertheless likely to be that of the large temple oval at Khafajah or Ubaid rather than that of the smaller temples that were contemporary and perhaps just as characteristic. The temple oval appears to have housed a society within a city, but many temples had no auxiliary buildings. More impressive even than the temple ovals were the great ziggurats erected on artificial mounds—at Uruk 13 meters high and visible for many kilometers. Again this was only one of several temples at the same site. In Ubaid, Eridu, and Uqair, for example, where temples were originally associated with residential settlements, the towns were later abandoned and only the temples with cemeteries were maintained.

Summary

It seems unlikely that Mesopotamian society took a single path as it approached the rigidly organized, hierarchal civilization of Early Dynastic times. Rather, we imagine that there was considerable experimentation and variety in the organization of society as people adapted to their physical environment and to the presence of other expanding communities.

Some towns and cities probably arose as the demographic solution to the problem of procuring and distributing resources. It would have made sense to have central "clearing houses." Similarly, it would have made sense to have the craftsmen who turned the raw materials into finished products live close to their supply (probably the temple stores). Temple centers are natural focal points of settlements. Cities and towns, however, are not the only demographic solutions to the problem of farming and maintaining irrigation canals. Both of these tasks could have been carried out by people living in more dispersed settlements. City life in Mesopotamia probably also presented other benefits. For example, as warfare came to be a recurrent threat, the psychological and physical security of a city must have been a comfort for many. Finally, to judge from some historical evidence, Mesopotamian cities were places of diversity and opportunity, no doubt desiderata for many people as long as they could also gain a suitable livelihood. . . .

Reprinted from *Americas,* monthly magazine published by the General Secretariat
of the Organization of American States in English, Spanish, and Portuguese. From
"The Olmec: America's First Civilization," by Marion Stirling, *Americas,* Vol. 23,
Nos. 6–7, 1971.

13 / The Olmec: America's First Civilization

MARION STIRLING

*This article deals with the development of early civilization in the New
World. The early Sumerian cultural traditions that we just read about
were quite different from the Olmec in certain respects, but the two
cultures do share some features. Common aspects include architecture,
permanent settlements based on agriculture, highly developed crafts, and
a theocratic state. A noticeable difference is a lack of urban settlements
in Olmec and the presence of city living in Sumer. Although the Olmec
way of life came to an abrupt end about* A.D. *200, Olmec art styles flourished in a wide area long after the temples of Olmec centers were mute.
The author discusses the nature of Olmec life.*

"Who were the Olmec? I have heard of the Maya, the Toltec, and the
Aztec, but I never heard of the Olmec."

Since my husband and I started working in Olmec sites, in eastern Mexico in 1939, I have been asked this question innumerable times. When I
answer that we think Olmec is the mother culture of Mesoamerica, the
next question is "Why?"

"Because they had a calendar and writing, military, political and religious organization. To achieve what they did, they must have had
accomplished artists, engineers and scientists. Their 'empire' spread to
Guerrero and the Pacific on the west and through Guatemala, El Salvador,
and perhaps Costa Rica on the southeast. They influenced later civilizations."

My answer is often greeted with surprise and disbelief. Actually, until
recently this was an unpopular theory among most archaeologists, especially those working on the Maya, who, because of their spectacular
achievements, were long regarded as the source of Mesoamerican civilization. In Mexico, famous anthropologist Alfonso Caso was the first to use
the term "mother culture," at the La Venta Congress in Tuxtla Gutiérrez
in 1942. Another staunch believer in the antiquity of the Olmec was the

Mexican artist Miguel Covarrubias, who based his conclusion largely on detailed studies of art styles.

Now, thanks to radiocarbon dating and intensive excavation by Robert Heizer and Philip Drucker at La Venta, Michael Coe at San Lorenzo, Alfonso Medellín at Laguna de Los Cerros, and Román Piña Chán, all doubts as to the antiquity of the Olmec have been removed. Just recently two books on the Olmec have appeared: *The Olmec World*, by Ignacio Bernal; and *America's First Civilization, Discovering the Olmec,* by Michael D. Coe.

The Olmec civilization developed in the tropical jungles of the southern Gulf Coast of Mexico, now Veracruz and Tabasco, and flourished from the thirteenth to the last century B.C. Bernal estimates the population at three hundred and fifty thousand in an area of seven thousand square miles.

Did the civilization rise in response to the challenge of the jungle or because of it? Caso gives many reasons for believing the Olmec had a true empire.

To most people the Olmec are best known for their remarkable stone sculpture. The colossal stone heads ranging in size from five feet to ten feet are the most impressive and best known features of Olmec culture. Some of the giant heads from San Lorenzo have toured the United States and visited such European cities as Rome, Moscow, and Paris. Pictures of them have appeared in many magazines advertising travel to Mexico.

There are now twelve known colossal heads: two from Tres Zapotes, four from La Venta, and six from San Lorenzo. Of these, on our National Geographic Society–Smithsonian Institution expeditions, we discovered eight; three at La Venta and five at San Lorenzo. The heads, carved from basalt, never had bodies. We believe they represent portraits of leaders. Others suggest they represent gods or decapitated ball game heroes, since they wear a sort of helmet. The art style is sometimes called "Baby Face" and sometimes described as Negroid, because the faces are round, with thick lips, flat broad noses and puffy eyes. Many descendants of this physical type are living in Mexico today. Another ethnic type, taller and with an aquiline nose, is shown on the stone monuments and pottery and jade figurines, but these may represent visitors.

Other stone monuments, many larger than the colossal heads, were altars and stelae, elaborately carved and decorated.

We don't know what the Olmec called themselves or where they came from. The name Olmec means "the rubber people," literally people from the land where rubber is produced. It was the name of a group living in southern Veracruz in historical times who had nothing to do with the prehistoric culture with which we are concerned. Attempts to change the name to "La Venta," the type site of the culture, have not been successful.

Scientific work has been carried on at La Venta in Tabasco and at Tres Zapotes, San Lorenzo and Laguna de Los Cerros in Veracruz. Of all the

Olmec sites excavated to date, La Venta is the most spectacular. It was a great ceremonial center, built on an island away from where people lived. The Olmec believed in doing things the hard way. Here there is a clay mound 103 feet high with ten alternating valleys and ridges, looking like a man-made cinder cone. In the ceremonial court in front of the mound, three huge pits were dug and thick serpentine floors laid down. On the bottom of one, $50 \times 61 \times 24$ feet deep, over one thousand tons of serpentine slabs had been neatly laid as a massive floor. To form a similar larger pit seventy-seven feet square, sixty thousand cubic feet of material had been excavated. Three large mosaic jaguar masks, made of green serpentine blocks, were deeply buried in a similar manner.

Almost immediately after installation, the pavements and masks were intentionally covered with a series of brilliantly colored clays. Basalt columns, weighing two tons each, form a stockade surrounding the principal court.

Tombs with rich offerings of jade were constructed to contain the remains of important individuals. The Olmec seemed to make a point of having no two tombs alike. Most unusual was a tomb of basalt columns containing the bones of two infants, and a treasure trove of jade offerings buried in cinnabar.

A sandstone sarcophagus with lid, in the form of a stylized jaguar, also contained jade offerings and was unique in Mexico until the sarcophagus in the Palenque tomb was found.

In a slab-lined stone cyst, jade ornaments were arranged as if placed on a burial. Still another rich tomb was covered by eleven basalt columns laid horizontally above. Among the treasures deposited in the tombs were objects of jade, quartz crystal, amethyst, turquoise, obsidian, ilmenite, magnetite, amber and pyrites.

Human figures represented on large stone monuments are usually males, wearing enormous headdresses, bead necklaces and ornaments. Various caches of jade and serpentine figurines and celts were buried as offerings in the court.

There are no volcanic rocks and there is no clay on the sandy island of La Venta. Tons of red, yellow, white and purple clay were carried in for the construction of the ceremonial court.

The vast quantity of stone of which the structures and monuments are made was probably transported by means of rafts along the navigable rivers. Five thousand tons of green serpentine used in constructing the buried massive offerings were brought to La Venta from Niltepic, on the Pacific side of the Isthmus, 350 river miles away. The nearest basalt from which the huge stone monuments were carved—some exceed thirty tons in weight—is fifty miles away in an air line. Transporting such burdens through rough country with neither wheels nor beasts of burden was a formidable task.

Such a frenzy of work indicates a highly developed social organization; an elite who ordered and a working class who obeyed. Also, it implies efficient agricultural practices, supplying an abundance of food.

The diet was probably similar to that of the region today: corn, beans and squash raised with slash and burn technique, supplemented to some extent by fish and wild game. Rainfall is heavy and many rivers cut through the land. There was never a shortage of water. Caso aptly calls the region the Mesopotamia of Mesoamerica.

In addition to their ability to carve gigantic monuments, the Olmec were undoubtedly the greatest craftsmen in the New World in working jade. They did not have gold or other metals. Jade was their most precious substance. The high esteem for jade persisted through three thousand years. Montezuma, the Aztec ruler, informed Cortez that one jade bead was worth a load of gold.

Jade is a generic term used to designate both jadeite and nephrite. The jade used by the Olmec was jadeite, basically a silicate of sodium and aluminum. The ancient Chinese jades were nephrite, a calcium magnesium silicate. It was not until the eighteenth century that the Chinese began to import jadeite from Burma.

Many of the Olmec jade carvings are real masterpieces. One much admired is a seated figure from La Venta wearing a hematite mirror on the breast. Also aesthetically striking are the figurines carved of translucent blue jade.

At La Venta, we found beads and ornaments of transparent green jade of "Imperial" quality, as beautiful as emerald. Blue jade was used during Olmec times but does not appear during the later periods.

Costa Rica is the only other area in the New World where blue jade is found in abundance and some jade carvings found in Costa Rica show Olmec traits. Since many of the Costa Rican jades are made from re-worked celts, we have speculated that the Olmec traded as far south as Costa Rica for the raw material, made celts, and traded them back for more raw material.

Jade being both valuable and indestructible, there are some interesting combinations of provenience and epochs in the jade caches. Some of the group of sixteen miniature human figures from La Venta may have been heirloom pieces when the offering was made. Four of the celts were made from an older object, probably an elaborately incised plaque. Many of the figurines had old breaks when deposited.

In the 782-piece jade cache at Cerro de las Mesas there were several heirloom pieces, some of which had been reworked. Many had been traded from distant places. One in blue jade is definitely related to the art style known in Costa Rica as the "Beak Bird."

Since there are no natural jade occurrences in the Gulf Coast area, the Olmec must have been indefatigable jade prospectors. The wide range of jade objects indicates that they came from many sources. In view of this it is remarkable that today but one certain source is known in Mesoamerica, that near Manzanales, Guatemala.

Even more remarkable than the carving of jade without metal tools is the polishing of concave magnifying mirrors from certain iron-rich ores. Both lapidarists and scientists marvel at the perfection of the reflecting surfaces of the magnetite and ilmenite mirrors, which are ground as if to optical specifications. Examination by microscope shows no trace of abrasives. Each mirror has two perforations on one edge and some stone figures show them being worn as chest pendants.

We know the Olmec had a knowledge of astronomy because the entire site of La Venta is laid out in a North–South line. Another proof of a knowledge of astronomy, as well as writing to keep records, is shown by the date on Stela C at Tres Zapotes, 31 B.C. (Thompson correlation) or 291 B.C. (Spinden correlation). When we found the dated monument in 1939 there was much discussion as to whether the date was contemporary. Among other objections, it was said to be too early. Now, with radiocarbon dates showing the culture extended thirteen centuries B.C., even the Spinden correlation of 291 B.C. is late.

A glyph with a bar and dot reading "6," carved in the living rock in an arroyo at Tres Zapotes, is an intriguing puzzle. It is possible that it may refer to Cycle 6 of the ancient calendar.

Olmec pottery in the key sites is not of good quality and was infrequently used in ceremonial offerings. The poor quality of the pottery may be due to the moist tropical soil, which also destroyed skeletal material and wooden objects. Highland sites, such as Tlatilco and Las Bocas, were important colonies of the Olmec and are noted for exceptionally fine pottery. Fine paste white, brown, red and black vessels are beautifully formed, polished, and decorated. They made musical instruments— whistles, ocarinas, and the like. Figurines realistically portray animals and birds, jaguar, deer, tapir, monkey, opossum, iguana, armadillo, and wild turkey.

The jaguar was their most important deity, in fact, so important that features of the jaguar are frequently superimposed on human representations. Many times, a jaguar mouth is shown, and the cleft head ornament typical of Olmec sculpture is probably derived from the cleft in the jaguar skull. In related cultures, the jaguar, or werejaguar, becomes the rain god. The theme of a human head in an eagle or a jaguar mouth was continued to Aztec times.

The Olmec did not build roads. They followed rivers and trails along natural routes and mountain passes. Sites showing Olmec influences are found in widely scattered localities along such routes. The only known examples of Olmec painting are found in the caves of Juxtlahuaca and Oxtotitlán in Guerrero not far from a possible trade route.

Olmec civilization did not effloresce without stimulation from other contemporaneous cultures, such as those in the Valley of Oaxaca, Chiapas, and the Pacific slopes of Guatemala. Proof it was a basic culture is the survival of many Olmec traits and traditions among the many cultures that succeeded them.

At the end of the Olmec era, near the first century B.C., the valley of Mexico was marginal and backward. Three hundred years later, the great civilization of Teotihuacán emerged, inheriting many Olmec traits but creating others based on a different economy—irrigation.

In Guatemala and Honduras, the Classic Maya developed their impressive civilization, improving on the writing, calendar and mathematical systems of the Olmec, and building enormous ceremonial centers with pyramids of stone and elaborate carvings.

We *do* know the Olmec had a bona fide civilization. They had imagination and energy and delighted in the unusual and the difficult. The vitality and ingenuity of their art style has never been surpassed.

We *don't* know the antecedents of the Olmec or what became of them after 200 B.C. Further archaeological work should eventually give us the answers to these important questions.

14 / Prehistory Down Under

D. J. MULVANEY

Although present-day Australian Aborigines are well studied, little was known of Australian prehistory until the 1960s. Mulvaney examines tools and other remains of early man recently excavated "down under" dating back to about 25,000 years ago. The so-called dark continent of prehistory is becoming illuminated as excavations continue. Mulvaney points out that Australia is a "unique laboratory" for the analysis of cultural and ecological factors in the examination of early stone-using hunting and gathering peoples for more than 25,000 years ago to the present. The ecological framework discussed by Hole in the earlier selection on Middle East civilization could effectively be employed with the remains of early man in Australia.

With a perspective of history that reflects their European origins, Australians are now celebrating the bicentennial of Capt. James Cook's "discovery" of Australia in April, 1770. When Cook took possession of the eastern half of the continent for his British sovereign, however, upward of 250,000 people had been in occupation of Australia for considerably more than 25,000 years. Prehistorians have a rewarding task in assigning a vital role to the Aborigines in the story of Australian settlement, and the evidence they are uncovering is impressive.

Australia, the only continent whose prehistory ended with the Industrial Revolution, possesses advantages that make it a unique laboratory for the study of ecological and cultural relationships that existed during the stone-using hunter–gatherer stage of human social organization. Superficially, at least, this society appears akin to long extinct Paleolithic communities in other continents. This explains its fascination for evolutionary social theorists of the nineteenth century, including Lewis Henry Morgan, whose *Ancient Society* borrowed from Australia, and Edward B. Tylor, who contributed a paper on "The Tasmanians as Representatives of Paleolithic Man."

Unfortunately, these early workers treated Aboriginal institutions and implements like butterflies impaled on a collector's board. They assumed that the Aborigines were living fossils whose customs, possessions, bodily form, and even mental capacity had survived unaltered since the dawn of mankind. Accordingly, they classified them rigidly. They assumed further that this arrested development persisted in a harsh land of unchanging environmental conditions. This attitude bred an intellectual scorn for the "poor, primitive savage," while the static and selective concept of both culture and environment was artificial and misleading.

Aboriginal society is undergoing close scrutiny today, but the conditioning philosophical notions of the investigators have changed. Aboriginal life and the natural environment are recognized as being dynamic, interrelated, and fluctuating. While the Aboriginal situation is still studied because it offers insight into, or is analogous to, life at a comparable economic subsistence level in Paleolithic times, this is an incidental consequence. The chief interest is in the Aborigines as people and in their past adaptations to the natural environment.

Fundamental research in Australia can contribute substantially to the sum of world prehistory. This is the only continent where nonagricultural/pastoral people have retained total occupancy into the "ethnographic present." Although rarely attempted, it has been possible (and in some regions, it still is) to record and analyze the role of an individual Aboriginal hunter; the technological and economic organization, as well as the artistic and ceremonial life, of entire communities; and the spiritual bonds and linguistic affiliations of those societies.

Archeologists can examine sites that were not disturbed by later agriculture or industry, where organic materials are frequently preserved. There are even unique examples of perishable Stone Age field monuments surviving. Impressive "canoe trees," for example, their trunks scarred where the bark has been removed to make watercraft, still line some waterways.

The unrivaled opportunity still exists to meet Stone Age men—to talk with the present occupants of an archeological site about its function, or to be led to a ceremonial or art site by its owners, who can explain its meaning. In these circumstances, it is possible to document aspects of ethnoarcheology—for example, the manufacture and use of tools by Aboriginal craftsmen and the resultant effects of wear—that are of concern to all prehistorians of the Stone Age.

The ethnographic specimens collected in museums, the relatively bulky written records and sketches by early explorers, settlers, and anthropologists, and the oral sources mentioned above facilitate ethnohistorical reconstruction. In this way, the pattern of Aboriginal life near the end of its prehistoric phase can be presented as a form of history. This evidence also contains valuable clues concerning the demographic situation at the time. Population estimates of these hunter–gatherer groups, although rather vague, are probably more reliable than figures for any comparable society in the past and are therefore relevant to any discussion of prehistoric world population densities.

Collated with the results of ecological research, such data also provide insight into the flora, fauna, and landscape immediately preceding the drastic impact of farmers and pastoralists. Of even greater significance is the possibility of eventually reconstructing the environment at the time of initial Aboriginal colonization. Then the role of the nomadic Aboriginal, his dog, and his firestick as factors in transforming plant and animal communities will be clarified. There are hints that these factors were far-reaching in their effect, and some authorities believe that, particularly through fires instigated by man, huge tracts of forestland were converted to open grasslands, and that the giant marsupial fauna became extinct only after man's arrival. But such theories require unequivocal proof, and field work to that end is in progress.

Australian prehistorians are at present preoccupied with a chronological leapfrog. Ten years ago the oldest carbon 14-dated Aboriginal site positively associated with man was about 8,500 years B.P. In 1962, my excavation at Kenniff Cave, Queensland, took prehistory firmly into late Pleistocene (Ice Age) times, with dates back to about 16,000 years. Then the work of other archeologists produced ages of 20,000 years and more for occupation in Arnhem Land, in the north, and at Koonalda Cave, on the Nullarbor Plain near the southern coastline. More recently, a cave at Burrill Lake, on the eastern seaboard south of Sydney, also proved to have been occupied 20,000 years ago.

Greater antiquity is probable, but until substantiated by further field work, it remains less securely based. There is presumed human association with an age of perhaps 26,000 years at Lake Menindee, in western New South Wales; a comparable antiquity is inferred at another site in that region, and field work is in progress. Just outside Melbourne, the Keilor soil pit produced a date of some 31,000 years, which the excavator, A. Gallus, associates with human occupation. He infers even greater antiquity for other finds, but his interpretation of the fractured stone at this site is disputed by some archeologists, who consider natural factors a possible explanation.

Within a few years, then, Australia's human time-span has been trebled, and the initial colonization is firmly based in the last major stage of the Pleistocene ice advance, if not earlier. This implies that at the time of this migration, sea levels were lower by 300 feet or more, and vast plains emerged from the seabed to the north of Australia, adding perhaps 10 percent to the area of the continent. New Guinea and Australia were connected, and the flat plains extended toward Indonesia, cutting the extent of water separating insular southeast Asia from Australia, but never bridging the ocean deep of Wallacea, the region of the Wallace Line of zoogeographic fame. Migrants therefore required some form of watercraft.

The most significant archeological discoveries within recent years concern human fossil remains. N. W. G. Macintosh, of Sydney University, has reappraised existing data, concluding that two basic groups are represented in the fossil record. One group (which includes the presumed terminal Pleistocene-aged Keilor cranium) possesses many characteristic modern features, implying that people with the morphology of modern Aborigines had reached southern Australia by the late Pleistocene.

The second group has many archaic features, and as their presumed age is comparable to that of the first group, it raises the possibility that they coexisted within the same region of Australia. This provides the background to recent significant discoveries by A. G. Thorne, also of Sydney University, who has located a number of fossils of the archaic group buried in a sand lunette not far from the Cohuna site, where an archaic cranium was found many years ago. So far, he has discovered seven individuals, and further finds are anticipated from large-scale, interdisciplinary excavation.

The deposit in which the burials occur is undated at present, but it is presumed to be at least 20,000 years old. The bones are heavily mineralized and carbonate encrusted. All individuals possessed very rugged features; the jaws and brow ridges were massive, the cranial bone was exceptionally thick, and the foreheads receded more than in any other known Australian specimens. Indeed, some of these characteristics suggest comparison with the Javanese fossils of *Pithecanthropus (Homo erectus),* whose order of antiquity is some half-million years.

Thorne's definitive report on these remains will constitute a landmark in Australian physical anthropology. Normally, a researcher has to interpret single and fragmentary fossil finds. In this case, with seven individuals already obtained from the one site, including postcranial bones, he has available for analysis a unique and challenging human population.

Australian prehistory contains other surprises. During 1964–65, in the course of research at The Australian National University, Carmel White excavated several sites in the Oenpelli area, Arnhem Land. In two of them, radiocarbon dates back 18,000 to 23,000 years were obtained, and in both instances this occupation was associated with the use of edge-ground axes. Such an antiquity for grinding techniques was unexpected, and interest was further enhanced because some of the axes were shaped in a tapering or waisted fashion, while others possessed deliberate grooves. These technological developments were once considered the type indicator of the New Stone Age.

Interest then focused on the antiquity of Aboriginal art. The deposit at Kenniff Cave contained ocher fragments throughout, and some indefinite esthetic purpose might be inferred from their presence even in Pleistocene levels. The real breakthrough in this regard was made at Koonalda Cave, a site used by prehistoric artisans as a flint quarry. In total darkness deep inside the cave, hundreds of square feet of linear finger tracings and grooves cover the soft limestone walls, in a style and arrangement reminiscent of some Paleolithic caves in France. A massive rock fall that crashed down against them coincidentally allowed a minimum age to be assigned to these designs. Subsequent flint miners, working in the dark, had tossed burned wooden torches onto this rubble, thereby piling up ideal radiocarbon samples against the future. This wood is older than 18,000 years, giving the wall art an age greater than many classic European Paleolithic art sites, and proving that the early Aborigines possessed an esthetic sense.

The motifs engraved on Koonalda's walls include simple finger tracings and linear incisions, but their purpose and interpretation are debatable. Across the continent, however, in a shelter at Ingaladdi, 200 miles south of Darwin, excavations recovered several sandstone fragments with similar abraded grooves. Presumably, they had disintegrated from the rock face, and when they fell, they scattered over the prehistoric habitation floor. Because an accumulating deposit later buried them below three feet of occupational debris, their minimum age is the age of the layer in which they were imbedded, and this dates from 5,000 to 7,000 years ago.

Whatever the purpose of these markings, further evidence for a remarkable stylistic continuity through time comes from the same district. Observations made during this century by anthropologists at a nearby Aboriginal ceremonial site at Delamere cattle ranch establish that similar abraded grooves were rubbed into the rock by Aboriginal participants during rain-making rituals. Calcite crystals were also used in these ceremonies, and it is therefore relevant that we excavated similar calcite crystals in the Ingaladdi deposit.

From studies of contemporary Aboriginal rituals the prehistorian also learns that more of the decorative devices are designed for destruction than for permanence on rock surfaces. Indeed, the time and trouble taken to produce perishable art forms—body painting, intricate ceremonial regalia destroyed during the ceremony, and large-scale ground paintings and sand drawings—far surpass that spent on the rock art by which Paleolithic societies are known.

A major survey and film record of central Australian rock art, undertaken by Robert Edwards of the South Australian Museum, has disclosed many engraved sites. From the extent of their patination and weathering, he inferred they were of great antiquity. The most remarkable of such galleries is in the remote sandstone Cleland Hills, west of Alice Springs. In addition to the familiar linear motifs of other sites, there are striking engraved human figures of some artistic merit, staring from the past with owlish gaze.

The Australian Institute of Aboriginal Studies recently sponsored a major salvage project at Mount Cameron West, in northwestern Tasmania. Work centered on a large gallery of art engraved upon soft eolianite, wind-deposited rock, situated on an exposed ocean beach. Excavations showed that drifting sand had covered many engraved rocks, and that previous human occupation of the site had resulted in an accumulation of midden against the lowest rocks. Radiocarbon dating of charcoal from this level, therefore, should provide a minimum age for the art. A consideration of interest to Edwards, who photographed the site, is that circles and other art forms on this monument are reminiscent of designs on those Central Australian sites to which he attributes great antiquity.

Tasmania is archeologically intriguing. The rising seas following the melting of the ice sheets made it an island some 10,000 years ago. As far as can be ascertained at present, its Aboriginal population arrived by land before that time and thereafter remained isolated from outside influences until the fatal impact of the European arrival in the late eighteenth century. Their way of life at that time was materially simpler than that of the mainland Aborigines, and excavations have shown that apparently their stone technology did not change significantly during the long duration of their occupation of Tasmania.

It seems justifiable to assume, therefore, that Tasmanian material culture, particularly its stone equipment, reflected the technological status attained by mainland Aboriginal society about the end of the Pleistocene. It is tempting also to infer that Tasmanian rock art was part of the "invisible baggage" of these early migrants. If the art style does prove to be so ancient, however, the possibility of continuity of tradition emerges. About A.D. 1800, the Tasmanians were seen to draw similar motifs on sheets of bark.

It has become a truism of Australian archeology that the older layers on many excavated mainland sites contain types of stone tools whose affinity with the Tasmanian material seems close. Both these early mainland collections and Tasmanian implements are made of cores or flakes. Blade tools are absent from Tasmanian collections. The distribution of a considerable variety of small and carefully trimmed blades and points is limited to continental Australia, where their first appearance, 6,000 to 7,000 years ago, came long after Tasmania became isolated.

This technological change from core and flake production to blade tools was vividly illustrated at Ingaladdi. The lower layers, which contained the engraved rocks, also produced numerous trimmed flakes (scrapers) and small cores that apparently had served as chopping or planing tools. The upper layers contained a different assemblage, consisting primarily of thousands of small, pointed blades, presumably projectile points, carefully retouched on one or both faces. This dichotomy between an earlier flake and core industry made on fairly large pieces, and a later, small blade and flake complex, has been reproduced at several excavated deposits across the continent, including those at Kenniff Cave and Burrill Lake. The form these tools take is subject to regional variation.

Another rock shelter that seems to follow this pattern is on the slopes of Mount Burr, an extinct volcano in southeastern South Australia. Men occupied it over 8,000 years ago, although the area was still volcanically active. Nearby, Mount Gambier last erupted little more than 4,000 years ago. This is a reminder that the Aborigines have adapted to many far-reaching environmental changes since their arrival in Australia: the seas rose and the coastline shrank, inland lakes dried up, major river systems flowed intermittently, and numerous volcanoes on the extensive south-eastern basalt plains became extinct.

Certain changes may have been assisted by the Aborigines. Early explorers commented upon their widespread practice of firing the countryside, and this regular burning, particularly of semiarid landscapes, may have produced drastic changes in vegetation cover, native fauna, and soil erosion.

Predatory man also introduced another scourge of native fauna, the dingo—a reddish-brown wild dog. It must have crossed the seas from Asia with man at an early date in the history of animal domestication. The earliest evidence for its presence in Australia consisted of a 3,000-year-old skeleton excavated at Fromm's Landing, South Australia. Subsequently, bones that may be 8,000 years old have been recovered at the Mount Burr shelter, so that dogs had reached the southern coast by that early date.

On present evidence, therefore, it appears that man, the hunter and food gatherer, probably arrived on this continent before the settlement of the New World. Even 20,000 years ago, he possessed artistic and technological skills that earlier prehistorians would not have attributed to him because they assumed that the Aborigines were so "primitive." In both adapting to and shaping the Australian environment, the Aborigines left traces that research can transform into prehistory.

15 / The Bog People of Denmark

PETER V. GLOB

What was the life of Iron Age man like in northern Europe 2,000 years ago? From the shallow depths of peat bogs in Denmark archeologists are able to reconstruct this way of life by examining the remains of remarkably well-preserved bodies with clothing, ornaments, grave furniture, food remains, and other items. This selection by Peter V. Glob describes the remarkable state of preservation of "Bog People" remains and their way of life as it was about 2,000 years ago.

One spring morning in 1950, two Danish farmworkers cutting peat at Tollund Fen in central Jutland discovered a body in the peat layer they had just uncovered. Looking down at the well-preserved features, they could only suppose that they had come across the victim of a recent murder.

The police were soon on the scene, and with them they brought representatives of the local museum, since well-preserved remains of Iron Age men were not unknown in the region. I was hastily summoned from Aarhus University and, that same evening, bent over the discovery, I found myself face to face with an Iron Age man who had been deposited in the peatbog some two thousand years earlier.

The dead man lay on his right side in a natural attitude of sleep. The head was to the west, with the face turned to the south; the legs were to the east. He lay fifty yards out from firm ground and had been covered by eight or nine feet of peat.

On his head he wore a pointed skin cap fastened securely under the chin by a hide thong, and round his waist was a smooth hide belt. Otherwise he was naked. His hair was cropped short and he was clean-shaven, although his chin and upper lip were covered with very short stubble.

Round his neck was a rope made of two leather thongs twisted together and drawn tight into his throat in a noose and then coiled like a snake over his shoulder and down across the back.

The Tollund man's head was remarkably well preserved, the best preserved human head, in fact, to have survived from antiquity in any part of the world. The dead man's lightly-closed eyes and half-closed lips give the face a distinctive expression, calling to mind the words of the world's oldest heroic epic, the *Gilgamesh,* "the dead and the sleeping, how they resemble one another."

A wooden crate was assembled on the site of the discovery so that the Tollund man could be removed to the National Museum in Copenhagen in exactly the position in which he was found.

The doctors and medico-legal experts who examined him in Copenhagen concluded that he had probably been hanged rather than strangled by the rope found round his neck. X-rays showed that the skull was undamaged and the brain intact but shrunken. The wisdom teeth had developed, indicating that the man must have been appreciably over twenty years old at the time of death.

An autopsy showed that the inner organs, such as the heart, lungs, and liver were well preserved as were the stomach and the large and small intestines, which contained traces of the dead man's last meal, eaten between 12 and 24 hours before death. Apparently this had consisted of a gruel prepared from barley, linseed, "gold of pleasure" and various other weeds, but there was no trace of any meat or fish.

After these exhaustive examinations, the head underwent conservation treatment, and was sent to the Silkeborg Museum, not far from Tollund, where it can be seen to this day. Dark in hue, the majestic, 2,000 year old head is still full of life; it astonishes the beholder and rivets his attention.

Barely two years after the discovery of the Tollund man, in April 1952, another body was discovered in a Jutland fen. This time it was in the Nebelgard Fen at Grauballe, about eleven miles east of Tollund. When I was called to the scene, the man's head and shoulders were sticking up out of the dark brown peat. I immediately arranged for the body to be transported to the Museum of Prehistory at Aarhus, still in the block of peat in which it lay.

The Grauballe man had been placed in his peat grave completely naked and no objects of any kind were found in the vicinity. Carbon 14 dating of the liver and muscle tissue and dating by pollen analysis placed the date of death between 210 A.D. and 410 A.D.

X-rays and examination of various bone tissues and the teeth established the Grauballe man's age at around thirty years.

There could be no doubt about the cause of death. A long cut ran round the throat practically from ear to ear, so deep that the gullet was completely severed.

The Grauballe man was perfectly preserved, though somewhat flattened by the over-lying peat. His hair was about six inches in length and short stubble on his chin and upper lip showed that he had been clean-shaven.

Radiography of the head showed that the brain was remarkably well preserved though a little shrunken. The two halves of the brain and its convolutions could be clearly seen in the X-rays.

His last meal was similar to that of the Tollund man, consisting of a gruel of grain and seed, but containing no trace of summer or autumn berries or other fruit or greenstuffs. There are thus grounds for thinking that both men met their deaths in winter or early spring, before everything had come into leaf. It may be deduced that they were both sacrificed and placed in the peat-bog as offerings at the mid-winter celebrations or the festivals of spring.

Examination of the beautifully preserved feet and hands revealed such clear line patterns that it was possible to take prints of several of his fingers, the oldest known fingerprints of any human being.

When investigation of the Grauballe man was completed, and before he was given conservation treatment, a plaster cast was made of him lying in exactly the position in which he was found in the peat-bog.

During the 1,500 years he had lain in the peat-bog a tanning process had been taking place which had preserved him up to our day. This process begun by nature was successfully completed in a laboratory by the "pit-tanning" technique, using oak bark, to which the body was subjected for just over a year and a half. Since then the Grauballe man has been exhibited in the Museum of Prehistory at Aarhus, where he lies just as he was found in the peat-bog.

The peat-bogs of north-west Europe have yielded up nearly 700 bodies of men, women and children preserved by nature for twenty centuries. Most of the bodies of these people, who lived during the early centuries of the Christian era, were found in Denmark, and more than half of them in the Jutland peninsula and the adjoining regions of north-west Germany. Other bog people have been found in England, Wales, Scotland and Ireland and, in smaller numbers, in Norway, Sweden and central Europe.

It is the acid in these peat-bogs, as well as the low oxygen content of bog water, which has tanned the skin and hair of the bodies and preserved them as though they had only recently been placed there.

But only very few of these bog people are still in a good state of preservation. Most of the bodies crumbled away as soon as they were exposed to the oxygen in the air, since no one seemed to know how to preserve them. A few have been saved by a careful drying process, in particular the body of a woman found at Haraldskjaer in Denmark, in 1837. The experts of the day thought that this might have been the body of the Norwegian Queen Gunhild who was murdered by being drowned in a peat-bog 900 years earlier.

But the body was later identified as that of an Iron Age woman dating back a further thousand years. Her body is still preserved and lies in the crypt of the church of St. Nicholas at Vejle, in Jutland, in an oak coffin personally presented by King Frederick VI.

Another early discovery, dating back to 1780, is that of a woman of

rank unearthed from a peat-bog near Drumkeragh Mountain in Ireland. She was dressed in a finely-woven red and green garment and a stole embroidered with figures, and she lay on three woollen blankets.

Other well-preserved bodies of bog people found in Denmark include those of a man and a woman, uncovered in Borre Fen at Himmerland, in the north of Jutland, near the site of an early Iron Age village in which they had probably lived.

The man had been placed in the peat-bog in a sitting position. The back of his head was crushed in and round his neck was a hemp rope fastened with a slip-knot. Both ends of the rope were skillfully bound and stitched with hide thongs to prevent them from unravelling. He had probably been hanged or strangled with this rope.

The dead man had been brought to the peat-bog naked except for the rope around his neck. Rolled up at his feet, however, were two capes, sewn together from pieces of light and dark sheepskin.

The woman lay face downwards on a sheet of birch bark. The upper part of her body was uncovered while the remainder was covered by a wollen blanket.

On an island in the same fen, an Iron Age village consisting of some twenty houses has been excavated. Like most Jutland peasant houses of two thousand years ago those of the village of Borre Fen were dwellings for both men and animals.

The houses varied in size and were clustered round the village street. The biggest house is eighty-eight feet long by twenty-three feet wide and the smallest is half this length and somewhat narrower. The walls were made of turf and the roofs of straw or heather thatch. The inhabitants lived in one half of the house round a central hearth while the animals occupied the other half.

Other bog people have been discovered in Schleswig-Holstein close to Jutland's southern border; they are now exhibited in the local museum of Gottorp castle in Schleswig. Among them are an elderly man and a young girl found in a peat-bog at Windeby farm in 1952.

Also to be seen at Gottorp castle is the head of a man wearing a curious hair style, described by the Roman historian Tacitus in his treatise on the German tribes, written at the time of the bog people, in the first century A.D. The reddish hair, originally blond, was eleven inches long. It was gathered at the right side into a skillfully contrived knot which, Tacitus tells us, was a style typical of the Swabian tribe. Similar knots are to be seen in Roman sculptures depicting the Germanic tribes.

Writing on human sacrifice among the Germani, Tacitus states that this was connected both with the punishment of crime and the ritual of spring worship of the gods. Concerning Germanic law, he writes that accusations and demands for the death penalty could be brought before the tribal assembly. Traitors and deserters were hung from a tree and cowards and evil-doers were plunged into the mud of the marshes.

Each year a dramatic ritual of worship was enacted to awaken the forces of nature and to ensure the germination of corn and the fertility of man and domestic animals.

Tacitus tells us that on an island in the ocean there was a holy grove where no man could set foot. In the grove was hidden a chariot in which none but a priest could ride in company with the goddess.

In this chariot, drawn by oxen, they drove through the countryside awakening life and fertility in all things. The goddess then retired to her divine abode. The chariot and the goddess were washed in a secret lake by slaves and ministrants who were then drowned in the lake.

The many people found in the peat-bogs may, therefore, have been placed there as punishment for crime or as sacrifices to the great goddess, whom Tacitus calls Nerthus, or Mother Earth.

During the centuries preceding and following the birth of Christ, such a goddess was worshipped in northern lands. She is depicted in several small bronzes wearing only two rings around her neck and sometimes in her ears and with her hands under her life-giving breasts.

The Mother goddess had already been worshipped in neolithic times. Her eyes look out at us from the clay pots of this period and her symbol is to be seen on slate pendants worn as amulets.

During the period of the bog people, in the late Iron Age, this goddess reigned supreme over all other gods and she is represented in highly stylized form on bronze jewel-pins. Many bracelets and necklaces have been discovered in the peat-bogs where they were placed as offerings.

A magnificent silver cauldron was found in a peat-bog near Gundestrup in Jutland. It is decorated with embossed figures representing, on the outside, gods and goddesses with their attendants and, on the inside, scenes showing the goddess surrounded by legendary beasts and human sacrifices.

The Gundestrup cauldron was made in south-east Europe, where it was captured as war booty, brought back to Denmark and placed as an offering in a peat-bog near Borre Fen. But several of the deities worshipped by the bog people of Denmark are represented on the cauldron.

The Tollund man and many of the other bog men, after their brief time as the companion and lover of the goddess, may have been sacrificed and placed in the peat-bogs in which they have been so remarkably preserved.

Part 3 / QUESTIONS AND PROBLEMS FOR DISCUSSION

1. Discuss the reasons Australia provides a unique setting for the study of ecological–cultural relationships in the stone-using hunting and gathering stage of early man.

2. What does late Paleolithic art tell us about the belief systems of early modern man?
3. In what ways does the first civilization in the New World differ from the first civilization in the Old World? In what ways are the two similar?
4. What do the peat-bog burial remains tell us about the life of man during the Iron Age in northern Europe?
5. When, from where, and how was the New World populated?

4/ MAN SPEAKS
IN MANY TONGUES

Man as an animal has been called many things—a political animal, a rational animal, a human animal, and so forth. He is all of these things, but above all he is a speaking animal. Man alone has the ability to communicate through the medium of language. Of all animals, man alone possesses the unique ability to symbolize and express previous experiences in the form of words. Although all men have this quality, there is a tremendous amount of variation in language—man speaks in many tongues. It is the diversity of languages as well as the common features of language that are of primary concern to the linguist. Anthropologists who study language do not have the final answer as to exactly how language started or the exact way it has developed, but all anthropologists agree that language is the most important element in man's cultural heritage. Language not only provides a system of symbolization for the parts of a culture (law, religion, economics, and such), but it is also the means by which the total cultural system is integrated and passed from generation to generation. Without language culture could not exist. This statement prompts the long-standing consideration of which developed first, culture or language. Although many anthropologists take the position that language preceded the development of early culture, it is also reasonable to take the position that both developed at about the same time. Here, then, we are able to see the strong overlap of the field of linguistics as it relates to the study of prehistory and the development of early man. The following selections show how anthropologists approach the study of how man speaks. Articles include the way anthropologists analyze sound, grammar, and the meaning of words; the way the element of time affects communication; and the way jargon affects the transmission of ideas through speech.

16 / Man Studies His Speech

PAUL BOHANNAN

We all know something about the language we speak, but how does man study his own speech? Paul Bohannan's selection answers this question, in part, by showing how the linguist places speech elements in an orderly fashion so that language can be studied in a scientific manner. Another aspect of speech is that different languages call attention to different types of social reality. "We speak as we think, and we think as we speak." Consider this statement carefully as you read Bohannan's comments on the Whorfian hypothesis, a startling idea on the interaction of language structure and the thinking process.

Language, by means of speech and highly abstract symbols, allows human beings to communicate abstract details to one another. Words and grammar enable us to call up in someone else the sort of sensations that are (so far as we can tell) analogous to our own, so that some sort of common goal or activity is possible.

All human beings speak, unless they are abnormal. Their speech represents or symbolizes the set of common understandings that is culture. Speech is a reflection of culture, because it is the means by which we symbolize all culture for purposes of communication. There are also other, more specialized, ways of symbolizing culture for communication. Gestures may be systematized and widely known—and may, in fact, communicate much even if they are not systematized. Music is a more general and less precise type of symbolization for communication than is art. Nevertheless, music can communicate emotion of a sort, a sense of order that challenges even mathematics, and if it is really good music, much more. However, language is both the most common and the most extensive symbol system.

But language is a two-edged sword: at the same time that it allows people to cut through the morass of sensation and communicate not merely gross impression but the intricacies of idea and interpretation, it also creates disjointed pieces and characteristic unions of them that imprison the mind within a single mode of perception. Language (or art) is the mold into which perception must be fitted if it is to be communicated. Any single language imprints its own "genius" on the message. We have already seen that the task of the anthropologist is to explore and illuminate the linguistic and cultural vise that holds firmly the minds of the people of his own society and of others.

Probably the most popular, because it is the most vivid, example for describing the cultural categories that the necessity to communicate creates in human perception is to compare the ways in which different peoples cut up colors into communicable units. The spectrum is a continuum of light waves, with frequencies that (when measured in length) increase at a continuous rate. That part of the continuum of waves that can be perceived by the human eye is called the spectrum. The longer waves we see as violet, the shorter as red; all the other colors of the spectrum fall between them. The perception of light, broken into colors, seems to be the same for all human beings except the color blind, and even they have the same range. But the ways different cultures organize these sensations for communication show some strange differences.

The Japanese, for example, have one word, *aoi,* which covers both blue and green ranges of the spectrum: actually, it means a sort of "nature color." The fact that the Japanese do not make a linguistic distinction does not mean that they cannot tell blue from green, because they obviously can, and can describe the differences in metaphors if they so desire. It means, rather, that the Japanese language, and hence Japanese culture as a whole, sees no need to make this distinction for purposes of ordinary living.

The noted Danish linguist Louis Hjelmslev has compared the color words of English and Welsh; in Figure 2 I have added the color words from the Tiv language. The Welsh word *glas* covers everything English

Tiv	English	Welsh
pupu	green	gwyrdd
	blue	
ii	gray	glas
	brown	llwyd
nyian	red	
	yellow	

FIGURE 2   Color words

would call blue, some of the colors English would call green, and some it would call gray. *Llwyd* takes up the rest of the gray and runs over into brown. In Tiv, on the other hand, all green, some blues, and some grays are *ii*. But very light blues and light grays are *pupu*. *Nyian*, which covers brown, also covers all warm colors through red to yellow. The distinction between *ii* and *pupu* actually is not in terms of color, but in terms of what we would call shade—darkness and lightness. Very light blue, gray, or white are all *pupu*. *Ii* means dark and covers all dark colors and black—unless there is a warm color present: brown, red, and yellow are all *nyian*. Tiv can distinguish colors and do color-blind tests, but their culture does not require—or allow—that they make some of the color distinctions that Westerners make. Westerners are among the most color-conscious of peoples.

Although colors provide the most obvious example, they are not unique in being culturally and not "naturally" determined segments of reality. Indeed, all human perception is of this sort.

As a second example, take the English, German, Danish, and Tiv words for wood and trees (Figure 3). German and English both have three words.

English	German	Danish	Tiv
tree	Baum	trae	kon
wood	Holz		
forest	Wald	skov	ika

FIGURE 3 Tree words

Tree and *Baum* cut the continuum in about the same place. But the English word "wood" has a wider field of meaning than the German word *Holz;* that is, a wood is, in English (Americans use the plural), a forest that is not very dense. This kind of "wood" and "forest" itself are both *Wald* in German. Speakers of Danish cut the same total field of meaning with two words instead of three. Tiv also use only two words, but they cut the field very differently. Obviously, distinction within a perceived field is a matter that is culturally conditioned, learned, and passed on. For purposes of communication, one way is probably as good as the next in a common-sense situation; but the points of precision are different from one language to the next. The "culture," following the language, shows a significant variation.

Differences in Structure

When one comes to the structure of ideas as reflected in sentences, the matter becomes even more complex:

jeg ved det ikke	Danish
I do not know	English
Je ne sais pas	French
en tieda	Finnish
naluvara	Eskimo

The meanings of these short sentences are all more or less the same—at least, they are translations of one another. But the ways in which the idea is cut up for communication varies widely. In Danish the first word, *jeg*, means "I," then *ved* (know, present indicative), then an object *det* (it), and finally a negative, *ikke*. Very straightforward and sensible, but different from English where the first word is "I," then a verbal concept of the sort that would be called a modal auxiliary in German—and which is not represented in the Danish sentence at all—then the negation, and only then the word "know" which tells us what it is all about—and there is no case in the verb, and no object in the sentence. In French, there is first "I," then a kind of negation that is, however, completely different from that of English or Danish because it does not function as a negative in all combinations, then "know" (first person, present indicative), and finally a very peculiar particle (*pas*) that some people claim is a negative but that can also mean "step" and that acts grammatically as an adverb; as in English, there is no object. In Finnish, there is first a verb signifying "not I" (*et* means thou not; *ei*, he not; *emme*, we not; and so on), followed by the concept "know" in a form that has imperative meanings in other combinations; there is no object. Finally, in Eskimo the whole thing is a verb —"not-knowing-am-I-it"—derived from *malo*, ignorance, with the suffix of the first person subject and the third person object.

The point is that people use different types of linguistic units for breaking up experience into communicable bits, as well as vastly different principles for putting the bits back together again. Obviously, most people do not think about such matters when they are talking. The regularities are epiphenomenal to the activities of communication. Nevertheless, they are always there, for if they were not, communication would not be possible.

It is the process of breaking up perception into linguistic chunks for communication that creates the image. The image, seen in another light, is itself the vise in which every mind is ruthlessly held. All sensations, all input of ideas or impression, must either be fitted into the categories of communication that are already in the mind, or they must remain uncommunicated (and hence not fully realized). The only alternative is that they break the mold of linguistic and ideational categories and establish a new outlook.

All too seldom are people aware that their images are limited by language and culture. They are easily aware of constant broadening created by learning but not so easily aware of the equally constant narrowing created concomitantly. The enlargement of knowledge is education; the concomitant narrowing and hardening of the mode of perception and communication is a form of what we have already called habituation.

Education itself can be divided into two elements. There is on the one hand the process of training in which culture, ideas, and technique are poured into the student, utilizing the pigeonholes of communication to which he has already become habituated. He looked at his new knowledge and techniques through the old glasses, in terms of the old pigeon-holes. But on the other hand there is another process that lies at the heart of a liberal education: creating awareness in a person of the fact that his image is limited by the pigeonholes of his culture and that he must seek actively for a means of increasing its scope and quality.

Grammar

The regularities that any language demands if it is to be a suitable vehicle for communication were first (so far as we know) discovered several thousand years ago, in India, by a scholar of genius named Pānini. He made the first grammar—of Sanskrit. His idea of lifting out the regularities of usage of a language from the various acts of speech and writing was a new and daring process. Pānini's achievement was that he created a system of analytical thought which allowed him to understand the phenomena of speech in a new way. The regularities were inherent in Sanskrit —the recurrences he picked out can be likened to recurrent chemical reactions. But they had never been picked out before. Grammar has changed Sanskrit very little more than the science of chemistry has changed oxidation. But grammar and chemistry provided a new and better way of understanding the phenomena each comprehends.

Let us hasten to add that the analogy between grammar and chemistry is of limited use. People speak, and the matrices of their thought allow for change at a very much more rapid rate than phenomena comprehended by the so-called rules of chemistry. However, the idea of selecting regularities in occurrences or events, and explaining them with a "theory," is a sound one.

The Greeks obviously seem to have known Pānini's grammar, but they misunderstood it. Instead of looking at his *method* of reducing regularities to a statement of rules, they took the rules he had worked out for Sanskrit and tried to make them work in Greek. Greek is the first language, thus, to have a bad grammar, given to it by people who took their model from another language. The mistake has been often repeated: for centuries English was forced into the categories of Latin grammar (which, by and large, do not fit) because grammarians had accepted the *result* of the works of Latin grammarians—the forms—rather than the *principles* of grammar making—the activity.

There are, then, three different levels of analysis to be considered. First are the regularities in the vocal events that occur when a language is spoken (or in manual events when it is written). There are, in the second place, the "rules" of Sanskrit grammar, which can be elicited from the original regularities and stated more or less as "scientific" laws. Third and most elusive, there is the idea of the activity involved in seeking and discovering rules in regularities, and of organizing them into consistent bodies of thought. The first is event, the second is science, and the third is scientific method—the epistemology of science. Science must always be based on regularities occurring in the data that are to be explained. Scientific epistemology—"the philosophy of science"—must always be based on the regularities in the activity of scientists. The first set of regularities is one in communication, the second one in science, the third one in philosophy.

The analogy from language to the rest of culture should be obvious: there are regularities of behavior that can be observed. With observation, the "rules" (in the sense of the statistical mean, not the morally required minimum) of behavior can be established by scientists by and for people who live by means of that culture; moreover, the people who live the culture have already established their own rules. This second, or scientific process leads to "ethnographic theory," if the purpose be to explain and translate a single culture, or to "ethnological theory" if the purpose be to compare many cultures. Finally, there is the science of anthropology, which is a set of rules for examining behavior and creating ethnological theory. Anthropology is thus, at its most abstract level, interested in determining how it is that people know what they know, whether it be on the psychic, the scientific, or the epistemological levels.

Linguistics

It has been said that the beginning of scientific linguistics can be dated from the rediscovery of Pānini's grammar in the eighteenth century. For millennia after the original creation of grammar, no new regularities in languages and speech were either discovered or sought. It is practically within our own time that the next great surge of progress in the study of language has come. The result is that linguistics is the most scientifically advanced branch of cultural anthropology: indeed, linguistics provides the model on which cultural analysis is proceeding. Cultural anthropology, which treats of culture in relation to people and society much as linguistics treats of the phenomena of language in relation to the intricacies of meaning, has found—at least for the moment—a mode of progress.

The "secret" of the success of linguistics is an open one: there are many different sorts or regularities that can be discovered in the same body of phenomena. Linguistics has discovered that the number of sounds used by any language is limited; phonetics and phonemics have resulted. The characteristic ways that sounds are combined to communicate chunks of meaning have given rise to the concept of the morphemic system; tones, if they are important, can be understood in terms of a tonic system. There are many other possible systems.

Any sound that a language uses is called a *phoneme*. Phonemes can be easily discovered: if changing the sound changes the meaning, there are two phonemes; if it does not, there is only one. Thus, in English r and l are separate phonemes because there is a difference in meaning between rim and lim(b). In many West African languages, these two sounds are not separate phonemes. Conversely, in many African languages an exploded "b" of the sort found in English and the imploded " " that an English speaker would not even notice are separate phonemes. There would be, that is, a change of meaning between boy and   oy. Phonemics is not composed solely of the observation of individual sounds, but also of the characteristic ways in which languages put these sounds together. For example, no word in English begins with "s-r," although the combination is a common one in Italian.

Linguistics has reduced speech, the most important means by which we communicate, to order and made it amenable to scientific description and discussion. We know a great deal about how phonemic systems change, and can predict with almost uncanny accuracy what will happen to a "k" sound if it begins to come into conflict with a broad "a." Predictions can be made in the rest of the system.

However, note that the basic *communication* has not been touched. Linguistics, at this level, is dealing with the regularities in the *instrument* of communication, not with the ideas it contains. It has been dealing with a part of what communications engineers would call the matrix or the code, not with what they would call the message.

A matrix is as good as its ability to carry a message. What linguists study are the differences among and the systems within which people speak with one another and communicate their ideas. By their own choice, linguists have limited themselves to language. But cultural anthropologists do something of the same thing. They study the matrices within which people live with one another and communicate their lives. Whatever reality may be, the data that the anthropologist must work with is communication through act, word, or some other form. Presumably, by studying the differences in the matrix from one culture to another, we can ultimately learn something about human perception and various images to which it gives rise.

Linguistics is an extremely important and practical branch of anthropology. Besides the fact that it deals scientifically with one of the universal aspects of culture, it is of immense value on two other grounds. First, as the most scientifically advanced of the cultural sciences, it provides a necessary model. People can dissociate themselves from their languages with a fair degree of ease; self-consciousness and *amour-propre* soon disappear from a consideration of it. Therefore, the scientization of linguistics has proceeded rapidly, and the analogy to the activities of linguists can provide many scientific guideposts for men who are investigating other aspects of culture. Second, and even more practical, a firm knowledge of linguistics dramatically reduces the time required to learn new languages, and is hence an indispensable tool for the fieldworker.

Semantics and the Whorfian Hypothesis

Benjamin Lee Whorf was a linguist so startlingly original that he is still persistently misunderstood by many members of his profession. He is misunderstood for precisely the same reasons that James Joyce or Picasso, say, were not accepted for many years by some critics or much of public. In order to communicate new and deeply original perceptions, they all had to go beyond traditional modes of communication. Sometimes communication of new insights is clumsy. That is the worst charge that can be leveled against Whorf: he tried to express, in terms of the old categories of semantics, some new ideas that had to burst them.

What has come to be known as the "Whorfian hypothesis"—Whorf, had he lived, might well have joined the ranks of Marx and Freud by stating, "I am no Whorfian"—is merely this: people break up not just their language, but by means of their language their whole culture into bits for purposes of communication. As they learn the "code" or matrix in the process of maturation, there is an automatic knowledge and response in perception. The code units are words, and most of the knowledge and perception—certainly all that is communicated—is seen in terms of these words. The words become categories of reality. The mode of putting them together becomes the "natural organization" of reality, and the point of education and thought is to discover that the "naturalness" is itself open to questioning and to change.

Besides the words, there are larger categories that form the grammatical elements: the "parts of speech." They are the manner in which we put these word categories together when we communicate. Whorf pointed out (what we had, on a more primitive level, already known) that all Indo-European languages break things into two big, inclusive grammatical categories. There are things and there are qualities. The qualities we call verbs, adjectives, and adverbs. The things we call nouns and pronouns. The other grammatical bits such as postpositions, prepositions, and conjunctions are hooks for tying the main units together in the right juxtapositions. Every sentence we utter has a subject and a predicate. But we can, as a result of Whorf, see that fact in a new light. Every idea that we have and express in English *must* be broken down into things and qualities. The universe, indeed, must be classified into two boxes: things and qualities.

It is not possible to divide words themselves into two groups, some for things and other for qualities. The word "man," for example, represents a thing. But if you say "he is a man," the word "man" is a quality. If you say "the ship is manned," the word "man" becomes a quality of the ship. You can take the word "run," which is a quality of some animal, and turn it into a noun or thing quite easily.

This particular system is not quite universal. The Salish languages apparently do not so break the world into two great segments for communication. These languages seem to be made entirely of concepts that represent entities interrelated or juxtaposed. "I go down the path" comes out "I foot path." The qualities may be inherent in the nouns, but the world is not broken up in the same way as for the Indo-European languages. The point is that the matrix affects thought and very often changes the intricacies of thought, but one can say anything in any language. It may not come out the same, but the meaning can be got across. However, the people who speak the language habitually may not understand what a foreign speaker says in the language, even though he says it correctly, if they do not have the ideas themselves in at least some attenuated form.

Thus, a language is not merely part of the culture, but it is also a reflection of the total culture. It is a reflection, more importantly perhaps, of the *organization* of that total culture. To be perceived it must be broken up into bits. To be used, the bits must be organized, and it is the organization that is important.

The Trap of Language

One of the best ways to see that any language provides a trap at the same time it provides a means of expression is to examine some of the problems that have come to light in the course of translations. The Bible is the most widely translated book with which we are intimately acquainted. It has been set into the languages of "civilized" and "primitive" peoples, and into all the linguistic families of the world. Eugene Nida has written a book called *God's Word in Man's Language,* which rehearses in some detail problems that have arisen in translating the Bible into some of these languages.

One of the most common problems is that language may mirror social ranking and social organization, and the social system of the Bible may not correspond in any detail. One vivid example can be taken from the Japanese. In that language, a writer cannot use direct quotation without at the same time indicating the relative social rank of the two persons involved. Japanese verb endings—and the verbs must have endings—always indicate whether the speaker is socially superior, inferior, or equal to the addressee. There are, moreover, several grades of superior and inferior. When Christ turned to the man he had cured and said, "Pick up thy bed and walk," what verb endings would he have used had he been speaking Japanese? Were Christ and the patient equals? Was one the social superior or inferior of the other? These are theological problems created by the processes of translation.

In the original Greek—and indeed in English—there is nothing in the grammar to indicate relative social position; at most there would be something in the vocabulary or the tone of voice. In Japanese, the matter of rank is always present in the grammar. The social structure must thus be known or assumed even to *speak* Japanese. The same is true of some American Indian languages and some of the African languages. What we do with manner and choice of words, they do with grammar. Introduction of social organization into the forms of a language creates a difficult translation problem, and elucidates the nature of the language trap.

Our languages may also stamp our notions of credibility and proof. "Truth" is for Westerners a complex but single idea. Most West African languages have two words for "truth." There is one kind meaning "social correctness" and another meaning "what actually happened." If I know perfectly well that my brother's wife committed adultery and my brother asks me about it, I can tell the socially correct "truth" and save everyone a lot of trouble, or I can tell the precise "truth" and create trouble. The truth of right action, in the Tiv language, is called *mimi*. The truth of verifiable occurrence is called *vough*. The antonym of both these words is *yie,* which must be translated "lie." *Mimi* may coincide with *vough*— but it may not. Among close personal acquaintances and kinsmen, it is moral to use *mimi;* among others, it is wise to use *vough*. In court cases, when an oath is taken by a witness before he gives evidence, he swears to speak *vough*. But the defendant and the plaintiff are, in most parts of Africa, refused the right to swear, because each is expected to tell his version of *mimi*.

One of Whorf's favorite examples of the tyranny of language is the concept of time. We assume time, velocity, matter. Time is something in our concepts, which the physicists call *t*. It has a beginning—at least until Einstein, we thought it would have an end. It runs forward in one direction, at a uniform rate. It "exists." The idea of its existence has become more pronounced in the last 200 years. Since time has entered the market, it has become money. Time is divided into hours; hours cost money. And time is running out.

The Hopi people of our own Southwest, whose language was analyzed by Whorf, do not have this kind of an idea of time. To put it into a metaphor, time is to them a sort of cylinder that turns over slowly. There is night on one side and day on the other; first night comes round and then, as the cylinder turns, day. Both recur. The recurrences can be counted. However, it is not possible to compute duration. Time, *t,* in our own idea, has duration—"five days." The Hopi language puts it, "day came five times." There is a difference, even though the message is much the same. "I left the fifth time day came around" means the same thing as "I stayed five days."

The same conceptualization occurs among some African peoples with reference to generation—there are constantly two generations. You name your children for your parents, and they are in some sense reincarnations of the parents. The same principle may be applied to three or more generations as to two.

Time is a necessary dimension of English grammar—present, past, and future tense. Every speaker who would assert existence must indicate either that something is happening now or that it happened in the past. Hopi does not demand such a built-in statement about time. Neither does Japanese. The distinction between past and present is not built into some languages, yet the distinction can be made with adverbs or some other such way, if it is desired. In English the distinction is one that must be made in the sheer process of description or narrative: speakers of English are stuck with tense, and hence with a limited concept of time, just as speakers of Japanese are stuck with a mode of social organization.

English, furthermore, cannot put a statement into the future without implicit prognostication. But the Hopi language can. Hopi divide the world into what Whorf calls the manifest and the nonmanifest. The manifest "tense" has absolutely nothing to say about the present, last week, or a decade since. It "is." Everything that one wishes, knows, but does not see, such as religious ideas, are categorized together with the future in the nonmanifest. In this case one can immediately see how wrong it would be to say that all religion is in "the future tense" in Hopi: that would be seeing it in our terms. Rather, certain religious phenomena are unmanifested and therefore are so indicated grammatically.

There is, also, another Hopi "tense" for things that are constant and immutable in the world. Therefore, we have manifest-mutable, manifest-immutable, and nonmanifest. It is as good a way of dividing the world up as is the Indo-European.

A similar set of statements can be made about space. Our own ideas of dimension and space are probably unique in the world. In 1732 a device called the sextant was invented. It changed the culture of the world far more than it is given credit for, in only a little over two centuries. With this instrument and some other surveying equipment and the idea that positions on the earth are fixed relatively to the stars, we have been able to put on paper, or on globes, a grid. We can then pick out a point on the grid that is referable to the stars. Then, with other devices we measure out other points on the grid. And the result is something called a map. Scientifically, modern maps are "correct." But they and the instruments that produce them have led to a very pronounced and definite way of viewing space. People who do not have the same gadgetry do not see space in this mechanistic way—most of them see it in terms of social relations, kinsmen, time, and effort. In the Tiv language the word *cha,* which is usually translated "far," has three referents: it is far if when you go someplace it takes you a long time to get there; it is far if the distance is great; and it is far if you go into an area where you are a stranger.

The Value of Whorfian Concepts

Whorf's ideas are so simple and so vital that it would seem that some of his critics willfully refuse to understand them. Simplicity often makes for difficulty in understanding, especially if what is simplified includes ideas that people would just as soon continue to be muddled about.

Whorf was searching for a language different enough from English to enable him to pin down his ideas. He found the language in Hopi. There have been two kinds of criticism of Whorf. One of these is the *pars-pro-toto* type of criticism—the critic proves that two or three of Whorf's points in Hopi were wrong, so he throws out the hypothesis. This is the baby-with-the-bath fallacy. The other type of criticism is the sidetrack type of criticism—to criticize Whorf for something he did not do: he did *not* try to establish a "relationship between language and culture" or between language and the rest of culture. He has been extensively criticized as if he had.

It may sound a little shocking to say that it is a matter of complete indifference whether Whorf's analyses of the nature of Hopi turn out to be right or wrong. But reconsider: he has allowed us to see something in English that we could not have seen had it not been for his ideas and his perceptions in Hopi. It would be "nicer" if Whorf's analyses of Hopi were correct. But in the long run, it is beside the point whether they are right or not. Whorf based his ideas on something that is very right in English—he illustrated it by contrast from Hopi. His vision into Hopi—correct or erroneous, it does not matter—allowed him to see some of the pigeonholes and integrating devices in English.

Whorf was stating something very simple, almost axiomatic: I cannot know the nature of reality, for I have no way of perceiving it save through my senses and the instrumental extensions of them that I create. Therefore, I must work with perceived reality, and the more I know about the nature of the perceiver, the more nearly I will ultimately know the reality. The proper subject for study—indeed the only possible subject for study—is, therefore, perception.

17 | The Voices of Time

EDWARD T. HALL

The selection by Bohannan dealt with the relation of language to human communication. However, human communication involves more than just words. Edward T. Hall gives us a glimpse of how nonverbal communication aids in a real exchange of human ideas. Man is an orderly animal who attempts to place events and activities within the framework of space and time. However, peoples of various cultures treat space and time differently. In order to effectively understand peoples of other cultures, we must first analyze how space and time are treated. In the following excerpt, Hall offers examples of how time, viewed differently from culture to culture, allows people to "talk" without the use of words.

Time talks. It speaks more plainly than words. The message it conveys comes through loud and clear. Because it is manipulated less consciously, it is subject to less distortion than the spoken language. It can shout the truth where words lie.

. . . .

American Time

People of the Western world, particularly Americans, tend to think of time as something fixed in nature, something around us and from which we cannot escape; an ever-present part of the environment, just like the air we breathe. That it might be experienced in any other way seems unnatural and strange, a feeling which is rarely modified even when we begin to discover how really differently it is handled by some other people. Within the West itself certain cultures rank time much lower in over-all importance than we do. In Latin America, for example, where time is treated rather cavalierly, one commonly hears the expression, "Our time or your time?" *"Hora americana, hora mejicana?"*

As a rule, Americans think of time as a road or a ribbon stretching into the future, along which one progresses. The road has segments or compartments which are to be kept discrete ("one thing at a time"). People who cannot schedule time are looked down upon as impractical. In at least some parts of Latin America, the North American (their term for us) finds himself annoyed when he has made an appointment with somebody, only to find a lot of other things going on at the same time. An old friend of mine of Spanish cultural heritage used to run his business according to the "Latino" system. This meant that up to fifteen people were in his office at one time. Business which might have been finished in a quarter of an hour sometimes took a whole day. He realized, of course, that the Anglo-Americans were disturbed by this and used to make some allowance for them, a dispensation which meant that they spent only an hour or so in his office when they had planned on a few minutes. The American concept of the discreteness of time and the necessity for scheduling was at variance with this amiable and seemingly confusing Latin system. However, if my friend had adhered to the American system he would have destroyed a vital part of his prosperity. People who came to do business with him also came to find out things and to visit each other. The ten to fifteen Spanish-Americans and Indians who used to sit around the office (among whom I later found myself after I had learned to relax a little) played their own part in a particular type of communications network.

Not only do we Americans segment and schedule time, but we look ahead and are oriented almost entirely toward the future. We like new things and are preoccupied with change. We want to know how to overcome resistance to change. In fact, scientific theories and even some pseudo-scientific ones, which incorporate a striking theory of change, are often given special attention.

Time with us is handled much like a material; we earn it, spend it, save it, waste it. To us it is somewhat immoral to have two things going on at the same time. In Latin America it is not uncommon for one man to have a number of simultaneous jobs which he either carries on from one desk or which he moves between, spending a small amount of time on each.

While we look to the future, our view of it is limited. The future to us is the foreseeable future, not the future of the South Asian that may involve centuries. Indeed, our perspective is so short as to inhibit the operation of a good many practical projects, such as sixty- and one-hundred-year conservation works requiring public support and public funds. Anyone who has worked in industry or in the government of the United States has heard the following: "Gentlemen, this is for the long term! Five or ten years."

For us a "long time" can be almost anything—ten or twenty years, two or three months, a few weeks, or even a couple of days. The South Asian, however, feels that it is perfectly realistic to think of a "long time" in terms of thousands of years or even an endless period. A colleague once described their conceptualization of time as follows: "Time is like a museum with endless corridors and alcoves. You, the viewer, are walking through the museum in the dark, holding a light to each scene as you pass it. God is the curator of the museum, and only He knows all that is in it. One lifetime represents one alcove."

The American's view of the future is linked to a view of the past, for tradition plays an equally limited part in American culture. As a whole, we push it aside or leave it to a few souls who are interested in the past for very special reasons. There are, of course, a few pockets, such as New England and the South, where tradition is emphasized. But in the realm of business, which is the dominant model of United States life, tradition is equated with *experience,* and experience is thought of as being very close to if not synonymous with know-how. Know-how is one of our prized possessions, so that when we look backward it is rarely to take pleasure in the past itself but usually to calculate the know-how, to assess the prognosis for success in the future.

Promptness is also valued highly in American life. If people are not prompt, it is often taken either as an insult or as an indication that they are not quite responsible. There are those, of a psychological bent, who would say that we are obsessed with time. They can point to individuals in American culture who are literally time-ridden. And even the rest of us feel very strongly about time because we have been taught to take it so seriously. We have stressed this aspect of culture and developed it to a point unequaled anywhere in the world, except, perhaps, in Switzerland and north Germany. Many people criticize our obsessional handling of time. They attribute ulcers and hypertension to the pressure engendered by such a system. Perhaps they are right.

Some Other Concepts of Time

Even within the very borders of the United States there are people who handle time in a way which is almost incomprehensible to those who have not made a major effort to understand it. The Pueblo Indians, for example, who live in the Southwest, have a sense of time which is at complete variance with the clock-bound habits of the ordinary American citizen. For the Pueblos events begin when the time is ripe and no sooner.

I can still remember a Christmas dance I attended some twenty-five years ago at one of the pueblos near the Rio Grande. I had to travel over bumpy roads for forty-five miles to get there. At seven thousand feet the ordeal of winter cold at one o'clock in the morning is almost unbearable. Shivering in the still darkness of the pueblo, I kept searching for a clue as to when the dance would begin.

Outside everything was impenetrably quiet. Occasionally there was the muffled beat of a deep pueblo drum, the opening of a door, or the piercing of the night's darkness with a shaft of light. In the church where the dance was to take place a few white townsfolk were huddled together on a balcony, groping for some clue which would suggest how much longer they were going to suffer. "Last year I heard they started at ten o'clock." "They can't start until the priest comes." "There is no way of telling when they will start." All this punctuated by chattering teeth and the stamping of feet to keep up circulation.

Suddenly an Indian opened the door, entered, and poked up the fire in the stove. Everyone nudged his neighbor: "Maybe they are going to begin now." Another hour passed. Another Indian came in from outside, walked across the nave of the church, and disappeared through another door. "Certainly now they will begin. After all, it's almost two o'clock." Someone guessed that they were just being ornery in the hope that the white men would go away. Another had a friend in the pueblo and went to his house to ask when the dance would begin. Nobody knew. Suddenly, when the whites were almost exhausted, there burst upon the night the deep sounds of the drums, rattles, and low male voices singing. Without warning the dance had begun.

After years of performances such as this, no white man in his right mind will hazard a guess as to when one of these ceremonial dances will begin. Those of us who have learned now know that the dance doesn't start at a particular time. It is geared to no schedule. It starts when "things" are ready!

.   .   .   .

Time does not heal on Truk! Past events stack up, placing an ever-increasing burden on the Trukese and weighing heavily on the present. They are, in fact, treated as though they had just occurred. This was borne out by something which happened shortly after the American occupation of the atoll at the end of World War II.

A villager arrived all out of breath at the military government head-quarters. He said that a murder had been committed in the village and that the murderer was running around loose. Quite naturally the military government officer became alarmed. He was about to dispatch M.P.s to arrest the culprit when he remembered that someone had warned him about acting precipitously when dealing with "natives." A little inquiry turned up the fact that the victim had been "fooling around" with the murderer's wife. Still more inquiry of a routine type, designed to establish the place and date of the crime, revealed that the murder had not occurred a few hours or even days ago, as one might expect, but seventeen years before. The murderer had been running around loose in the village all this time.

A further example of how time does not heal on Truk is that of a land dispute that started with the German occupation in the 1890s, was carried on down through the Japanese occupation, and was still current and acrimonious when the Americans arrived in 1946.

Prior to Missionary Moses' arrival on Uman in 1867 life on Truk was characterized by violent and bloody warfare. Villages, instead of being built on the shore where life was a little easier, were placed on the sides of mountains where they could be better protected. Attacks would come without notice and often without apparent provocation. Or a fight might start if a man stole a coconut from a tree that was not his or waylaid a woman and took advantage of her. Years later someone would start thinking about the wrong and decide that it still had not been righted. A village would be attacked again in the middle of the night.

When charges were brought against a chief for things he had done to his people, every little slight, every minor graft would be listed; nothing would be forgotten. Damages would be asked for everything. It seemed preposterous to us Americans, particularly when we looked at the lists of charges. "How could a chief be so corrupt?" "How could the people remember so much?"

Though the Truk islanders carry the accumulated burden of time past on their shoulders, they show an almost total inability to grasp the notion that two events can take place at the same time when they are any distance apart. When the Japanese occupied Truk at the end of World War I they took Artie Moses, chief of the island of Uman, to Tokyo. Artie was made to send a wireless message back to his people as a demonstration of the wizardry of Japanese technology. His family refused to believe that he had sent it, that he had said anything at all, though they knew he was in Tokyo. Places at a distance are very real to them, but people who are away are very much away, and any interaction with them is unthinkable.

An entirely different handling of time is reported by the anthropologist Paul Bohannan for the Tiv, a primitive people who live in Nigeria. Like the Navajo, they point to the sun to indicate a general time of day, and they also observe the movement of the moon as it waxes and wanes. What is different is the way they use and experience time. For the Tiv, time is like a capsule. There is a time for visiting, for cooking, or for working; and when one is in one of these times, one does not shift to another.

The Tiv equivalent of the week lasts five to seven days. It is not tied into periodic natural events, such as the phases of the moon. The day of the week is named after the things which are being sold in the nearest "market." If we had the equivalent, Monday would be "automobiles" in Washington, D.C., "furniture" in Baltimore, and "yard goods" in New York. Each of these might be followed by the days for appliances, liquor, and diamonds in the respective cities. This would mean that as you traveled about the day of the week would keep changing, depending on where you were.

A requisite of our own temporal system is that the components must add up: Sixty seconds have to equal one minute, sixty minutes one hour. The American is perplexed by people who do not do this. The African specialist Henri Alexandre Junod, reporting on the Thonga, tells of a medicine man who had memorized a seventy-year chronology and could detail the events of each and every year in sequence. Yet this same man spoke of the period he had memorized as an "era" which he computed at "four months and eight hundred years' duration." The usual reaction to this story and others like it is that the man was primitive, like a child, and did not understand what he was saying, because how could seventy years possibly be the same as eight hundred? As students of culture we can no longer dismiss other conceptualizations of reality by saying that they are childlike. We must go much deeper. In the case of the Thonga it seems that a "chronology" is one thing and an "era" something else quite different, and there is no relation between the two in operational terms.

If these distinctions between European-American time and other conceptions of time seem to draw too heavily on primitive peoples, let me mention two other examples—from cultures which are as civilized, if not as industrialized, as our own. In comparing the United States with Iran and Afghanistan very great differences in the handling of time appear. The American attitude toward appointments is an example. Once while in Tehran I had an opportunity to observe some young Iranians making plans for a party. After plans were made to pick up everyone at appointed times and places everything began to fall apart. People would leave messages that they were unable to take so-and-so or were going somewhere else, knowing full well that the person who had been given the message couldn't possibly deliver it. One girl was left stranded on a street corner, and no one seemed to be concerned about it. One of my informants explained that he himself had had many similar experiences. Once he had made eleven appointments to meet a friend. Each time one of them failed to show up. The twelfth time they swore they would both be there, that nothing would interfere. The friend failed to arrive. After waiting for forty-five minutes my informant phoned his friend and found him still at home. The following conversation is an approximation of what took place:

"Is that you, Abdul?" "Yes." "Why aren't you here? I thought we were to meet for sure." "Oh, but it was raining," said Abdul with a sort of whining intonation that is very common in Parsi.

If present appointments are treated rather cavalierly, the past in Iran takes on a very great importance. People look back on what they feel are the wonders of the past and the great ages of Persian culture. Yet the future seems to have little reality or certainty to it. Businessmen have been known to invest hundreds of thousands of dollars in factories of various sorts without making the slightest plan as to how to use them. A complete woolen mill was bought and shipped to Tehran before the buyer had raised enough money to erect it, to buy supplies, or even to train personnel. When American teams of technicians came to help Iran's economy they constantly had to cope with what seemed to them an almost total lack of planning.

Moving east from Iran to Afghanistan, one gets farther afield from American time concepts. A few years ago in Kabul a man appeared, looking for his brother. He asked all the merchants of the market place if they had seen his brother and told them where he was staying in case his brother arrived and wanted to find him. The next year he was back and repeated the performance. By this time one of the members of the American embassy had heard about his inquiries and asked if he had found his brother. The man answered that he and his brother had agreed to meet in Kabul, but neither of them had said what year.

From "Right You Are If You Say You Are—Obscurely," *TIME* Essay from *TIME*, December 30, 1966, pp. 71–72. Reprinted by permission from *TIME, The Weekly Newsmagazine;* © Time Inc., 1966.

18 / Right You Are If You Say You Are—Obscurely

T I M E Magazine

Have you ever asked a question only to be baffled by a reply consisting of a seemingly endless string of incomprehensible utterances? If so, you may have been "jargonized." The previous selections by Bohannan and Hall speak of effective communication. This article forcefully demonstrates the way in which jargon can decrease effective communication. The central theme of the article is to show how individuals in a given profession, trade, or specialized activity are able to establish and maintain influence and authority in their fields by the careful use of words. Although the article gives the impression that jargon itself is a barrier to language fluency, the reader should keep in mind that jargon can be an effective tool in the expression of ideas. It is the abuse, *not the use, of jargon that causes confusion in a language system.*

The scene is the office of the dean of admissions at Instant College. A pale adolescent approaches the dean, who is appropriately clad in flowing white memos.

STUDENT: Y-you sent for me, sir?

DEAN: Yes, my boy. We've decided to accept you as a student here at Instant.

STUDENT: Sir, I can't tell you how pleased I am. I mean, my high school average is 65, I got straight Ds in mathematics, confuse the Norman Conquest with D-day, have a sub-average IQ, and got turned down by every other college in America. Yet in spite of all of this, you've accepted me.

DEAN: Not in spite of it, boy! Because of it!

STUDENT (*dimly*): Sir?

DEAN: Don't you see? You're a challenge. We're starting with nothing —you. Yet before we're through, corporations will seek your advice, little magazines will print your monographs on such arcane subjects as forensic medicine and epistemology, newspapers will publish your utterances as you enplane for conferences abroad.

STUDENT: Me?

DEAN: You. Because you will be an Expert.

STUDENT: An expert what?

DEAN: Just an Expert.

STUDENT: But sir, I don't know anything and I can't learn much. Not in four years, anyway.

DEAN: Why, my boy, we'll have you out of here in an hour. All you need is the catalyst that instantly transforms the lowest common denominator, you, into an Expert.

STUDENT: Money? Power? Intellect? Charm?

DEAN: No. These things are but children's toys compared to Jargon.

STUDENT: Jargon?

DEAN (*turning to his textbook*): The dictionary calls it "confused, unintelligible language: gibberish, a dialect regarded as barbarous or outlandish." But we at Instant call it the Expert's Ultimate Weapon. In 1967, it will hypnotize friends, quash enemies and intimidate whole nations. Follow me.

A school bell rings, and the entire faculty enters: Dr. Gummidge, professor of sociology; the Rev. Mr. Logos, head of the theological seminary; Dr. Beazle, head of the medical school; Mr. Flap, instructor in government; and finally, General Redstone, chief of the ROTC. Dr. Gummidge steps forward, conducts the student to an uncomfortable chair, mills about him like a lonely crowd, and begins.

GUMMIDGE: Remember Gummidge's Law and you will never be Found Out: The amount of expertise varies in inverse proportion to the number of statements understood by the General Public.

STUDENT: In other words?

GUMMIDGE: In other words, never say "In other words." That will force you to clarify your statements. Keep all pronunciamentos orotund and hazy. Suppose your mother comes to school and asks how you are doing. Do I reply: "He is at the bottom of his class—lazy and good-for-nothing"?

STUDENT: Why not? Everyone else does.

GUMMIDGE: I am not everyone else. I reply: "The student in question is performing minimally for his peer group and is an emerging underachiever."

STUDENT: Wow!

GUMMIDGE: Exactly. If you are poor, I refer to you as disadvantaged; if you live in a slum, you are in a culturally deprived environment.

STUDENT: If I want to get out of a crowded class?

GUMMIDGE: You seek a more favorable pupil-teacher ratio, plus a decentralized learning center in the multiversity.

STUDENT: If I'm learning a language by conversing in it?

GUMMIDGE: That's the aural–oral method. Say it aloud.

The student does and is completely incomprehensible. A cheer goes up from the faculty.

GUMMIDGE: From now on, you must never speak; you must verbalize.

STUDENT: Must I verbalize Jargon only to my peer group?

GUMMIDGE: Not at all. You can now use it even when addressing pre-schoolers. In his book *Translations from the English,* Robert Paul Smith offers these samples: "He shows a real ability in plastic conception." That means he can make a snake out of clay. "He's rather slow in group integration and reacts negatively to aggressive stimulus." He cries easily. And "He does seem to have developed late in large-muscle control." He falls on his head frequently.

STUDENT (*awestruck*): I'll never be able to do it.

GUMMIDGE: Of course you will. The uninitiated are easily impressed. It's all rather like the ignorant woman who learns that her friend's son has graduated from medical school. "How's your boy?" she asks. The friend clucks sadly: "He's a practicing homosexual." "Wonderful!" cries the first. "Where's his office?" Do I make myself clear?

STUDENT: No, sir.

GUMMIDGE: Fine. Now open your textbook to the David Riesman chapter. Here is the eminent sociologist writing about Jargon: "Phrases such as 'achievement-oriented' or 'need-achievement' were, if I am not mistaken, invented by colleagues and friends of mine, Harry Murray and David C. McClelland . . . It has occurred to me that they may be driven by a kind of asceticism precisely because they are poetic men of feeling who . . . have chosen to deal with soft data in a hard way." Now then, my boy, is there any better example of flapdoodle than that?

STUDENT: Well, how about these samples from Harvard Sociologist Talcott Parsons: "Adaptation, goal-attainment, integration and pattern maintenance."

GUMMIDGE: Yes, first rate. Even I practice them, just as Horowitz plays the scales. Try them in a sentence. Two men open a store. Someone provides the cash. What's that?

STUDENT: Adaptation?

GUMMIDGE: And then they entice customers—

STUDENT: Goal-attainment.

GUMMIDGE: They set up a sales staff—

STUDENT: Integration.

GUMMIDGE: And they don't steal from the cash register.

STUDENT: They agree to maintain the wider values of the culture. That's pattern maintenance.

GUMMIDGE: Perfect. See how complicated you can make things? Imagine what damage you can wreak in the schools where a situation is no longer practical, it is viable; where a pupil is no longer unmanageable, but alienated. Get it?

STUDENT: Got it.

GUMMIDGE: Do books have words and pictures?

STUDENT: No, sir, they have verbal symbols and visual representations.

GUMMIDGE: You're on your way. For your final exam, read and commit to memory the 23rd Psalm Jargonized by Alan Simpson, president of Vassar College.

STUDENT (*droning*): "The Lord is my external-internal integrative mechanism. I shall not be deprived of gratifications for my viscerogenic hungers or my need-dispositions. He motivates me to orient myself towards a nonsocial object with effective significance."

The student falls into a dreamlike trance during which Professor Gummidge tiptoes off and is replaced by the Rev. Mr. Logos, who continues the psalm.

LOGOS: "He positions me in a nondecisional situation. He maximizes my adjustment . . ." (*As the student wakes up*): I'm the Reverend Mr. Logos. Bless you, my son.

STUDENT: I see you're wearing a turned-around collar and a *yarmulke*. Just what is your religion?

LOGOS: I am a theologian. Does that answer you?

STUDENT: No.

LOGOS: Splendid. How would you refer to a priest disagreeing with a minister?

STUDENT: As two guys arguing?

LOGOS: No, no, no! Religious leaders never argue, they have dialogues, or I–Thou relationships.

STUDENT: If their studies are mainly about Jesus?

LOGOS: They are Christocentrically oriented. If they are interpreting the Bible, hermeneutics is the term.

STUDENT: Can you predict what words will be In for the theological year ahead?

LOGOS: Certainly. Demythologizing, optimism, theology of hope, *engagé* and commitment.

STUDENT: I like dialectic theology and conceptualism.

LOGOS: Forget them. They're all Out. Concentrate on phenomenology, sociological inspiration, ethical activism, crisis of authority.

STUDENT: Suppose someone realizes that I don't have the faintest idea what I'm talking about?

LOGOS: Then accuse him of objectification. If he doesn't go away, ask him what he did before he got religion, before his ultimate faith-concern, or better still, *Selbstverständnis*.

STUDENT: But that's not even English.

LOGOS: All the better. Many influential theologians wrote in German—Bultmann, Bonhoeffer, Barth—and German not only offers us a chance to obfuscate, it adds a tangy foreign flavor. For instance, there is *Historie,* meaning bare facts, *Geschichte,* meaning interpretive history.

STUDENT: Sort of like the difference between *The World Almanac* and Toynbee.

LOGOS: Remember Gummidge's Law: don't clarify!

STUDENT: Sorry.

LOGOS: Don't let it happen again. *Vorverständnis* is one of my favorites. It means presupposition. *Wissenschaft* is far better than saying simply discipline or science, and anxiety sounds much deeper if you say *Angst*. If you grow weary of German, there is always Greek—almost everyone has seen *Never on Sunday*—with such splendid specimens as *kerygma* (message of the Scriptures) and *agape* (divine love).

STUDENT (*writing furiously*): Are you sure Jargon *really* works? In religion, I mean?

LOGOS: Does it? I quote from a distinguished cleric: "I can't make heads or tails out of a great deal of what Tillich says." The confessor is Dr. Billy Graham himself.

At this, the Rev. Mr. Logos is borne away by the laity to edit a book of his sermons entitled Through Exegesis and Hermeneutics We Arrive at Kerygma. *In his place steps Dr. Beazle, who takes the student's blood pressure, temperature, hemoglobin count and wallet.*

BEAZLE: Now what kind of medical career do you want, physical or psychiatric?

STUDENT: I don't know. I never thought about it.

BEAZLE: That's a good start. Suppose we begin with plain everyday medicine. Was it not Herman Melville who wrote: "A man of true science uses but few hard words, and those only when none other will answer his purpose; whereas the smatterer in science thinks that by mouthing hard words he proves that he understands hard things." Now you don't want to be an ordinary man of true science when you can be a full-fledged Smatterer, do you?

STUDENT: I guess not.

BEAZLE: Very well, remember never to let the patient be fully aware of what is wrong. Even tonsillitis can be described as a malign hypertrophied condition that affects nares and pharynx and may result in paraphonia clausa. It was I, you know, who wrote the sign seen in hospitals: "Illumination is required to be extinguished on these premises on the termination of daily activities."

STUDENT: Which means—

BEAZLE: Put out the lights when you leave.

STUDENT: Marvelous.

BEAZLE: It was nothing, really. We medical men have been confounding patients for years. As far back as 1699, the physician and poet Samuel Garth wrote: "The patient's ears remorseless he assails/Murders with jargon where his medicine fails." Still, physical medicine is nothing compared with psychiatry. There's where we Jargonists truly have our day.

Suppose a man loses his wife and is unable to love anyone because he is sad. What do I tell him?

STUDENT: Cheer up, there are lots of fish in the—?

BEAZLE (*interrupting*): Of course not. I intone: You have suffered an object loss in which you had an over-cathesis of libido and have been unable to decathect the libido and invest it in a new object. Do you follow me?

STUDENT: I think so.

BEAZLE: Then be warned: the public is on our trail; they now have learned the meanings of the "oses" and the "itises." You had better replace them with "inadequacies," and "dependencies," tell the man who acts out fantasies that he is "role playing," speak of the creation of a child as "exclusive electivity of dynamic specificity."

STUDENT: And when the child is born?

BEAZLE: His development proceeds through "mutual synthesis carried on through a functional zone of mutuality."

STUDENT: In short, he grows up.

BEAZLE: In long, he proceeds in a continuous unidirectional ever-varying interplay of organism and environment.

STUDENT: If a patient is unhappy?

BEAZLE: He is having an identity crisis.

STUDENT: But suppose he's just unhappy?

BEAZLE: No one is just unhappy. Psych harder!

STUDENT: I'll start immediately. I will follow Lionel Trilling's dictum: no one will fall in love and get married as long as I'm present.

BEAZLE: What will they do?

STUDENT: Their libidinal impulses being reciprocal, they will integrate their individual erotic drives and bring them within the same frame of reference. How am I doing?

BEAZLE: Not badly, but I can still understand you.

STUDENT: Sorry. Day by day I will grow more obscure, until my patients and I completely fail to communicate.

BEAZLE: Oh, if only I could believe that! Smog, confuse, obfuscate! *He exits, to invent a cure for clarity and lucidity which he will sell to nine leading pharmaceutical firms. Mr. Flap and General Redstone come forward.*

FLAP: Order of magnitude, expedite, implement, reorient, interoccupational mobility, mission oriented—

REDSTONE: Component forces, readiness levels, destruct—

STUDENT: Excuse me—

REDSTONE (*ignoring him*): Credibility, paramilitary department—wide contingency plans, pre-emptive war, scenario, remote area conflict . . .

FLAP: Expedite, channels, maximize, bureau potential—

STUDENT: Gentlemen, please, I—

DEAN: It's no good, son. Once the civilian and the military start arguing it can go on for years.

REDSTONE: Circular error probability, target systems, pipeline requirements, deterrent gaps . . . counterinsurgency . . . soft target . . . *The general grinds to a halt. Two enlisted men enter, paint him a neutral olive drab and carry him off to the Pentagon, where he will replace a computer.*

FLAP (*running down*): Extended care facilities . . . oligopoly . . . input . . . phasein . . . interlocking intervention. . . . (*He creaks, coughs and crawls into a filing cabinet.*)

DEAN (*handing the student a diploma printed on sheep-like vinyl*): We've done all we can for you, son. In George Orwell's paraphrase: "The race is not to the swift—nor the battle to the strong . . . but time and chance—."

STUDENT: I know. "Objective considerations of contemporary phenomena compels the conclusion that success or failure in competitive activities exhibits no tendency to be commensurate with innate capacity, but that a considerable element of the unpredictable must be taken into account."

DEAN: Exactly. (*Moist of eye, he pats the new graduate on the head.*) You can now take your pick of careers in medicine, religion, business and geopolitics—as well as wine-tasting and art criticism. And if you fail at everything, there's a job for you at Instant College. (*Calling after him as the student exits.*) And remember, it is better to curse one candle than to light the darkness. . . .

He extinguishes the lights, leaving the audience in blackness as
THE CURTAIN FALLS

Part 4 / QUESTIONS AND PROBLEMS FOR DISCUSSION

1. Language is a unique feature that creates for us our own sociocultural reality. What does this statement mean in terms of the Whorfian hypothesis?
2. What does Hall mean when he says that "time talks"? Use examples from your own experiences to illustrate Hall's point.
3. In the development of man, did language precede culture or did culture come before language? Develop an argument that you think might support either a "yes" or a "no" answer.
4. Make a list and discuss how the meanings of certain words or phrases would be altered if we had a more relaxed attitude than we do toward the concept of time.
5. Read an academic article and select which jargon words contribute to and which jargon words detract from effective communication. On what basis did you choose the words you did?

5/ OF COURSE I HAVE CULTURE! BUT WHAT IS IT?

How can you have something and not know what it is? A fair question to ask but a difficult one to answer, especially when it is asked about culture. The reason for this is that the concept of culture is so central to all aspects of anthropology that persons in each field of anthropology have separate definitions which stress the emphasis of their particular field. The task of defining culture in a universally accepted statement might be likened to the task of having all religious leaders in the world agree upon a single definition of a Supreme Being—quite a gargantuan task, even without considering whether or not it would be desirable.

Culture is not just an interesting or quaint idea of behavior studied by anthropologists. It is not merely the study of unusual sex customs of the Samoans in the South Pacific. It is a pattern into which we all are born that restricts and allows us to behave in certain acceptable ways in our work-a-day life. How much do we know of our own culture, let alone an alien one? Very little.

Rather than say specifically what culture is, let me illustrate what the lack of culture is. It is a 12-year-old girl raised in Seattle, Walla Walla, or any other city, provided in life only with food, water, and protection from physical harm. She does not speak; she eats food with her hands; she does not love; she does not hate; she uses the most elemental techniques of waste elimination; she does not relate to other people in any human way. This girl is a biological being but not a human being. Psychologists would call her an autistic child. She is a being without learned behavior—she has no culture. The concept of culture, then, includes shared learned behavior patterns which people use to interpret the world about them and act purposefully within it.

What is culture? No definitive answer is given here. One reason for this position is that there are almost as many definitions of culture as there are anthropologists. So, instead of compiling a lengthy list of definitions, it might be more beneficial if the following selections speak for themselves. You, the reader, can attempt to answer the question of what culture is after reading about Thompson's "secret"; how Ishi, the Indian, reacts to a totally strange way of life; how Don, the Hopi, becomes a man; how the Nacirema regard their physical bodies; and how the Navaho people react to rapid cultural change.

19 / The Secret of Culture

LAURA THOMPSON

What is "culture"? We can't see it, touch it, or smell it; but we can define it. Or can we? The definition of this underlying concept in anthropology has been defined in dozens of ways, but few persons seem to agree what culture is. Is there a secret to culture? In this article Laura Thompson discusses how difficult it is to work out a universally accepted definition of the term. Thompson holds that the secret to understanding culture is to view it as a "group problem-solving device." In this light she presents culture as being a way in which different groups of people adapt to their total environment in terms of how they cope with the problems their environment presents to them. The reader should keep in mind this use of the term "culture" and how it either agrees with or conflicts with the use of the concept as it appears in other contexts.

We live in an era when significant scientific gains are being made toward improving human welfare. Ecologists and other scientists are helping man to increase his control over his environment. Psychologists and psychiatrists are discovering the meaning of behavior even at the unconscious level. Social scientists are beginning to fathom the dynamics of society from a universal viewpoint. And biologists are uncovering the hidden mechanisms of genetics and human variability.

In our search for improved welfare on a global scale, however, there remains a focal area about which our information is confused and fragmentary, even misleading: the realm of culture. Crucial data relating to the cultural factor are often missing from decision-making considerations in antipoverty and economic development projects, city and regional planning, population control and nutrition, political and military strategy. Absence of cultural sophistication also handicaps communication between nations, diplomatic negotiations, and the drafting of international treaties. Until decision makers gain a deeper understanding of cultural differences we shall probably continue trying to solve human problems by such unavailing and costly methods as fighting alien customs and ideologies with bullets and bombs.

Why are cultural phenomena so often neglected and so grossly misunderstood? In view of the basic role of culture in human behavior, what can be done to remedy the situation?

A widespread notion precluding cultural sophistication is that "after all, human nature is the same all over the world" and that all we need do to understand other peoples is to project our own feelings and ideas onto them. The basic flaw in this approach stems from the fact that, to an overwhelming extent, human nature is culturally molded nature. Studies by anthropologists, biologists, geneticists, linguists, archaeologists, and psychologists all conclude that most human problems are cultural problems. Our knowledge of the role of culture in human development is expanding rapidly, and if we are to assess man's character and aspirations or predict his behavior, an understanding of the culture of his social groups is crucial. Besides enhancing our understanding of human behavior, a thorough grasp of the nature of culture enables us to exercise a measure of control over our destiny. Without such grasp we remain inept and helpless. Despite the extraordinary technical achievements of modern man, our schemes for human betterment turn out to be impractical and unrealistic.

Culture: A Difficult Concept

The concept of culture is not a simple one. The term stems from the Latin, *cultivare,* to till or cultivate. Webster's primary definition is "the art or practice of cultivating; manner or method of cultivating; tillage." It is not surprising, therefore, that "culture" is frequently interpreted to mean refinement or civilization. This meaning recalls the German term *Kultur,* the ideal of a classical education based on study of Greek, Latin, and the humanities. In the eighteenth century the notion of culture as *Kultur* became basic to education in Europe, especially in the Anglo-Saxon countries, and a "civilized" man was judged by his knowledge of history, languages, literature, and the arts. As science and technology developed, this notion played a part in the establishment of a rigid separation between the sciences and the humanities.

On the other hand, many people think of culture as a thing of "shreds and patches," an aggregation of discrete items that are associated by historical chance and that do not make sense as a whole. For example, a person may profess a religious code of ethics on the Sabbath and a totally different, pragmatic code for the remainder of the week. According to the "shreds and patches" notion, he may deplore the moral discrepancy but will not perceive it as symptomatic of a cultural malaise. He will not link psychological stress with cultural ambivalence.

Another approach treats a culture as though it were a mechanical system. If a part, that is, a culture "trait," breaks down or wears out, we need merely replace it with a new one. For example, government officials often attempt to alter the culture of their constituents by this sort of cultural repair. Disinfectants are substituted for magical incantations; taxes for chiefly tribute; and stooges for troublesome native leaders banished to a distant province.

On the other hand, if the entire indigenous culture is condemned, attempts may be made simply to substitute another model, usually some version of Western technological civilization. The history of the American administration of the Pueblo Indians of Arizona and New Mexico between about 1850 and 1930 well illustrates an attempt to implement this conception of culture.

Although the fallacies of past approaches to culture are becoming apparent, often in highly dramatic ways, deeply ingrained habits of feeling and thought linger on and confuse us. How may we transform them into concepts consistent with the findings of modern scientific research?

Many scholars have worked on this problem—Alfred North Whitehead, John Dewey, F. S. C. Northrop, Ernst Cassirer, Nicolai Hartmann, C. S. Peirce, Lancelot Law Whyte, and Pierre Teilhard de Chardin, to mention a few. Each has made his contribution, and, little by little, a new image of man has begun to emerge. Hermann Wein has suggested that the work of certain American philosophers and anthropologists—Charles Morris, Clyde Kluckhohn, and John Collier, among others—is helping to build this new image. We might add the names of geneticist Theodocius Dobzhansky, biologists George Gaylord Simpson and Sir Julian Huxley, ecologists Marston Bates and Alfred E. Emerson, social psychiatrist Alexander H. Leighton, semanticist Alfred Korzybski, linguists Edward Sapir and Benjamin Lee Whorf, economic historian Karl Polanyi, and theoretical anthropologists Dorothy Lee and David Bidney.

Under such scrutiny the concept of culture is undergoing radical revision. Anthropologists are struggling to move out of a primarily descriptive, natural-history phase of scientific endeavor to a more mature phase of deductively formulated theory. Traditional definitions of a culture as a sum total of elements, traits, and patterns have long been outmoded. The view of culture as a mechanical-type system is also obsolete. But anthropologists are having difficulty developing a working concept of culture adequate to the complex, multidimensional requirements of modern biocultural research, which involves several disciplines focused on the behavior of human communities.

In a critical review of concepts and definitions of culture, A. L. Kroeber and Clyde Kluckhohn came to the conclusion that we do not yet have an adequate theory of culture. If we are to ameliorate world problems, however, we must systematically implement a scientifically viable, universally applicable concept of culture.

Culture as Coping

As we know, *Homo sapiens* is a relatively unspecialized species. Man's complex symbolizing brain differentiates him from the rest of the animal world. Culture, then, is the brainchild of man. Viewed holistically a culture is the supreme creation of a human community—the product of its deep-seated urge to fulfill and perpetuate itself.

My thesis is that, whatever else a culture may be, it is primarily a group problem-solving device instituted by a human community to cope with its basic practical problems. This is the secret of culture. From today's perspective it is the essential pragmatic fact about the cultures of mankind.

This thesis, of course, is not new. Similar notions have been expressed by many students of culture, including W. G. Sumner and A. G. Keller, Clellan S. Ford, A. L. Kroeber and Clyde Kluckhohn, Kimball Young, John J. Honigmann, and others. But the problem-solving function of culture is by no means fully accepted by all students of culture; nor have the implications of culture's problem-solving role been spelled out.

From *Ishi in Two Worlds,* by Theodora Kroeber, 1961, pp. 3–10. Originally published by the University of California Press; reprinted by permission of The Regents of the University of California.

20 / Outside the Slaughter House

THEODORA KROEBER

So now you have a brief idea of what culture is and you probably feel relatively safe in knowing that you have one. But how would you react if plucked from your surroundings and placed in a totally alien and more complex cultural tradition? Could you function properly? Would you be psychologically disoriented? How would you communicate? Your cultural traditions would become "curiosities" within the context of the more complex cultural system. Essentially this is what happened to Ishi, the last of the Yahi Indians of California. Ishi was thrown into the complex cultural system of contemporary America of little more than sixty years ago. He was then known as the "last wild Indian." His cultural activities of flaking stone tools and making wooden bows became "curiosities" to those thousands of people who viewed him as he worked in a museum. The following selection by Theodora Kroeber recalls Ishi's first contact and his reactions to an alien world.

The story of Ishi begins for us early in the morning of the twenty-ninth day of August in the year 1911 and in the corral of a slaughter house. It begins with the sharp barking of dogs which roused the sleeping butchers. In the dawn light they saw a man at bay, crouching against the corral fence—Ishi.

They called off the dogs. Then, in some considerable excitement, they telephoned the sheriff in Oroville two or three miles away to say that they were holding a wild man and would he please come and take him off their hands. Sheriff and deputies arrived shortly, approaching the corral with guns at the ready. The wild man made no move to resist capture, quietly allowing himself to be handcuffed.

The sheriff, J. B. Webber, saw that the man was an Indian, and that he was at the limit of exhaustion and fear. He could learn nothing further, since his prisoner understood no English. Not knowing what to do with him, he motioned the Indian into the wagon with himself and his deputies, drove him to the county jail in Oroville, and locked him up in the cell for the insane. There, Sheriff Webber reasoned, while he tried to discover something more about his captive he could at least protect him from the excited curiosity of the townspeople and the outsiders who were already pouring in from miles around to see the wild man.

The wild man was emaciated to starvation, his hair was burned off close to his head, he was naked except for a ragged scrap of ancient covered-wagon canvas which he wore around his shoulders like a poncho. He was a man of middle height, the long bones, painfully apparent, were straight, strong, and not heavy, the skin color somewhat paler in tone than the full copper characteristic of most Indians. The black eyes were wary and guarded now, but were set wide in a broad face, the mouth was generous and agreeably molded. For the rest, the Indian's extreme fatigue and fright heightened a sensitiveness which was always there, while it masked the usual mobility and expressiveness of the features.

It should be said that the sheriff's action in locking Ishi up was neither stupid nor brutal given the circumstances. Until sheriff Webber took the unwonted measure of keeping them out by force people filled the jail to gaze through the bars of his cell at the captive. Later, Ishi spoke with some diffidence of this, his first contact with white men. He said that he was put up in a fine house where he was kindly treated and well fed by a big chief. That he would eat nothing and drink nothing during his first days of captivity Ishi did not say. Such was the case; nor did he allow himself to sleep at first. Quite possibly it was a time of such strain and terror that he suppressed all memory of it. Or he may have felt that it was unkind to recall his suspicions which proved in the event groundless, for Ishi expected in those first days to be put to death. He knew of white men only that they were the murderers of his own people. It was natural that he should expect, once in their power, to be shot or hanged or killed by poisoning.

Meanwhile, local Indians and half-breeds as well as Mexicans and Spaniards tried to talk to the prisoner in Maidu, Wintu, and Spanish. Ishi listened patiently but uncomprehendingly, and when he spoke it was in a tongue which meant no more to the Indians there than to the whites.

The story of the capture of a wild Indian became headline news in the local valley papers, and reached the San Francisco dailies in forms more or less lurid and elaborated. The story in the *San Francisco Call* was accompanied by a picture, the first of many to come later. In another newspaper story, a Maidu Indian, Conway by name, "issued a statement" that he had conversed with the wild man. Conway's moment of publicity was brief since the wild man understood nothing of what he said.

These accounts were read by Professors Kroeber and Waterman, anthropologists at the University of California, who were at once alerted to the human drama behind the event and to its possible importance, the more particularly because it recalled to them an earlier episode on San Nicolas Island, one of the Channel Islands of the Pacific Ocean some seventy miles offshore from Santa Barbara.

In 1835, the padres of Mission Santa Barbara transferred the San Nicolas Indians to the mainland. A few minutes after the boat, which was carrying the Indians, had put off from the island, it was found that one baby had been left behind. It is not easy to land a boat on San Nicolas; the captain decided against returning for the baby; the baby's mother jumped overboard, and was last seen swimming toward the island. Half-hearted efforts made to find her in subsequent weeks were unsuccessful: it was believed that she had drowned in the rough surf. In 1853, eighteen years later, seal hunters in the Channel waters reported seeing a woman on San Nicolas, and a boatload of men from Santa Barbara went in search of her. They found her, a last survivor of her tribe. Her baby, as well as all her people who had been removed to the Mission, had died. She lived only a few months after her "rescue" and died without anyone having been able to communicate with her, leaving to posterity this skeletal outline of her grim story, and four words which someone remembered from her lost language and recorded as she said them. It so happens that these four words identify her language as having been Shoshonean, related to Indian languages of the Los Angeles area, not to those of Santa Barbara.

Another reason for the anthropologists' particular interest in the wild man was that three years earlier, in 1908, some surveyors working a few miles north of Oroville had surprised and routed a little band of Indians. After hearing of this incident, Waterman with two guides had spent several weeks in an unsuccessful search for the Indians: the wild man of Oroville might well be one of them.

On August 31, 1911, Kroeber sent the following telegram: "Sheriff Butte County. Newspapers report capture wild Indian speaking language other tribes totally unable understand. Please confirm or deny by collect telegram and if story correct hold Indian till arrival Professor State University who will take charge and be responsible for him. Matter important account aboriginal history."

The sheriff's office must have confirmed the report promptly: Waterman took the train to Oroville the same day. That he and Kroeber correctly "guessed" Ishi's tribe and language was no *tour de force* of intuition. The guess was based on field work with Indians all up and down California; they knew that Oroville was adjacent to country which formerly belonged to the Yana Indians; presumably the strange Indian would be a Yana. He might even be from the southernmost tribe of Yana, believed to be extinct. If this were true, neither they nor anyone so far as they knew could speak his language. But if he were a Northern or Central Yana, there were files of expertly recorded vocabularies for those dialects from two old Yanas, Batwi, called Sam, and Chidaimiya, called Betty Brown.

With a copy of Batwi's and Chidaimiya's vocabularies in his pocket, Waterman arrived in Oroville where he identified himself to Sheriff Webber and was taken to visit the wild man. Waterman found a weary, badgered Indian sitting in his cell, wearing the butcher's apron he had been given at the slaughter house, courteously making what answer he could in his own language to a barrage of questions thrown at him in English, Spanish, and assorted Indian from a miscellaneous set of visitors.

Waterman sat down beside Ishi, and with his phonetically transcribed list of Northern and Central Yana words before him, began to read from it, repeating each word, pronouncing it as well as he knew how. Ishi was attentive but unresponding until, discouragingly far down the list, Waterman said *siwini*, which means yellow pine, at the same time tapping the pine framework of the cot on which they sat. Recognition lighted up the Indian's face. Waterman said the magic word again; Ishi repeated it after him, correcting his pronunciation, and for the next moments the two of them banged at the wood of the cot, telling each other over and over, *siwini, siwini!*

With the difficult first sound recognition achieved, others followed. Ishi was indeed one of the lost tribe, a Yahi; in other words, he was from the southernmost Yana. Waterman was learning that the unknown Yahi dialect differed considerably but not to the point of unintelligibility from the two northern ones of his list. Together he and Ishi tried out more and more words and phrases: they were beginning to communicate. After a while Ishi ventured to ask Waterman, *I ne ma Yahi?* "Are you an Indian?" Waterman answered that he was. The hunted look left Ishi's eyes—here was a friend. He knew as well as did his friend that Waterman was not an Indian. The question was a tentative and subtle way of reassuring and being reassured, not an easy thing to do when the meaningful shared sounds are few. Between meetings with Ishi, Waterman wrote to Kroeber from Oroville:

> This man [Ishi] is undoubtedly wild. He has pieces of deer thong in place of ornaments in the lobes of his ears and a wooden plug in the septum of his nose. He recognizes most of my Yana words and a fair proportion of his own seem to be identical [with mine]. Some of his, however, are either quite different or else my pronunciation of them is very bad, because he doesn't respond to them except by pointing to his ears and asking to have them repeated. "No!" *k'u'i*—it is not—is one. "Yes!" *ähä*, pleases him immensely. I think I get a few endings that don't occur in Northern Yana on nouns, for example. Phonetically, he has some of the prettiest cracked consonants I ever heard in my life. He will be a splendid informant, especially for phonetics, for he speaks very clearly. I have not communicated with him successfully enough to get his story, but what can I expect? He has a yarn to tell about his woman, who had a baby on her back and seems to have been drowned, except that he is so *cheerful* about it.

Waterman misunderstood. In the excitement and relief of having someone to talk to, Ishi poured out confidences and recollections which Waterman could by no means comprehend even with the aid of an elaborate pantomime. Ishi's seeming pleasure was not in the recollected event, but was rather a near hysteria induced by human interchange of speech and feelings too long denied.

Waterman's letters continue:

> We had a lot of conversation this morning about deer hunting and making acorn soup, but I got as far as my list of words would take me. If I am not mistaken, he's full of religion—bathing at sunrise, putting out pinches of tobacco where the lightning strikes, etc. I'll try rattlesnake on him when I go back after lunch. It was a picnic to see him open his eyes when he heard Yana from me. And he looked over my shoulder at the paper in a most mystified way. He knew at once where I got my inspiration. . . . We showed him some arrows last night, and we could hardly get them away from him. He showed us how he flaked the points, singed the edges of the feathering, and put on the sinew wrappings.

Even before Waterman had established a thin line of communication with Ishi, the sheriff had become convinced that his prisoner was neither insane nor dangerous. There were no charges against him; he did not properly belong in jail. The question was, what in place of the shelter of the jail was there for him? Waterman offered to take him to San Francisco. Phones and telegraph wires were kept busy for the next forty-eight hours between Oroville and San Francisco, where the University's Museum of Anthropology then was, and between the museum and Washington, D.C.

While these negotiations were going forward, the sheriff, at Waterman's suggestion, sent a deputy to Redding to find and bring back with him the old man, Batwi, to act as interpreter–companion to Ishi. Batwi came, and although he patronized Ishi outrageously, he was for the present a help. He and Ishi could communicate in Yana, not without some difficulty, but quite fully. Meanwhile, the Indian Bureau in Washington telegraphed permission for Ishi to go to the University's museum whose staff was to be responsible for him at least until there was opportunity for fuller investigation. The sheriff of Butte County was greatly relieved; he at once made out a receipt of release from the jail to the University. This remarkable document seems not to have survived the years of moving and storing in odd corners which has been the fate of the museum files and specimens.

In any case, Waterman, Batwi, and Ishi, with the release and government permission, left Oroville on Labor Day, September 4, arriving in San Francisco somewhat before midnight. There remained to Ishi four years and seven months of life, years which were to pass within the shelter of the museum walls at the Affiliated Colleges, or in the hospital next door when he was sick.

Ishi was the last wild Indian in North America, a man of Stone Age culture subjected for the first time when he was past middle age to twentieth-century culture. He was content that it should be so, participating as fully as he could in the new life. Before examining more closely those astounding few years and what one Stone Age man contributed in so short a time to our understanding of man as such, let us go back to the years of childhood, young manhood, and middle age—almost a whole lifetime. These were years spent by him without experience or understanding of a way of life other than that of a tiny fugitive band of fewer than a dozen souls at most, opposing their ancient Yahi skills and beliefs to an unknown but hostile outside world.

There came the time—months, perhaps two or three years before August, 1911—when Ishi was the only one remaining of the little band, violence from without, old age and illness from within, having brought death to the others.

Ishi's arrival at the slaughter house was the culmination of unprecedented behavior on his part. A few days earlier, without hope, indifferent whether he lived or died, he had started on an aimless trek in a more or less southerly direction which took him into country he did not know. Exhaustion was added to grief and loneliness. He lay down in the corral because he could go no farther. He was then about forty miles from home, a man without living kin or friends, a man who had probably never been beyond the borders of his own tribal territory.

Our task is to piece together all that is known of Ishi's life before that day: from his own account of it; from what was learned of it on a camping trip with him in his own home country; and from the miscellany of rumor and fact and speculation as reported by surveyors, ranchers, rangers, and other white residents of Butte and Tehama counties. It is an episodic story, incomplete, and loosely strung across lacunae of time, ignorance, and events too painful for Ishi to relive in memory.

That Ishi should have crossed the boundaries of his homeland, and continued on into the unknown, means to be sure that he had also reached and crossed certain physical and psychic limits. But to begin to understand how profoundly disturbed he must have been, we must know how aberrant such behavior was, not for Ishi the man merely, but for Ishi the Yahi. His life becomes more of a piece if we step back from it, as from the detail of a face or feature in a painting, to focus briefly on the whole of the canvas, bringing its background and pattern into perspective. To understand Ishi's values and behavior and belief, and his way of life, we must know in a broad and general way something of his heritage: the land and people of Indian California.

21 / The Making of a Man

LEO W. SIMMONS

Becoming an adult is a transition we all go through. But how do we know when we are an adult? Do we even know what adulthood is? Adulthood may be loosely described as that stage in life where an individual achieves maturity (physically or culturally defined) and participates in the broader aspects of one's cultural system. In this selection the reader is admitted to Don Talayesva's life when he becomes a man. Don's lively autobiography relates how it feels to be caught between two cultural traditions, the Hopi life-style of the southwestern United States and the Anglo-American life-style which threatens his native beliefs. Don recreates his life for us. He allows us to smell the sunshine in the view from his mesa as he becomes a man.

I could not put off initiation into the Wowochim. My father, grandfather, and two great-uncles urged me to forget about school and become a man. They said it would please the gods, prepare me for ceremonial work, put me in line to become Chief of the Sun Clan, and fit me for a higher place in life after death. Talasvuyauoma, the big War Chief, advised me to join the men's society without delay. My ceremonial father, clan fathers, mother, godmother, clan mothers, and other relatives encouraged me; and they implied that any boy who did not seek membership in the Wowochim proved himself to be either incompetent or kahopi. They said that only hopeless cripples like Naquima or young men who had been spoiled by Christianity failed to take this important step into manhood.

. . . .

The eighth day of the Soyal was a long tiresome task. Early in the morning the Soyal Chief took the black pahos to the other kivas, and each person who had prepared a hihikwispi put corn meal and pollen upon it and held it to the rising sun, saying "Breathe on this." He then carried it to the house of his relatives, letting them breathe on it for protection against sore throats and coughs. After prayers at the edge of the mesa and breakfast in the kiva, we were sent to the spring to bathe and then home for head washing. As soon as my mother had washed my head, I collected corn ears and meal from neighbors and took them to the kiva, where the officers were smoking and drying their hair. The large altar frame was set up in the north end of the kiva, back of a sand field forty inches wide and thirty-two deep. A priest made holes in the moist sand, blew a puff of smoke into each hole, and closed it. Semicircles and lines were drawn on the sand to represent rain. Many sacred objects, including a quartz crystal *tiponi* (sacred emblem of authority), were placed about the altar. Corn ears of various colors were piled back of the altar frame, and the Special Officers took a little corn pollen, held it solemnly to their lips, and sprinkled it over the altar and the sacred emblems.

About noon we dressed in our Kele costumes and prepared to begin our prayer songs. The Soyalmana entered, dressed in a red, white, and blue blanket, an embroidered ceremonial robe, and turquoise ear pendants. After she sat down on the east bench four young men began to dress in fancy Katcina costumes with sash, kilt, and beads, and put bright feathers on their heads. White clay was daubed on their feet, hands, shoulders, and hair. The Soyal Chief and other priests sat down before the altar near a tray of pahos, smoked, and then spat honey on the altar and sacred objects and into their hands to rub their bodies. Two priests shook gourd rattles for half an hour, while a third sprinkled corn meal and pollen. Then one blew a bone whistle, facing the altar, several smoked, and we all sat in silence until the four costumed men leaned against the ladder in succession, went through vigorous motions as in sexual copulation with the ladder, and departed to collect more colored corn ears for the altar.

The Chief Assistant was erecting a small altar in the southwest corner of the deeper part of the kiva, while many Soyal members went to their homes and returned with meal, some of which was placed in four large trays in a row between the fireplace and the large altar. On the trays were placed thin black pahos, and, between them, the bundles of hihikwispi. A few priests were singing around the smaller altar. Special Officers from the other kivas entered with their initiates, and two Kwan members in costume sprinkled meal upon the altars and sat down opposite the ladder, where they smoked native cigarettes, each resting an arm around the nearest ladder pole. The War Chief, with shield, bow, and tomahawk, sat southeast of the ladder, smoking and guarding the kiva entrance. We Keles sat on the elevated portion of the kiva. Three special women, who had attended the previous ceremonies, entered and took their seats, while the Soyalmana retained her position on the east bench. When the singing and rattling had commenced again at the small altar, the four messengers who had collected the corn took up the large trays of meal and pahos, hung the bunches of hihikwispi over their left shoulders, circled inside the kiva four times, ascended the ladder and circled outside four times, and then started in file to the Oraibi spring to deposit the offerings. While they were on this errand, two masked Katcinas (Mastops) appeared from the Kwan kiva with their bodies painted black and covered with white handprints. They wore old skin kilts, had dry grass wreaths around their necks, and wore large black masks decorated with white dots, hooked marks, cornhusk pendants for ears, two white drawings of frogs on the back, and a bunch of eagle feathers and red horsehair on top. From their belts dangled bunches of cow hoofs, which rattled when they ran among the spectators, seizing women from behind and going through vigorous motions of copulation. After each conquest a Katcina would run to the kiva, jabber in a disguised voice, and set out to catch another woman. They finally entered the kiva and sat down east of the ladder, where many Soyal members sprinkled them with corn meal and gave them prayer feathers asking for rain. The Katcinas put their prayer offerings in a sack and departed. Singing and rattling continued at the small altar, and a man kept whistling into a bowl of water in the southeast corner. The War Chief handed us a crystal to suck four times and hold to our hearts, while he bit off pieces of root, chewed them, and spat on his shield, seeming to paint it. He held in one hand a white corn ear and the six old eagle feathers used in the Medicine Making ceremony. The four messengers returned from the spring and received our thanks.

Near sunset the priests from other kivas brought in their plaques of pahos and placed them near the large altar. After having smoked, the Chief Assistant rubbed his hands with corn meal, took up his tiponi, rubbed meal on it, stepped north of the four empty trays which had been returned by the messengers, sprinkled meal on the pahos, waved his tiponi to the southeast, and prayed. We all responded with "*Kwaikwai*," spat on our hands, rubbed our bodies, and ended a long ceremony which had been necessary in order that we Hopi might not disappear from the earth.

The leaders of the Kwan, Ahl, and Tao societies took their initiates back to their kivas. We removed our Kele costumes, dressed, and went to our houses for food—salted stew this time, for the fast was broken. The stew was excellent and made our eyes shine with health. The officers ate after us on the lower floor and then invited us down to eat some more, signifying that at the next harvest we would have food enough and to spare. The food which remained was carefully saved to symbolize our frugality. In the evening we again performed our Medicine Making ceremony of the fourth day and followed it with the Hawk ceremony of the fifth day, with some elaborations.

Just after midnight the Chief Assistant and the Soyalmana left the kiva. Soon the Screen Priest and his Assistant brought in a large buckskin stretched on a frame. Painted on the screen was the picture of Muyingwu, the god of germination. He held in his right hand a growing cornstalk and in his left an emblem of authority (*Monwikuru*). On his head were symbols of clouds, with falling rain and rays of lightning. Under the cornstalk was a symbol of the moon and on the other side of Muyingwu was a symbol of the sun. To both sides of the screen were attached artificial flowers, and to the lower part were fastened watermelon, muskmelon, squash, cotton, pumpkin, corn, and other seeds. Eagle feathers below and red horsehair on the sides and base represented rays of the sun.

Screeching was heard outside and the Chief Assistant entered with the Soyalmana, dressed in elaborate costume consisting of a ceremonial blanket held in place by a knotted belt, a man's Katcina kilt tied over her left shoulder, and numerous strands of beads around her neck and yarn around her wrists. The Chief Assistant sat down east of the ladder, then moved forward, squatted, screeched, and waved the wings, while the Mana followed in an upright position as both worked their way around the screen. A tray with two corn ears, some corn meal, and pahos was handed to the Soyal Chief, who prayed over it. The officers smoked and one priest blew smoke back of the screen. The Soyal Chief received the tray, after four other priests had prayed over it, stooped down, and scraped with a corn ear all the seeds from the screen into the tray together with the artificial flowers on the edge. When he stood up and prayed, the Assistant Chief led the Mana from the kiva, the screen was removed, and the tray placed near the altar.

The War Chief took the medicine bowl and left the kiva, but soon returned with the Star and Sun Priest. We all stood up as they entered, and the War Chief sprinkled medicine from the bowl, while someone beat a drum in muffled tone. Men from other kivas entered in costumes. The Star Priest, representing the Sun god that I had seen in my dream as a boy, was barefoot and dressed in a Katcina kilt and sash, ankle bands, and turtle-shell rattles on each leg, green arm bands, a buckskin, and numerous strands of beads. His body was unpainted except for lines of white dots running from the point of the big toe up and around the front of the leg, from the heel over the calves, from the thumb along the front of his arms to the shoulder and down to the nipples; and from the hands along the outside of the arms to the shoulder and down each side of the back. His headdress consisted of a frame of leather bands, to the front of which was attached a four-pointed star and to the sides artificial flowers. In his right hand was a long crook, in the middle of which was fastened a black corn ear; in his left were seven corn ears. He danced backward and forward to the beating of the drum, talking rapidly and incoherently. The Soyal Chief stood west of the fireplace, holding a paho and meal tray from which he occasionally sprinkled meal upon the Sun god. To his left stood the Assistant Chief in a white blanket and with face painted white. All at once the Sun god leaped toward the Soyal Chief, handed him the crook and the corn ear, and received from the Assistant Chief a rawhide sun symbol fastened to a stick which had been concealed under the white blanket. The god took hold of the stick with both hands, shook it, and danced north of the fireplace, sideways from east to west and back, twirling the sun symbol rapidly, clockwise. Someone screamed and a song was intoned. The beating of the drum became louder and louder, as the Sun god danced and leaped about in a marvelous manner. As the song ended he leaped toward the Soyal Chief and ascended the ladder. The Special Officers began to smoke over the corn ear and the crook which the god had left with the Soyal Chief.

In a short time officers from the other societies came for their pahos which had been consecrated on the altar and in the ceremony. Loma-vuyaoma of the Fire Clan prepared to take a special offering to the shrine of Masau'u, a journey which required a brave heart. He sat by the fireplace and smoked, while every member of the Soyal, including us Keles, placed a paho on an old plaque for Masau'u. Special piki made by members of the Fire Clan was placed on the plaque, together with a piece of raw rabbit meat, some mountain tobacco, and corn meal. When Lomavuyaoma lifted the plaque to go, we all said in unison, "With your brave, happy heart take our pahos over there and deliver our message to Masau'u." When he returned from his mission, we said, "Kwaikwai." He sat down and smoked, relating how when he deposited the plaque and prayed, he heard a strong breath coming from the shrine, which signified that Masau'u who guards our village had heard our petition and received our offerings.

In a short time Katcinas (Quoqulum) in yellow masks and red horse-hair came from the Ahl kiva and danced for us. A priest was sent with offerings to the Sun shrine (Tawaki) on top of a high mesa about three miles southeast of Oraibi. It was to be a hard journey for him, because he had to run fast, present the offering just as the Sun god peeped over the horizon, and return swiftly. This prayer offering was very important because the Sun god is chief over all, and gives heat and light, without which there would be no life.

I was taken by my ceremonial father to the house of his sister Solemana to have my head washed again and to receive another name. She held the mother-corn ear before me and said, "My sweetheart, now I name you Tanackmainewa, which means the shining feathers of the Road-Runner. Take this name, look up to our Sun god, and call it loudly to him who is your uncle." This name did not stick like the Wowochim name, which seemed to be glued to me.

Before dawn we took our prayer offerings to our relatives who had washed their heads and were ready with happy hearts for the Paho Planting ceremony. At sunrise the entire village, including babies on their mothers' backs, assembled at the east edge of the mesa, thrust many hundreds of pahos into the ground, and sprinkled them with meal. The people who belonged to my father's clan placed their pahos at a spot called Bow Height (*Awatobi*), because the Sand Clan came from Awatobi, a village now in ruins. Many men and boys, including myself, placed pahos on the Antelope shrine in order to have success in hunting. As we returned to the village, one could see hundreds of willow switches standing three or four feet high with seven or eight turkey, hawk, eagle, or other soft feathers attached to them three or four inches apart. No chicken or crow feathers were ever used. Fathers who had sons less than a year old planted little crooked pahos for them in order that they might thrive, be happy, and live long. Most of the prayer feathers were fastened to the long sticks for our departed dear ones. The short double pahos were made for all the dead and for the Six-Point-Cloud-People who send rain. It is our belief that the spirit gods and our ancestors come with outstretched hands, seeking pahos in exchange for the blessings of health and long life, and that if they find none they turn away sorrowful. We know that they take with them only the souls of the pahos.

We ate breakfast in our own houses, distributed our prayer feathers among our friends, and attached them to animals, and other objects of value. I gave pahos to several people, tied them to the Katcina masks, to the ceiling of our house, to the necks of our dogs and burrows, and to branches of the fruit trees. During the forenoon Katcina masks were painted, the altar taken down and stored, and the sand in the kiva sprinkled with meal and thrown in a gully to wash down over the fields.

In early afternoon fifteen or twenty Quoqulum Katcina and five or six "females" entered the village from the south. They went to every kiva, where one of them made four lines of corn meal and meal paths leading out in four directions. This was to "open the kiva" and arouse the Spirit Katcinas from their long rest in order that they might visit us again. The Quoqulum Katcinas sang and danced several times, and then made corn-meal paths leading southeast from the village as far as their meal lasted. When the paths were completed they returned, and the Father of the Katcina (a Powamu member) took the rattles from their legs, sprinkled the Katcinas with meal, and gave each a soft prayer feather to take to the Six-Point-Cloud-People. They departed southward over the cliff to the Katcina shrine, where they deposited the feathers, prayed, undressed, and returned to the Ahl kiva with their masks concealed from the children.

We Soyal members returned to the kiva, where the Special Officers smoked and made prayer feathers to use in a rabbit hunt. They made them for the divine mothers of rabbits and chicken hawks because these deities are good hunters. The ceremonial father of the Soyalmana was Hunter Chief. He went through the kivas announcing the place to build the cere-monial fire and begin the hunt. We smoked and went to our houses for supper, but returned to the kiva to sleep, because love-making was taboo for four days more.

We hunted rabbits for three days, leaving the catch in the house of the Soyalmana. On the fourth we arose and went to the east edge of the mesa to pray, returned to the kiva, dressed, and went to our houses to get our heads washed before sunrise, according to Hopi rule. It is our belief that whoever washes his or her head on this day will be among the first to taste the ripe melons in summer. The Sun god had reached his winter home four days before—when we planted the pahos—and was now turning back to his summer house, leading us along his trail.

In mid-afternoon we prepared for a shower bath and a feast. Our folks made unsalted gravy which we took with our dancing outfits to the kiva. There we painted our bodies with whitewash in stripes, dressed in Katcina costumes, and formed a line, taking the gravy in little plaques. The ceremonial father of Sadie (the Soyalmana) took a pot—with two cooked rabbits partly exposed—and led about forty of us into the house of the Soyalmana. On each side of the door were two tubs of water, with a woman standing behind each holding a plaque. We undressed quickly and ran out between the tubs, where the women dashed cold water over us, washing off the white paint. After our bath we reëntered the house and threw out great quantities of food to the scrambling spectators. The bath signified rains, and the distribution of food a good harvest. We returned to the kiva, dried and dressed ourselves, and had a feast of rabbit stew. After the meal my old uncle, Kayayeptewa, told a long story of our history to which we were supposed to pay close attention. But some of the men seemed restless for love-making and joked in undertones—for they were free of the ceremony and could return to their wives and sweethearts.

I had learned a great lesson and now knew that the ceremonies handed down by our fathers mean life and security, both now and hereafter. I regretted that I had ever joined the Y.M.C.A. and decided to set myself against Christianity once and for all. I could see that the old people were right when they insisted that Jesus Christ might do for modern Whites in a good climate, but that the Hopi gods had brought success to us in the desert ever since the world began.

From "Body Ritual among the Nacirema," by Horace Miner, *American Anthropologist,* Vol. 58, No. 3, June, 1956, pp. 503–507. Reproduced by permission of the American Anthropological Association and the author.

22 / Body Ritual among the Nacirema

HORACE MINER

Why do we take pride in our own life-style? Nearly every member of every society believes his way of life is better than that of others. This ethnocentric attitude is a result of being unable to be objective when look-ing at the "strange customs" of other peoples. Anthropology stresses how important it is to be able to interpret beliefs and customs of another cul-ture in terms of the belief system of that cultural tradition and not to interpret other customs in view of our own beliefs. The concept of cultural relativism is difficult to achieve. To illustrate this point, consider the following article by Horace Miner, in which he describes the customs of the Nacirema. While reading this selection keep in mind how you feel about these customs and why you feel the way you do.

The anthropologist has become so familiar with the diversity of ways in which different peoples behave in similar situations that he is not apt to be surprised by even the most exotic customs. In fact, if all of the logically possible combinations of behavior have not been found somewhere in the world, he is apt to suspect that they must be present in some yet un-described tribe. . . . In this light, the magical beliefs and practices of the Nacirema present such unusual aspects that it seems desirable to de-scribe them as an example of the extremes to which human behavior can go.

Professor Linton first brought the ritual of the Nacirema to the attention of anthropologists twenty years ago, but the culture of this people is still very poorly understood. They are a North American group living in the territory between the Canadian Cree, the Yaqui and Tarahumare of Mexico, and the Carib and Arawak of the Antilles. Little is known of their origin, although tradition states that they came from the east. According to Naci-rema mythology, their nation was originated by a culture hero, Notgnihsaw, who is otherwise known for two great feats of strength—the throwing of a piece of wampum across the river Pa-To-Mac and the chopping down of a cherry tree in which the Spirit of Truth resided.

Nacirema culture is characterized by a highly developed market economy which has evolved in a rich natural habitat. While much of the people's time is devoted to economic pursuits, a large part of the fruits of these labors and a considerable portion of the day are spent in ritual activity. The focus of this activity is the human body, the appearance and health of which loom as a dominant concern in the ethos of the people. While such a concern is certainly not unusual, its ceremonial aspects and associated philosophy are unique.

The fundamental belief underlying the whole system appears to be that the human body is ugly and that its natural tendency is to debility and disease. Incarcerated in such a body, man's only hope is to avert these characteristics through the use of the powerful influences of ritual and ceremony. Every household has one or more shrines devoted to this purpose. The more powerful individuals in the society have several shrines in their houses and, in fact, the opulence of a house is often referred to in terms of the number of such ritual centers it possesses. Most houses are of wattle and daub construction, but the shrine rooms of the more wealthy are walled with stone. Poorer families imitate the rich by applying pottery plaques to their shrine walls.

While each family has at least one such shrine, the rituals associated with it are not family ceremonies but are private and secret. The rites are normally only discussed with children, and then only during the period when they are being initiated into these mysteries. I was able, however, to establish sufficient rapport with the natives to examine these shrines and to have the rituals described to me.

The focal point of the shrine is a box or chest which is built into the wall. In this chest are kept the many charms and magical potions without which no native believes he could live. These preparations are secured from a variety of specialized practitioners. The most powerful of these are the medicine men, whose assistance must be rewarded with substantial gifts. However, the medicine men do not provide the curative potions for their clients, but decide what the ingredients should be and then write them down in an ancient and secret language. This writing is understood only by the medicine men and by the herbalists who, for another gift, provide the required charm.

The charm is not disposed of after it has served its purpose, but is placed in the charm-box of the household shrine. As these magical materials are specific for certain ills, and the real or imagined maladies of the people are many, the charm-box is usually full to overflowing. The magical packets are so numerous that people forget what their purposes were and fear to use them again. While the natives are very vague on this point, we can only assume that the idea in retaining all the old magical materials is that their presence in the charm-box, before which the body rituals are conducted, will in some way protect the worshipper.

Beneath the charm-box is a small font. Each day every member of the family, in succession, enters the shrine room, bows his head before the charm-box, mingles different sorts of holy water in the font, and proceeds with a brief rite of ablution. The holy waters are secured from the Water Temple of the community, where the priests conduct elaborate ceremonies to make the liquid ritually pure.

In the hierarchy of magical practitioners, and below the medicine men in prestige, are specialists whose designation is best translated "holy-mouth-men." The Nacirema have an almost pathological horror of and fascination with the mouth, the condition of which is believed to have a supernatural influence on all social relationships. Were it not for the rituals of the mouth, they believe that their teeth would fall out, their gums bleed, their jaws shrink, their friends desert them, and their lovers reject them. They also believe that a strong relationship exists between oral and moral characteristics. For example, there is a ritual ablution of the mouth for children which is supposed to improve their moral fiber.

The daily body ritual performed by everyone includes a mouth-rite. Despite the fact that these people are so punctilious about care of the mouth, this rite involves a practice which strikes the uninitiated stranger as revolting. It was reported to me that the ritual consists of inserting a small bundle of hog hair into the mouth, along with certain magical powders, and then moving the bundle in a highly formalized series of gestures.

In addition to the private mouth-rite, the people seek out a holy-mouth-man once or twice a year. These practitioners have an impressive set of paraphernalia, consisting of a variety of augers, awls, probes, and prods. The use of these objects in the exorcism of the evils of the mouth involves almost unbelievable ritual torture of the client. The holy-mouth-man opens the client's mouth and, using the above-mentioned tools, enlarges any holes which decay may have created in the teeth. Magical materials are put into these holes. If there are no naturally occurring holes in the teeth, large sections of one or more teeth are gouged out so that the supernatural substance can be applied. In the client's view, the purpose of these ministrations is to arrest decay and to draw friends. The extremely sacred and traditional character of the rite is evident in the fact that the natives return to the holy-mouth-men year after year, despite the fact that their teeth continue to decay.

It is to be hoped that, when a thorough study of the Nacirema is made, there will be careful inquiry into the personality structure of these people. One has but to watch the gleam in the eye of a holy-mouth-man, as he jabs an awl into an exposed nerve, to suspect a certain amount of sadism is involved. If this can be established, a very interesting pattern emerges, for most of the population shows definite masochistic tendencies. It was to these that Professor Linton referred in discussing a distinctive part of the daily body ritual which is performed only by men. This part of the rite involves scraping and lacerating the surface of the face with a sharp instrument. Special women's rites are performed only four times during each lunar month, but what they lack in frequency is made up in barbarity. As part of this ceremony, women bake their heads in small ovens for about an hour. The theoretically interesting point is that what seems to be a preponderantly masochistic people have developed sadistic specialists.

The medicine men have an imposing temple, or *latipso,* in every community of any size. The more elaborate ceremonies required to treat very sick patients can only be performed at this temple. These ceremonies involve not only the thaumaturge but a permanent group of vestal maidens who move sedately about the temple chambers in distinctive costume and headdress.

The *latipso* ceremonies are so harsh that it is phenomenal that a fair proportion of the really sick natives who enter the temple ever recover. Small children whose indoctrination is still incomplete have been known to resist attempts to take them to the temple because "that is where you go to die." Despite this fact, sick adults are not only willing but eager to undergo the protracted ritual purification, if they can afford to do so. No matter how ill the supplicant or how grave the emergency, the guardians of many temples will not admit a client if he cannot give a rich gift to the custodian. Even after one has gained admission and survived the ceremonies, the guardians will not permit the neophyte to leave until he makes still another gift.

The supplicant entering the temple is first stripped of his or her clothes. In every-day life the Nacirema avoids exposure of his body and its natural functions. Bathing and excretory acts are performed only in the secrecy of the household shrine, where they are ritualized as part of the body-rites. Psychological shock results from the fact that body secrecy is suddenly lost upon entry into the *latipso.* A man, whose own wife has never seen him in an excretory act, suddenly finds himself naked and assisted by a vestal maiden while he performs his natural functions into a sacred vessel. This sort of ceremonial treatment is necessitated by the fact that the excreta are used by a diviner to ascertain the course and nature of the client's sickness. Female clients, on the other hand, find their naked bodies are subjected to the scrutiny, manipulation and prodding of the medicine men.

Few supplicants in the temple are well enough to do anything but lie on their hard beds. The daily ceremonies, like the rites of the holy-mouth-men, involve discomfort and torture. With ritual precision, the vestals awaken their miserable charges each dawn and roll them about on their beds of pain while performing ablutions, in the formal movements of which the maidens are highly trained. At other times they insert magic wands in the supplicant's mouth or force him to eat substances which are supposed to be healing. From time to time the medicine men come to their clients and jab magically treated needles into their flesh. The fact that these temple ceremonies may not cure, and may even kill the neophyte, in no way decreases the people's faith in the medicine men.

There remains one other kind of practitioner, known as a "listener."

This witch-doctor has the power to exorcise the devils that lodge in the heads of people who have been bewitched. The Nacirema believe that parents bewitch their own children. Mothers are particularly suspected of putting a curse on children while teaching them the secret body rituals. The counter-magic of the witch-doctor is unusual in its lack of ritual. The patient simply tells the "listener" all his troubles and fears, beginning with the earliest difficulties he can remember. The memory displayed by the Nacirema in these exorcism sessions is truly remarkable. It is not uncommon for the patient to bemoan the rejection he felt upon being weaned as a babe, and a few individuals even see their troubles going back to the traumatic effects of their own birth.

In conclusion, mention must be made of certain practices which have their base in native esthetics but which depend upon the pervasive aversion to the natural body and its functions. There are ritual fasts to make fat people thin and ceremonial feasts to make thin people fat. Still other rites are used to make women's breasts larger if they are small, and smaller if they are large. General dissatisfaction with breast shape is symbolized in the fact that the ideal form is virtually outside the range of human variation. A few women afflicted with almost inhuman hypermammary development are so idolized that they make a handsome living by simply going from village to village and permitting the natives to stare at them for a fee.

Reference has already been made to the fact that excretory functions are ritualized, routinized, and relegated to secrecy. Natural reproductive functions are similarly distorted. Intercourse is taboo as a topic and scheduled as an act. Efforts are made to avoid pregnancy by the use of magical materials or by limiting intercourse to certain phases of the moon. Conception is actually very infrequent. When pregnant, women dress so as to hide their condition. Parturition takes place in secret, without friends or relatives to assist, and the majority of women do not nurse their infants.

Our review of the ritual life of the Nacirema has certainly shown them to be a magic-ridden people. It is hard to understand how they have managed to exist so long under the burdens which they have imposed upon themselves. But even such exotic customs as these take on real meaning when they are viewed with the insight provided by Malinowski when he wrote:

> Looking from far and above, from our high places of safety in the developed civilization, it is easy to see all the crudity and irrelevance of magic. But without its power and guidance early man could not have mastered his practical difficulties as he has done, nor could man have advanced to the higher stages of civilization.

From *Innovation: The Basis of Cultural Change,* by Homer G. Barnett, 1953, pp. 7–10. Reprinted by permission of the McGraw-Hill Book Company.

23 / What Is an Innovation?

HOMER G. BARNETT

How does a culture change? Simple, say many textbooks—through diffusion and invention. Then this traditional approach proceeds to make distinctions between different types of diffusion (independent and parallel) and invention (basic and derived). The approach has merit in that it provides convenient terms for describing the many ways a culture changes. However, such a rigid system of terms tends to obscure the realization that all these terms are merely variations on a single theme. The following selection from Barnett's book points out that all types of diffusion and invention involve one basic common process—the innovative process. Barnett's use of the term "innovation" provides the synthesis approach to cultural change. Everyone may not be involved in diffusion; everyone may not be an inventor; but everyone is an innovator. The reader should carefully consider what an innovator is and how he himself is an innovator while carrying out daily routine activities.

An innovation is here defined as any thought, behavior, or thing that is new because it is qualitatively different from existing forms. Strictly speaking, every innovation is an idea, or a constellation of ideas; but some innovations by their nature must remain mental organizations only, whereas others may be given overt and tangible expression. "Innovation" is therefore a comprehensive term covering all kinds of mental constructs, whether they can be given sensible representation or not. A novelty is understood in the same way; hence, "innovation" and "novelty" are hereafter used synonymously, the choice of one term over the other being dictated solely by lexical propriety. To a limited extent "invention" is also used as a synonym for "innovation." There would be no objection to a consistent equation of these two terms were it not that popular usage puts a more restricted meaning upon invention than is intended for the word innovation. For most people an invention is a thing, and the label seems inappropriate when applied to novel behavior patterns, theories, and social relations. While maintaining that there is no psychological distinction between the conception of a new object and a new act or theory, the present study retains the conventional implications of the term "invention." When it is used it means simply a technological innovation, a new thing. Custom has also governed the use of the term "discovery." It is fruitless to try to establish a rigorous and meaningful distinction between "discovery" and "invention," and nothing is to be gained by redefining the two words. On the contrary, communication is facilitated by conforming to ordinary usage. Beyond this purpose no significance should be attached to the differential employment of "invention" and "discovery." Both are names for innovations.

Some authors attempt to draw a distinction between "basic" and "derived" or "elaborating" inventions. While this approach may have some value, it is likely to be more misleading than enlightening. This is definitely so if it alleges or suggests that there are two kinds of inventions and that they result from different conditions and mental processes. It is impossible to characterize major and minor concepts in terms of the concepts themselves, yet this approach is likely to carry that implication. Actually when such a distinction is made it rests on other grounds, and the evaluation is to a large extent subjective. If "basic" means "important," any attempt to use the characteristics of inventions themselves as a measure of their relative importance turns out to be an estimate of the attitudes toward them, and this estimate varies by individual and with context. The same novelty will be regarded in one situation as trivial, whereas in another it will assume major significance. The devising of a whistle to call farm hands to dinner might strike most people as a rather unimportant novelty, although it would not if its purpose were to announce dinner to formally invited guests. A new type of wrench would undoubtedly be regarded as more important by a mechanic than by a lawyer; and new technological developments generally are more highly valued by Americans than by many other people.

There are objective grounds for saying that one invention is more basic than another if the criterion is the social effects that they have; but this cannot be adduced from the qualities which characterize them. If it could, we would be much wiser than we are about the future consequences of a given innovation. Also, if by basic and derived it is meant that some inventions provide a stimulus for more subsequent inventions than do others, there is an unquestioned basis for making a distinction. But, again, this has nothing to do with the properties of the inventions themselves; or at least none that can be demonstrated in advance of developments. If new ideas do have such inherent qualities they appear only in retrospect, which means that external factors play a necessary part in determining what they are. It is, in fact, evident that the time–place setting of an invention instills it with whatever possibilities it might have for future development.

All in all the distinction between basic and secondary inventions is an artificial one that contributes more confusion than clarity to an understanding of cultural change. All innovations have antecedents. All are therefore derived from others. Consequently, each one may be considered to be an elaboration, even though not all are basic to others. Certainly in point of creative processes, which is our main concern here, there is no difference between an invention such as the wheel that has subsequently entered into the creation of many others and one such as the hairpin that has figured in relatively few developments. The conception of something new is independent of the consequences of its conception.

This conclusion is related to the contention that new ideas are a much more common occurrence than they are usually supposed to be. Unless some arbitrary and external standard is set up, it is not possible to segregate what we laud as inventions from other new ideas. Whether a novelty is striking or shocking or is a minor or a major departure from previous patterns has nothing to do with the mental processes which brought the idea of it into existence. The innovative act is the same; "radical" or "minor" are expressions of attitudes toward certain of its consequences. When this evaluative attitude is discounted, it will appear that innovations, whether major or minor, whether of private or public significance, and whether of ephemeral or lasting utility, are constantly being made. Everyone is an innovator, whether popular definitions allow him that recognition or not.

In defining an innovation as something that is qualitatively new, emphasis is placed upon reorganization rather than upon quantitative variation as the criterion of a novelty. Innovation does not result from the addition or subtraction of parts. It takes place only when there is a recombination of them. Psychologically this is a process of substitution, not one of addition or subtraction, although the product, the novelty, may be described as having a greater or lesser number of parts than some antecedent form. The essence of change, however, lies in the restructuring of the parts so that a new pattern results, a pattern the distinctness of which cannot be characterized merely in terms of an increase or decrease in the number of its component elements. This limitation clearly excludes from the category of innovations the many instances of change that consist solely of a multiplication or an extension of the dimensions of an existing thing. The manipulation of parts that can be treated as mathematical units produces an entirely different result from that which occurs when incommensurable variables are added, dropped, or interchanged.

While quantitative variations in themselves are not to be reckoned as innovations, it is true that they may be employed with innovative results. Such employment is, in fact, a very common occurrence. The requirement, again, is reorganization, which can be entirely independent of numerical variation. Thus, the man who increases the size or number of sails on a boat has created nothing qualitatively new if quantity alone, and not proportion or arrangement, is involved. If, however, an added sail is so placed that the configuration it forms with others is different, there has been an innovation. The same applies to the sail itself; changing its size is not innovative, whereas changing its shape by disproportionate extensions is. The addition of one molecule of water to another produces nothing qualitatively new, but the addition of one atom of oxygen to H_2O does. The removal of one of the four legs of a stool is not in itself innovative. It becomes so if the arrangement of the remaining three legs is altered so that a tripod support, for example, replaces the original four-post pattern. In all such instances of innovation, even though quantitative changes are necessarily involved, those changes are not the critical factor. The definitive characteristic of a novelty is its newness with respect to the interrelationships of its parts, not their number. Irrespective of whether or not quantitative changes are entailed, all innovations are qualitative departures from habitual patterns.

The materials for all innovations come from two major sources. There is, first of all, the cultural inventory that is available to the innovator. This includes all the ideas of things, techniques, behaviors, and ideas that he knows to pertain to human beings, whether they belong only to his own particular ethnic group or to others. Then there are the nonartificial elements of the innovator's experience, those that exist independent of human ingenuity or control. They include, most obviously, the objects and phenomena of nature. But they also include the natural man himself, his physical and mental attributes, as a thing or other part of the inescapably given universe of phenomena. It is important to bear this fact in mind, for innovators do treat human beings as they do other objects in nature. They invent by drawing upon the physical properties of man as they do by using the physical properties of iron and heat. Furthermore, they manipulate the psychical and psychosomatic attributes of themselves as they do the immaterial aspects of the rest of their experience. They take, as their material, ideas and the ideas of ideas. They treat persons not only as objects but as volitional, feeling, vacillating elements. The manipulation of these intangibles is indeed the height of innovative ingenuity.

24 / Watch Out, You Might Assimilate

KEITH L. PEARSON

Picture a Pueblo Indian house held together by sun-dried adobe bricks and modern concrete blocks. The house has a dirt floor but is furnished with an aluminum window and Teflon-coated cooking utensils. The Pueblo life-style is in a state of marked cultural change. In this article Pearson brings the question of how a culture changes from the theoretical level of Barnett to specific examples in the southwestern United States. Through intensive diffusion people in contact with the Euro-American world have often had to exchange former livelihoods for wage labor. Pearson notes this and elaborates how the new economic system altered more extensive social–political relationships of the Pueblos. The reader should note the changes in the Pueblo way of life brought about by culture borrowing (diffusion) and view these changes in the light of Barnett's more inclusive concept of innovation.

In front of a wind-worn adobe wall two Indian boys try out their newly bought "click-clacks," and the sharp tat-tat-tat of plastic balls smacking together—proof of their growing proficiency—echoes through the Santa Clara pueblo. A miniskirted young woman pauses in the street to watch the boys practice. A red pickup truck pulls up, and the driver blows the horn, adding more noise. At all age levels, the 40,000 Pueblo Indians living in the Rio Grande region, including the residents of Santa Clara, glaringly reveal their assimilation into the present-day culture of the United States.

A casual observer—such as a disappointed tourist—seeing that these Indians had abandoned most of their heritage, would predict that any remnants of the Pueblo Indian culture will be gone in a few years. But such a pessimistic prognosis would be wrong. The Pueblo Indians have prevailed as a cultural entity for thousands of years, they possess a strong cultural structure today, and I believe they will maintain their identity for generations to come. This can be seen by looking at the people, their history, and their handling of contemporary problems, rather than by focusing solely on their architecture and public ceremonies.

The Pueblo people have consistently constructed societies capable of successful adaptation to severe ecological and environmental changes. They are dynamic, not helpless; they are creators, not simply the pawns of other societies.

The prehistoric and historic records attest to this view. About one thousand years ago there was a severe and prolonged drought in the southwestern United States, causing dramatic changes in the life-styles of the area's peoples, including several groups that were ancestors of the Pueblo Indians. Along the Rio Grande, groups of people using irrigation systems for their farms began to settle in the region. They are known as the Tanoans, a name derived from their language. Their irrigation systems, complicated networks of canals, dams, and floodgates insured the success of their crops even during droughts.

The people who built these irrigation systems had also developed a social organization that could mobilize workers for canal construction, maintenance, and repairs, They had devised communal methods for making public decisions about land use and planting as well as water control.

Archeologists consider the Tanoans to have been the earliest permanent village, or pueblo, residents of the area. They were not, of course, the only people who made use of the riverine resource. From time to time, hunting bands camped along the waterways, and other groups entered the region for trade purposes. The Tanoans undoubtedly interacted with the hunting and trading groups, exchanging ideas as well as material goods.

During the fourteenth century, another group of pueblo people appeared in the Rio Grande region. These people, who spoke a language known as Keresan, farmed without irrigation systems. Their social organization emphasized kinship alignments instead of political leadership. Their view of the world stressed the need for man to cooperate with, not take control over, nature. The Keresans believed that their survival was directly controlled by deities whose nature they sought to define. Their genius lay in the creation of philosophical systems, while the Tanoans excelled in technological devices.

The arrival of the Keresans at the Rio Grande changed the human environment, and both village groups had to adapt. While Tanoan religious activity began to reflect Keresan theology, the Keresans adopted some of the Tanoan ideas of man's place in the natural world. Both groups revised some of their socioreligious practices. Changes were made in their systems of social organization, material possessions, and technologies.

In the late fifteenth century, a third group appeared in the Rio Grande region. This group, composed of people who spoke a language known as Athapascan, again altered the environmental situation. The Navaho and Apache, contemporary names for the Athapascans, were hunters who generally lived in the highlands. Although small-scale raiding occurred, the villagers did not attempt to drive out the newcomers. A trading pattern developed between the highland and valley groups. For meat, deerskins, and wild foods from the Athapascans, the villagers exchanged corn and other farm-grown vegetables, cotton, and manufactured goods. Because the trade was beneficial to the villagers as well as to the hunters, the adaptation was positive.

When the Spanish took control of the Rio Grande Valley in the late sixteenth century, they imposed rigorous policies of military conquest, colonization, and the establishment of an administrative government. Spanish missionaries and soldiers forced Pueblo men to build churches or chapels in the villages. Minor violations of Spanish rules were punished with imprisonment, enslavement, or physical mutilation. Villages that persisted in practicing traditional ways were frequently attacked and often destroyed.

The Spanish placed extraordinary pressures on the Puebloan adaptive techniques. On the one hand, the Indians were required to either accept the Spanish religion, economy, form of government, language, and social organization or be killed. On the other hand, if they accepted these traits, thus giving up their own cultures, Puebloan life as such would cease to exist. Their positive response to these conditions is almost incredible.

The explanation for their survival is not to be found in Puebloan conservatism, as is often claimed, but in their adaptiveness and their ability to select the beneficial aspects of Spanish culture, while rejecting the detrimental. For example, the Spanish missionaries demanded that the Puebloans observe the special days of the Catholic liturgical calendar. The villagers, particularly the Keresans, had their own calendrical sequence for religious ceremonies. Adoption of the Catholic schedule could have had severe theological implications for the Keresans. But the Keresans found that the Catholic calendar, like their own, was geared to a seasonal cycle. With a few minor revisions they were able to hold their animal, corn, and other observances on the days the missionaries considered important. Thus, the Puebloans held a deer dance at Christmas, an eagle dance on Epiphany, and other religious ceremonies on certain saints' days.

When the Spanish imposed their administrative structure on the pueblos, the residents shuffled and redefined the Spanish system. In a recent publication on the Pueblo Indians, the late Prof. Edward Dozier observed that official governmental positions forced on the villagers by the Spanish gave Puebloans the opportunity "to conduct secular matters separately, while their ceremonial activities [remained] under the direction of leaders unknown to outsiders."

During the three hundred years of Spanish domination, Puebloan culture changed extensively. Many villages were abandoned; others were relocated. All the villages came to have Catholic churches in their territories. New crops, textiles, species of livestock, crafts, and forms of labor were accepted. Spanish became the common language. The Puebloans of the nineteenth century were not the same as they had been three hundred years earlier. Even their name derived from *pueblo,* the Spanish word for village.

But they were still culturally and socially distinct from the Spanish. It is in this ability to retain their distinct identity, while constantly incorporating extensive changes into their society, that the adaptive success of the Puebloan people can be seen.

The United States assumed control of the Rio Grande region in the 1840's. The new government brought restrictions on land and land use, a strong effort to eradicate Puebloan traditions through religious and educational policies, and a rapid increase in the non-Indian population. Again, Puebloan survival was seriously threatened.

The villagers, proceeding slowly and cautiously, began to make the necessary adjustments. English replaced Spanish as the common language. Wage work, instead of farming or livestock raising, gradually became the primary type of livelihood. As technology progressed, the people accepted such things as electricity and electrical appliances, plumbing, roads, automotive vehicles, hospitals, and medical technology.

The villages changed. New houses were built from new kinds of materials. Old houses were remodeled. Concrete blocks were used when adobe bricks began to crumble. Glass windows were installed in ancient walls. Doorways with wooden doors replaced rooftop entrances. Stairways were built and ladders discarded.

The villagers changed. Women made pottery for tourists instead of for home use. With the profits, they bought glassware and modern cookware. Men, whose working time was once determined by the sun, geared their work day to their employer's time clock. Their walk to the fields was replaced by a ride in a car pool to an office or factory.

The villages and villagers of the 1970's are much different from those of the 1840's. But the women with the Teflon-coated cookware and the men in the car pool are Pueblo Indians. They take pride in their distinctive identity.

The process of creative adaptation is associated with anguish, frustration, and pain. It is by no means automatic. It succeeds or fails on the basis of human decisions, which are frequently reached only after extended discussion, bitter arguments, and severe criticism. To overlook the fact that the Puebloans, in order to adapt, have had to continually immerse themselves in this kind of procedure is to disregard their humanity.

An idea of the drama involved can be given by considering the villagers' reactions to some of the problems confronting them today.

Poverty is a problem common to all the villages. Unemployment is high; income is low. Further, income statistics are often misleading because the Puebloans' value system more or less obligates a person to share his income with relatives. Thus a Puebloan worker's paycheck is widely distributed.

The villagers sense that unless it is eliminated, poverty could signal the end of their traditions. They also realize that possibilities for a solution are extremely limited. The chances of persuading industries to locate on their land are remote. There are not enough jobs even in such towns as Santa Fe, Los Alamos, and Albuquerque. The alternative of leaving the village to work in Phoenix, Los Angeles, Denver, or other cities is often rejected. To leave the village is to end their tradition.

Efforts toward a solution of their problem have generated emotionally charged discussions in all the villages. Villagers have been polarized into progressive and conservative factions. The utilization of outside consultants has caused disagreements. Some of the people feel that consultants are needed; others maintain that, because they are not aware of village life and traditions, outsiders are useless. Fighting has erupted in the council chambers. Friendships have been broken.

Nevertheless, decisions have been reached. Some of these reflect a great degree of caution. Others are imaginative and surprising. None has escaped severe criticism.

The villagers of Taos, Santa Clara, and Jemez have decided to develop recreational facilities for tourists. The residents of Santa Clara have already developed a recreation area complete with campsites and stocked fishing lakes. The people of Jemez are planning a large dam, which will provide flood control as well as recreational facilities. Taos, considered by many to be one of the most conservative of the villages, recently announced plans for building a tourist center that would include a large motel and possibly a museum.

The Acoma people, located on a 250,000-acre reservation about 60 miles west of Albuquerque, could not commute to jobs without great expense. To resolve their poverty situation, the Acoma are trying to interest mining companies in surveying their reservation for uranium deposits.

After a long sequence of complicated and bitterly criticized decisions, the people of Tesuque and Cochiti have leased large amounts of land for new housing developments. Tesuque people approved an arrangement whereby 1,300 acres of land would be leased for 99 years to a development corporation that plans to build a new community. Cochiti village residents recently leased 7,500 acres of land for similar purposes. The corporation in this case intends to build a city for some 50,000 inhabitants.

These different decisions may or may not alleviate the poverty problem, but they do illustrate creative adaptation, an often painful process whereby a society accepts new customs and practices, yet maintains a core of traditions that keeps it distinctive as a group.

Population growth is another village problem. The number of Pueblo Indians has increased enormously in the past century. Dozier estimated that there are at least 40,000, the great majority living in the Rio Grande region.

One reason for the overcrowded villages is that while there are many more people than there were a century ago, there are fewer villages. In addition, inadequate water resources have prevented expansion.

Resolution of the population problem entails more than simply building new houses. Such village traditions as ownership rights are involved: houses may be regarded as the property of the corporate group of villagers, a clan group, or the family. Other traditions specify who can live within the confines of the village. In some cases, eligibility is restricted to native-born people. In other villages, people born outside the area, as long as they are either Puebloan or married to Puebloans, are welcome.

The problems of poverty and population growth have forced the villagers to make decisions that have broad implications. Will a large village population decrease the effectiveness of the Pueblo social organization? Is it better for a village to limit its numbers or to allow expansion? A larger village population can command greater attention from the outside world. Is this desirable?

Before decisions about these matters were reached, villages were again the scenes of arguments, accusations, bitterness, and criticism. Anguish accompanied the creative responses. Some of the villages decided to allow large housing projects. In the Acoma area about 100 houses are being built. In Santa Clara, 75 new houses will be constructed. Several villages have so far opposed any new house construction.

Poverty and population growth are only two of the many problems demanding decisions from the villagers. Matters such as land rights, land claims, religious activities, education, the formulation of village constitutions, and participation in federal programs illustrate the complexity of the situations. Each of these will create frictions and factions before it is resolved.

The Puebloan villages are not sleepy, peaceful, quiet places. The Puebloan process of creative adaptation can be chaotic. However, it is in accord with their tradition of recognizing and respecting differences. Each person and group in a village is encouraged to express an opinion on any issue. Formulating a decision in an atmosphere of disagreement and conflicting opinion is a difficult task. However, a decision made under such circumstances stands a good chance of being widely accepted and highly respected.

The Puebloans today may be facing some of the most difficult problems that the members of their culture have ever had to resolve. But through the process of creative adaptation, the Pueblo Indians will prevail.

Part 5 / QUESTIONS AND PROBLEMS FOR DISCUSSION

1. What do you see as some of the major difficulties in agreeing upon a universally accepted definition of the concept of culture?

2. The process of "becoming an adult" varies in content from society to society. Compare some ways that the Hopi use with those used in your own society.
3. According to Horace Miner the Nacirema people are strongly obsessed about the beautification of the human body. Do you think Miner was being very objective in making this statement? Why?
4. What is an innovation? How is the innovative process used in both invention and diffusion?
5. The Pueblo Indians as discussed in Pearson's article are undergoing the process of assimilation. What difficulties do you see the Pueblo Indians faced with in attempting to maintain their distinctive culture?

6/ WHY DO YOU DO IT THAT WAY?

Somewhere near the windswept, barren ice shelf of the Arctic Ocean an aging Eskimo man hands his favorite bone-handled knife to his son and says "It is time." Out of duty, but with love, the son thrusts the knife blade into the vital organs of his father. As the last gasp of life leaves the aged man's body, the son and his family move on to continue living. Later in life the son will make the same request of his son. And so it goes. What is being done here? In the Eskimo world this is not murder. It is a form of population control. The aged man, no longer able to fish and hunt, willingly gives his life so that the rest of the family members will have adequate shares of food. The Eskimo son is well aware that he is doing the right thing and he has no fear of punishment. This is a lesson in cultural diversity. Having dealt with the nature of culture in the previous section, attention is now focused on cultural diversity, or "Why do you do it that way?"

One of the more fascinating things about taking an introductory anthropology course is knowing some of the facts of cultural diversity. We know, for example, that the aversion to eating termites or grubs in our cultural surroundings is learned and not instinctive. Many peoples in the world eat insects with sheer delight. We might ask ourselves why some people believe they will die if an individual several miles away points a bone at them. Why do some people eat the flesh of their slain enemies? Why can a person marry one individual and not another when both appear to be equally related? The questions of how and why peoples do things differently from us tantalize the minds of both the introductory student and the professional anthropologist.

We know that groups of people behave differently. What we need to be told is that Americans, Samoans, Eskimos, Turks, and Nigerians differ as a result of being born into different cultural traditions rather than because they are of different racial groups. We need to be told this because it has far-reaching implications regarding how we relate to people. Most of our difficulties in dealing with people are a result of our own ignorance. When the anthropologist points this out he is either ignored or listened to skeptically. He may even be seen as a threat to our safe and secure way of life. He draws people to a pool of still water and asks them to look in and see themselves; what they see they often do not like. What they see and do not like is that they have much in common with peoples whom they thought were basically "inferior" in way of life. It is not an accident that the anthropologist chooses to study groups with different life-styles, for only by so doing can he point out that conformity to one's life-style acts as a blinder toward a realization that the basic similarities of mankind overshadow the specific differences of human behavior.

People begin to learn at birth. This learning process is by and large a subconscious activity, and what we learn (behavioral patterns) becomes so much a part of us that it is assumed to be the only "right way" to behave. The things we learn to eat and wear, and what we believe, often becomes the "right way." Then, sometimes later we discover that other peoples eat different things, wear other kinds of clothes, and believe a bit differently. Too often the first tendency is to become either confused or bewildered and wonder why other peoples do not behave as we do. However, upon further analysis we might wonder if other peoples think us strange for not behaving the way they do, since they also believe that their way of life is the "right way" to live. Then we realize that as we are born into our family, so we are born into our culture. With this in mind, when we come across things that are different from the way we have been taught, we should ask ourselves, "Why is it done this way?" And keep in mind that "it is done this way" because it is a satisfactory means of behavior for the people of that particular cultural tradition.

From "The Autobiography of a Winnebago Indian," by Paul Radin, *University of California Publications in American Archaeology and Ethnology,* Vol. 16:7, 1920. Originally published by the University of California Press; reprinted by permission of The Regents of the University of California.

25 / I Eat Peyote

PAUL RADIN

A Winnebago Indian sits in his lodge chewing a peyote button. Why is he doing this? It would be easy enough for an objective observer to answer this question, but in the following article this question and others are answered in a Winnebago's own words. The usefulness of this "inside view" approach has long been recognized. It provides feelings, thoughts, and atmosphere that cannot be reached by the observer or even the participant–observer. Paul Radin has recorded the autobiography of a Winnebago Indian and in this selection gives us an unusual insight into the first experiences of an Indian with peyote and his ultimate conversion to the peyote religion. Radin's writing style allows us to ease into the inner thoughts of a Winnebago Indian.

Then my father and mother asked me to come to the Missouri River (Nebraska) but I had been told that my father and mother had eaten peyote and I did not like it. I had been told that these peyote eaters were doing wrong, and therefore I disliked them; I had heard that they were doing everything that was wicked. For these reasons we did not like them. About this time they sent me money for my ticket and since my brothers and sisters told me to go, I went. Just as I was about to start, my youngest sister, the one to whom we always listened most attentively, said to me, "Older brother, do not you indulge in this medicine eating (peyote) of which so much is said." I promised. Then I started out.

As soon as I arrived (in Nebraska) I met some people who had not joined the peyote eaters and who said to me, "Your relatives are eating the peyote and they sent for you that you also might eat it. Your mother, your father, and your younger sister, they are all eating it." Thus they spoke to me. Then they told me of some of the bad things it was reported that these people had done. I felt ashamed and I wished I had not come in the first place. Then I said that I was going to eat the medicine.

After that I saw my father, mother, and sister. They were glad. Then we all went to where they were staying. My father and I walked (alone).

Then he told me about the peyote eating. "It does not amount to anything, all this that they are doing, although they do stop drinking. It is also said that sick people get well. We were told about this and so we joined, and, sure enough, we are practically well, your mother as well as I. It is said that they offer prayers to Earthmaker (God)," he said. He kept on talking. "They are rather foolish. They cry when they feel very happy about anything. They throw away all of the medicines that they possess and know. They give up all the blessings they received while fasting and they give up all the spirits that blessed them in their fasts. They also stop smoking and chewing tobacco. They stop giving feasts, and they stop making offerings of tobacco. Indeed they burn up their holy things. They burn up their war-bundles. They are bad people. They give up the Medicine Dance. They burn up their medicine bags and even cut up their otter-skin bags. They say they are praying to Earthmaker (God) and they do so standing and crying. They claim that they hold nothing holy except Earthmaker (God). They claim that all the things that they are stopping are those of the bad spirit (the devil), and that the bad spirit (the devil) has deceived them; that there are no spirits who can bless; that there is no other spirit except Earthmaker (God)." Then I said, "Say, they certainly speak foolishly." I felt very angry towards them. "You will hear them for they are going to have a meeting tonight. Their songs are very strange. They use a very small drum," said he. Then I felt a very strong desire to see them.

After a while we arrived. At night they had their ceremony. At first I sat outside and listened to them. I was rather fond of them. I stayed in that country and the young peyote eaters were exceedingly friendly to me. They would give me a little money now and then and they treated me with tender regard. They did everything that they thought would make me feel good, and in consequence I used to speak as though I liked their ceremony. However I was only deceiving them. I only said it, because they were so good to me. I thought they acted in this way because (the peyote) was deceiving them.

Soon after that my parents returned to Wisconsin, but when they left they said they would come back in a little while. So I was left there with my relatives who were all peyote followers. For that reason they left me there. Whenever I went among the non-peyote people I used to say all sorts of things about the peyote people and when I returned to the peyote people, I used to say all sorts of things about the others.

I had a friend who was a peyote man and he said to me, "My friend, I wish very much that you should eat the peyote." Thus he spoke and I answered him, "My friend, I will do it, but not until I get accustomed to the people of this country. Then I will do it. The only thing that worries me is the fact that they are making fun of you. And in addition, I am not quite used to them." I spoke dishonestly.

I was staying at the place where my sister lived. She had gone to Oklahoma; she was a peyote follower. After a while she returned. I was then living with a number of women. This was the second time (there) and from them I obtained some money. Once I got drunk there and was locked up for six days. After my sister returned she and the others paid more attention than ever to me. Especially was this true of my brother-in-law. They gave me horses and a vehicle. They really treated me very tenderly. I knew that they did all this because they wished me to eat the peyote. I, in my turn, was very kind to them. I thought that I was fooling them and they thought that they were converting me. I told them that I believed in the peyote because they were treating me so nicely.

After a while we moved to a certain place where they were to have a large peyote meeting. I knew they were doing this in order to get me to join. Then I said to my younger sister, "I would be quite willing to eat this peyote (ordinarily), but I don't like the woman with whom I am living just now and I think I will leave her. That is why I do not want to join now, for I understand that when married people eat medicine (peyote) they will always have to stay together. Therefore I will join when I am married to some woman permanently." Then my brother-in-law came and she told him what I had said, and he said to me, "You are right in what you say. The woman with whom you are staying is a married woman and you can not continue living with her. It is null and void (this marriage) and we know it. You had better join now. It will be the same as if you were single. We will pray for you as though you were single. After you have joined this ceremony, then you can marry any woman whom you have a right to marry (legally). So, do join tonight. It is best. For some time we have been desirous of your joining but we have not said anything to you. It is Earthmaker's (God's) blessing to you that you have been thinking of this," said he.

I Eat Peyote

There I sat inside the meeting-place with them. One man acted as leader. We were to do whatever he ordered. The regalia were placed before him. I wanted to sit in some place on the side, because I thought I might get to crying like the others. I felt ashamed of myself.

Then the leader arose and talked. He said that this was an affair of Earthmaker's (God's), and that he (the leader) could do nothing on his own initiative; that Earthmaker (God) was going to conduct the ceremony. Then he said that the medicine (peyote) was holy and that he would turn us all over to it; that he had turned himself over to it and wished now to turn all of us over to it. He said further, "I am a very pitiable (figure) in this ceremony, so when you pray to Earthmaker, pray also for me. Now let us all rise and pray to Earthmaker (God)." We all rose. Then he prayed. He prayed for the sick, and he prayed for those who did not yet know Earthmaker. He said that they were to be pitied. When he had finished we sat down. Then the peyote was passed around. They gave me five. My brother-in-law said to me, "If you speak to this medicine (peyote), it will give you whatever you ask of it. Then you must pray to Earthmaker, and then you must eat the medicine." However I ate them (the peyote) immediately for I did not know what to ask for and I did not know what to say in a prayer to Earthmaker (God). So I ate the peyote just as they were. They were very bitter and had a taste difficult to describe. I wondered what would happen to me. After a while I was given five more and I also ate them. They tasted rather bitter. Now I was very quiet. The peyote rather weakened me. Then I listened very attentively to the singing. I liked it very much. I felt as though I were partly asleep. I felt different from (my normal self), but when I (looked around) and examined myself, I saw nothing wrong about myself. However I felt different from (my normal self). Before this I used to dislike the songs. Now I liked the leader's singing very much. I liked to listen to him.

They were all sitting very quietly. They were doing nothing except singing. Each man sang four songs and then passed the regalia to the next one. (Each one) held a stick and an eagle's tail feather in one hand and a small gourd rattle, which they used to shake while singing, in the other. One of (those) present used to do the drumming. Thus objects would pass around until they came back to the leader, who would then sing four songs. When these were finished, he would place the various (things) on the ground, rise, and pray to Earthmaker (God). Then he called upon one or two to speak. They said that Earthmaker (God) was good and that the peyote was good, and that whosoever ate this medicine (peyote) would be able to free himself from the bad spirit (the devil); for they said that Earthmaker forbids us to commit sins. When this was over they sang again.

After midnight, every once in a while, (I heard) someone cry. In some cases they would go up to the leader and talk with him. He would stand up and pray with them. They told me what they were saying. They said that they were asking (people) to pray for them, as they were sorry for their sins and that they might be prevented from committing them again. That is what they were saying. They cried very loudly. I was rather frightened. (I noticed also) that when I closed my eyes and sat still, I began to see strange things. I did not get sleepy in the least. Thus the light (of morning) came upon me. In the morning, as the sun rose, they stopped. They all got up and prayed to Earthmaker (God) and then they stopped.

During the daytime, I did not get sleepy in the least. My actions were a little different (from my usual ones). Then they said, "Tonight they are going to have another meeting. Let us go over. They say that is the best (thing) to do and thus you can learn it (the ceremony) right away. It is said that their spirits wander over all the earth and the heavens also. All this you will learn and see," they said. "At times they die and remain dead all night and all day. When in this condition they sometimes see Earthmaker (God), it is said." One would also be able to see where the bad spirit lived, it was said.

So we went there again. I doubted all this. I thought that what they were saying was untrue. However, I went along anyhow. When we got there I had already eaten some peyote, for I had taken three during the day. Now near the peyote meeting an (Indian) feast was being given and I went there instead. When I reached the place, I saw a long lodge. The noise was terrific. They were beating an enormous drum. The sound almost raised me in the air, so (pleasurably) loud did it sound to me. Not so (pleasurable) had things appeared at those affairs (peyote meetings) that I had lately been attending. There I danced all night and I flirted with the women. About day I left and when I got back the peyote meeting was still going on. When I got back they told me to sit down at a certain place. They treated me very kindly. There I again ate peyote. I heard that they were going to have another meeting nearby on the evening of the same day. We continued eating peyote the whole day at the place where we were staying. We were staying at the house of one of my relatives. Some of the boys there taught me a few songs. "Say, when you learn how to sing, you will be the best singer, for you are a good singer as it is. You have a good voice," they said to me. I thought so myself.

The Effects of the Peyote

That night we went to the place where the peyote meeting was to take place. They gave me a place to sit and treated me very kindly. "Well, he has come," they even said when I got there, "make a place for him." I thought they regarded me as a great man. John Rave, the leader, was to conduct the (ceremony). I ate five peyote. Then my brother-in-law and my sister came and gave themselves up. They asked me to stand there with them. I did not like it, but I did it nevertheless. "Why should I give myself up? I am not in earnest, and I intend to stop this as soon as I get back to Wisconsin. I am only doing this because they have given me presents," I thought. "I might just as well get up, since it doesn't mean anything to me." So I stood up. The leader began to talk and I (suddenly) began to feel sick. It got worse and worse and finally I lost consciousness entirely. When I recovered I was lying flat on my back. Those with whom I had been standing, were still standing there. I had (as a matter of fact) regained consciousness as soon as I fell down. I felt like leaving the place that night, but I did not do it. I was quite tired out. "Why have I done this?" I said to myself. "I promised (my sister) that I would not do it." So I thought and then I tried to leave, but could not. I suffered intensely. At last daylight came upon me. Now I thought that they regarded me as one who had had a trance and found out something.

Then we went home and they showed me a passage in the Bible where it said that it was a shame for any man to wear long hair. That is what it said, they told me. I looked at the passage. I was not a man learned in books, but I wanted to give the impression that I knew how to read, so I told them to cut my hair, for I wore it long at that time. After my hair was cut I took out a lot of medicine that I happened to have in my pockets. These were courting medicines. There were many small bundles of them. All these, together with my hair, I gave to my brother-in-law. Then I cried and my brother-in-law also cried. Then he thanked me. He told me that I understood and that I had done well. He told me that Earthmaker (God) alone was holy; that all the things (blessings and medicines) that I possessed, were false; that I had been fooled by the bad spirit (devil). He told me that I had now freed myself from much of this (bad influence). My relatives expressed their thanks fervently.

On the fourth night they had another meeting and I went to it again. There I again ate (peyote). I enjoyed it and I sang along with them. I wanted to sing immediately. Some young men were singing and I enjoyed it, so I prayed to Earthmaker asking him to let me learn to sing right away. That was all I asked for. My brother-in-law was with me all the time. At that meeting all the things I had given my brother-in-law were burned up.

The fact that he (my brother-in-law) told me that I understood, pleased me, and I felt good when daylight came. (As a matter of fact) I had not received any knowledge. However I thought it was the proper way to act, so I did it.

After that I would attend meetings every once in a while and I looked around for a woman whom I might marry permanently. Before long that was the only thing I thought of when I attended the meetings.

I Am Converted

On one occasion we were to have a meeting of men and I went to the meeting with a woman, with whom I thought of going around the next day. That was (the only) reason I went with her. When we arrived, the one who was to lead, asked me to sit near him. There he placed me. He urged me to eat a lot of peyote, so I did. The leaders (of the ceremony) always place the regalia in front of themselves; they also had a peyote placed there. The one this leader placed in front of himself this time, was a very small one. "Why does he have a very small one there?" I thought to myself. I did not think much about it.

It was now late at night and I had eaten a lot of peyote and felt rather tired. I suffered considerably. After a while I looked at the peyote and there stood an eagle with outspread wings. It was as beautiful a sight as one could behold. Each of the feathers seemed to have a mark. The eagle stood looking at me. I looked around thinking that perhaps there was something the matter with my sight. Then I looked again and it was really there. I then looked in a different direction and it disappeared.

Only the small peyote remained. I looked around at the other people but they all had their heads bowed and were singing. I was very much surprised.

Some time after this (I saw) a lion lying in the same place (where I had seen the eagle). I watched it very closely. It was alive and looking at me. I looked at it very closely and when I turned my eyes away just the least little bit, it disappeared. "I suppose they all know this and I am just beginning to know of it," I thought. Then I saw a small person (at the same place). He wore blue clothes and a shining brimmed cap. He had on a soldier's uniform. He was sitting on the arm of the person who was drumming, and he looked at every one. He was a little man, perfect (in all proportions). Finally I lost sight of him. I was very much surprised indeed. I sat very quietly. "This is what it is," I thought, "this is what they all probably see and I am just beginning to find out."

Then I prayed to Earthmaker (God): *"This, your ceremony, let me hereafter perform."*

As I looked again, I saw a flag. I looked more carefully and (I saw) the house full of flags. They had the most beautiful marks on them. In the middle (of the room) there was a very large flag and it was a live one; it was moving. In the doorway there was another one not entirely visible. I had never seen anything so beautiful in all my life before.

Then again I prayed to Earthmaker (God). I bowed my head and closed my eyes and began (to speak). I said many things that I would ordinarily never have spoken about. As I prayed, I was aware of something above me and there he was; Earthmaker (God) to whom I was praying, he it was. That which is called the soul, that is it, that is what one calls Earthmaker (God). Now this is what I felt and saw. The one called Earthmaker (God) is a spirit and that is what I felt and saw. All of us sitting there, we had all together one spirit or soul; at least that is what I learned. I instantly became the spirit and I was their spirit or soul. Whatever they thought of, I (immediately) knew it. I did not have to speak to them and get an answer to know what their thoughts had been. Then I thought of a certain place, far away, and immediately I was there; I was my thought.

I looked around and noticed how everything seemed about me, and when I opened my eyes I was myself in the body again. From this time on, I thought, thus I shall be. This is the way they are, and I am only just beginning to be that way. "All those that heed Earthmaker (God) must be thus," I thought. "I would not need any more food," I thought, "for was I not my spirit? Nor would I have any more use of my body," I felt. "My corporeal affairs are over," I felt.

Then they stopped and left for it was just dawning. Then someone spoke to me. I did not answer for I thought they were just fooling and that they were all like myself, and that (therefore) it was unnecessary for me to talk to them. So when they spoke to me I only answered with a smile. "They are just saying this to me because (they realize) that I have just found out," I thought. That was why I did not answer. I did not speak to anyone until noon. Then I had to leave the house to perform one of nature's duties and someone followed me. It was my friend. He said, "My friend, what troubles you that makes you act as you do?" "Well, there's no need of your saying anything for you know it beforehand," I said.

Then I immediately got over my trance and again got into my (normal) condition so that he would have to speak to me before I knew his thoughts. I became like my former self. It became necessary for me to speak to him.

Then I spoke to him and said, "My friend, let us hitch up these horses and then I will go wherever you like, for you wish to speak to me and I also want to go around and talk to you." Thus I spoke to him. "If I were to tell you all that I have learned, I would never be able to stop at all, so much have I learned," I said to him. "However, I would enjoy telling some of it." "Good," said he. He liked it (what I told him) very much. "That is what I am anxious to hear," said he. Then we went after the horses. We caught one of them, but we could not get the other. He got away from us and we could not find him. We hunted everywhere for the horse but could not discover where he had run to. Long afterwards we found it among the whites.

Now since that time (of my conversion) no matter where I am I always think of this religion. I still remember it and I think I will remember it as long as I live. It is the only thing that I have been aware of in all my life.

26 / Can a "Root Doctor" Actually Put a Hex On or Is It All a Great Put-on?

MIKE MICHAELSON

The previous selection illustrated in part how Winnebago Indians deal with the supernatural aspects of life. We turn now to a different way of dealing with similar supernatural aspects. It has often been noted that individuals in primitive societies have died as a direct result of a "voodoo" or "hex." Although we generally regard witchcraft as a part of underdeveloped societies, we only have to look in our own backyard to find the "witch doctor" at work. In this selection Michaelson examines activities of the "root doctor" and the reactions of hexed victims as they occur in the southeastern United States. It is easy to notice many similarities in the practice of witchcraft, whether in East Africa or in the United States. In most societies there are some individuals who use witchcraft either to explain unusual events or to bring about desired reactions. While reading this article the reader should keep in mind that there is a recent rise in the belief of witchcraft in the United States. How would you attempt to explain the widespread belief in witchcraft in a supposedly sophisticated society?

From out of South Carolina's Low Country she had come, 17 years old and frightened because of the terrible weakness and the trouble she was having with her breathing. Now, gaunt and dull-eyed, she huddled under a coarse hospital gown, bewildered at the turn of events of the last three weeks that had shuttled her from the medical service of the Medical University of South Carolina, Charleston, to its department of psychiatry.

"All I know, doctor," she says to R. Ramsey Mellette, Jr., M.D., director of the child psychiatry unit, "is I sure do feel bad. I lost weight, feel tired all the time, don't hold no hope 'bout nothin'."

Knowing that physical examinations had failed to turn up any primary organic cause for her disability . . . knowing that conventional psychotherapy was not helping . . . knowing the nature of the community she had come from—poor, predominantly black, influenced by the work of three practicing witch doctors . . . Dr. Mellette gradually leads up to the one question he feels will cut to the core of the problem: "Do you," he says, looking the girl in the eye, "have a bad root on you?"

The question seems to unlock the girl's soul and her story tumbles out. She had unsurped another girl's boyfriend and was convinced the irate girl had exacted terrible vengeance, paying a local root doctor—a woman reputed to have great powers—to put a "death root" on her rival. (These practitioners are known as "root doctors" or "root workers" because of the roots of trees and plants they use to make their "roots" or spells.)

But now it is too late. The girl's psychotic depression is too deep, her deterioration too advanced to bring about a reversal. Within weeks she dies—one more mysterious fatality that root doctors explain away so easily and which modern medicine wrestles so earnestly to understand.

Can such sorcery really work? If not, why do so many hex victims become mysteriously ill and sometimes die? Medical science doesn't yet have all the answers, but it is coming to grips with witchcraft and restoring the health of some of its victims.

Autosuggestion can be so overpowering, says Dr. Mellette, "that a person is unable to think of anything else." As a simple illustration, the psychiatrist points to the person who lies awake at night obsessed with his own heartbeat or with the unbearable thirst which finally drives him to fetch a drink.

"Those who let the hex become an obsession," he adds, "usually deteriorate until it actually takes over. It's autosuggestion of the strongest kind and it can kill those who let it."

Witchcraft, Dr. Mellette explains, is widespread in the southeastern United States. And while it flourishes primarily along the sparsely populated coastline from Wilmington, North Carolina, to Jacksonville, Florida, it is found, too, in that region's cities—Charleston, Savannah, Brunswick.

For a fee, a root doctor can be found who will manufacture a "root" to accomplish either good or evil. "The bad type—the hexes," explains Dr. Mellette, "are designed to cause weakness, suffering, misery, confusion, impotence, pain, sickness and death. The good or 'white' type have to do with attraction, potency, success, recovery and protection from bad roots."

This particular brand of witchcraft, he explains, came over from Africa with slaves and thrives among their descendants. "Belief in its powers," says Dr. Mellette, "may now be held by as many as 50 percent of the black population of the Low Country [the misty, marshy sea islands strung along the Georgia/Carolinas coastline]."

Root medicine, however, is by no means the exclusive domain of blacks. Nor does the Low Country have sole claim to it.

"You'll find root work of one kind or another in any urban area in the United States that has a large black population," notes Dr. Hazel

Weidman, associate professor of social anthropology with the department of psychiatry at the University of Miami Medical School. Dr. Weidman, who under a $180,000 grant is studying the effects of root work and faith healing in Miami's Afro-Cuban cult, estimates that about one-third of the black patients treated at Miami's Jackson Memorial Hospital psychiatric center insist they are hex victims.

Root work is practiced right next door to some of the largest and most prestigious medical centers, says Dr. Weidman. "Yet medical people are not trained to look for it," she says. "It's difficult even to get them to ask the patient if he has been hexed. But when the question is raised, you really get an incredible response from some of these people. Usually, though, their problem is disregarded. They're given drugs, protected in the hospital, and if they can pull themselves together well enough, sent home—with the same beliefs."

Successful dehexing, says Dr. Weidman, must involve: (1) recognition of a hexed patient; (2) an understanding of how a root doctor works; (3) development of a treatment approach which embraces both psychotherapeutic and "root" techniques. "We are barely getting to the first step of recognizing these people as being hexed," says Dr. Weidman. "And those who do recognize them are still looked at askance by traditional practitioners who believe that insight therapy is the be-all and end-all of psychiatric treatment."

In Hartford, Connecticut, a two-year study directed by psychiatrist Dr. Ronald Wintrob at the Connecticut School of Medicine has uncovered close to 30 patients who say they have a knowledge of root work, and about 10 of them believe their own illnesses are influenced by it. "A primary task in therapy," says Dr. Wintrob, "is to recognize the patient's legitimate right to believe in a hex, just as we may believe that people are the victims of circumstances and fate. The patient's belief also has to be given prominence in the treatment plan," Dr. Wintrob emphasizes, "even to the extent of encouraging him to go to a root worker for tandem treatment—if he feels that unless he gets that treatment he can't recover."

Belief in root work is widespread, says Dr. Wintrob, "not only among those who live in or who migrated from the South, but also among those born in the North." New Jersey, for example, is said to harbor a particularly potent brand. "This is the real 'bad news' kind," says Dr. Mellette, who is currently treating two patients who returned south from New Jersey to have "bad" roots removed.

Public health nurses in Louisiana encounter victims of voodoo hexes, while in Chicago, root workers offer their services through classified advertisements in the *Daily Defender*. Most major cities have at least one store where the do-it-yourself believer can buy the "root" equivalent of patent medicine. A drugstore in downtown Charleston has a large display of such preparations, ranging from good-luck powder to "dragon's blood" and cans of "graveyard dust."

To get an understanding of how a root doctor operates, I had driven with Dr. Mellette the 60 miles from his Charleston office to the historic coastal town of Beaufort, population 3,500. Four root doctors are known to operate in the area, and we are being granted an audience with one of them—a rare privilege, we have been told.

We wait uneasily in the car parked across the street from the root doctor's house. Except for a wire fence and a red sign warning of a dog, the small, frame bungalow is like any other on the nondescript narrow backstreet. Our contact, a former local sheriff, J. E. (Ed) McTeer, Sr., has gone ahead to set things up, instructing us not to follow until he signals.

"Doctor" Eagle is in consultation with a client. The woman has driven more than 100 miles from Augusta, Georgia, to seek his widely-known mystical services.

For a fee that could run as high as $200, Dr. Eagle will intervene in matters ranging from troublesome aches and pains to delicate *affaires d'amour*. He has awesome power, it is whispered, to induce or remove a hex—either good or evil.

Waiting in the car, feeling somewhat foolish about my anxieties, I look to my guide for reassurance. The psychiatrist is playing it straight, watching intently for the sheriff's sign.

Ramsey Mellette has studied the root cult more or less as a hobby for more than 20 years. He was exposed to it first as a child growing up in the Low Country, then as a young attendant in a psychiatric hospital. However, his full professional life helping disturbed children leaves little time for his fascinating avocation.

At last, Eagle's "patient" comes out. She is a heavily built white woman wearing an outmoded fur-trimmed coat. Then Ed McTeer is on the steps, beckoning, and we hurry to his side.

We enter Dr. Eagle's living room. It is sparsely furnished, decorated with pictures of the Kennedys and Dr. Martin Luther King, Jr., and dominated by a color TV set. Two black women are sitting on the couch, absorbed in "The Newlywed Game," as they await Dr. Eagle's counsel.

The root man, known legally as P. C. Washington, works out of his bedroom. It is cluttered with personal, religious and patriotic bric-a-brac and stacks of mysterious containers. A vague scent of incense pervades the room, while a small oil burner keeps it uncomfortably warm. Outside, a rooster, apparently unaware it is almost noon, adds his periodic crowing to the theatrical effect.

Dr. Eagle is an elderly, emaciated black man, probably well past 70 years of age. His collar hangs loose on his thin neck, his faded, canary-colored sweater is bunched around him. He is toothless. His eyes, although they tend to water now with his years, are dark and penetrating. Dr. Eagle has been plying his nebulous craft since 1939.

His reputation is known throughout the area. "I know Percy Washington to be an astute judge of character," Louis J. Roempke, Jr., M.D., a local family practitioner, has said. "As a natural-born psychologist, he saw a good opportunity to make a living for himself. And when he sort of looks straight through you and chants in his 'unknown tongue' [a rhythmic mixture of biblical phrases, witches' curses and sea-island dialect], well, if you were the impressionable kind, I guess you might really feel the whammy had been put on you."

Whammy-inducing apparently is a profitable occupation. Dr. Eagle refers obliquely to real estate holdings, and when notorious root worker "Dr." Bug once ran afoul of the law, the result was the discovery by FBI agents of a trunk containing close to $13,000 in small bills.

Usually, though, root doctors are artfully adept at avoiding encounters with the law. Careful not to dispense medication illegally, they avoid oral "cures" in favor of "powerful" root bags and lucky lodestones their clients can carry, and mystical powders they can sprinkle on themselves.

Root doctors are wary, too, about illicit use of the mails. Ed McTeer recalls a time when "Dr." Buzzard, probably the most famous of all root men, decided to cash a year's accumulation of mail-order receipts. "He had this thick bunch of money orders," says McTeer, "and when the postmistress told him he'd have to sign a received payment slip, he destroyed every one of them. That's how careful root doctors are."

After 37 years as sheriff of Beaufort County, Ed McTeer probably knows more about Low Country root medicine than any other man alive. In fact, because of his special interest in witchcraft, he has acquired a reputation as a practitioner of "white magic." Many times, local physicians have referred to him for "de-hexing" patients seemingly beyond the range of physical medicine. As McTeer produced "cures" with his own mysterious preparations, his reputation, even among the root doctors, soared.

Now in his late 60's, McTeer is a tall, gaunt man. He wears his thin, snowy-white hair brushed back and is a fastidious dresser.

"I grew up in this atmosphere of superstition and witchcraft," McTeer explains. "When I succeeded my father as high sheriff, I saw people going raving crazy, burning down their houses and sometimes dying because they believed a hex had been put on them. That's when I became involved.

"Over the years I have convinced them that I can take off a spell, but that if I practiced black magic I would lose this power. I tell them, too, that if I took even one hen egg—two cents—the spell would turn on me. This gets me off the hook for not accepting a fee for helping them.

"Recently, I was asked to help a woman who claims she can't walk in the back yard without her whole leg burning up. She believes someone has buried a root on her."

When a root is buried near a house, misfortune is supposed to befall the occupants. Dr. Stanley F. Morse, Jr., a Beaufort family practitioner, tells of a patient who collapsed and died of pneumonia after being out all night in the winter rain and cold frantically trying to uncover a concealed root.

McTeer tells his "clients" that, yes, there is a root on them: "I tell them they've got dirt from a criminal's grave in their root, and that tonight I'm going to get the dirt from a minister's grave and that will kill it as dead as a frog.

"To help a person like that you've got to convince him you are working for good against evil and have the power to be stronger than the person who put on the hex. If you convince him, you can help him—and cure him."

In 26 years of practicing medicine in Beaufort, Dr. Morse has seen many root victims. The veteran GP also believes in fighting fire with fire or, as he puts it, "counteracting faith with faith."

One of the means used by Dr. Morse to dehex root victims involves methylene blue, a clinically used dye. "I give them these pills and say that one of three things will happen. I tell them that if in the next 24 hours the color of their urine remains unchanged, they are to come back and we'll try again. If it turns red, I tell them they're doomed, that no one can help. But if it turns blue, I tell them the root is off and they'll never have to worry again."

Use of the placebo effect to counteract a hex is endorsed by Dr. E. Fuller Torrey, special assistant to the director for international activities at the National Institute of Mental Health. "There's a technique used extensively in East Africa," he says, "involving injections of calcium gluconate. It makes the body tingle for a short time and, while this is physiologically harmless, it is most powerful against a hex." He stresses, however, that this technique should be used *in addition* to therapy directed at resolving the patient's underlying conflicts.

Calcium gluconate was an important weapon in the dehexing armamentarium of a doctor in Albemarle, in south-central North Carolina. Dr. Essex C. Noel, III, was in general practice there for 11 years, during which time he encountered many victims of root work. He describes these disorders as "psycho-physiologic"—not unlike colitis or gastric ulcers. They can cause structural damage and could become life-threatening.

"If a person sincerely believes that his condition is the result of someone working a hex on him," says Dr. Noel, "the therapeutic relief also must be related to that which produced the problem. Often I found that if patients felt we were using a good strong 'medicine' to 'burn' this hex out, it was quite effective. Of course, it is always necessary to first eliminate the possibility of physical pathology."

When Dr. Mellette's hexed patients fail to respond to normal therapy, he too may resort to such innocuous—but effective—agents. He sometimes prescribes a regimen of nicotinic acid. This induces—on cue—a burning sensation which can be ascribed to a powerful counter-hex.

Dr. Mellette, who has treated some 30 root victims, says that such unorthodox therapy works in about three-fourths of the cases. It may be more effective, he suggests, when dispensed with exaggerated histrionics—

keeping the tablets in a crumpled, yellowing envelope and producing it surreptitiously from an obscure desk drawer.

"Of course," he adds, "you would only resort to something like this after exhausting all the traditional ways—hypnosis, electro-shock, drug therapy—of dealing with obsessions, depressions and the schizophrenic process, because a root victim may involve shades of each of these."

Sometimes in witchcraft cases there is an unaccountable factor—a string of strange coincidences. Ask Dr. Mellette to explain the unexplainable and he'll tell you that whenever he finds time to pursue his hobby, "something usually happens."

Once he was caught photographing a house with a blue-painted trim. (Some Low Country folk still paint window frames blue to ward off evil spirits and paper their walls with comic sheets to divert such spirits as do gain entry.) Next day he was felled with an attack of acute appendicitis.

He gave a slide presentation on witchcraft to a women's psychiatric auxiliary group, and within 15 minutes a prominent member fell and fractured her hip. Another time, the ceiling of his study caved in after newspapermen interviewed him there.

"All coincidences," says Dr. Mellette with a wide grin. "But I'm getting extremely tired of coincidences."

Maybe that's why he's playing it straight now as we have our audience with Dr. Eagle. The bearded, wild-haired root man is at work assuring us of riches as he squirts us with a heavily perfumed aerosol spray called "Silver and Gold."

"Somebody cross you up, I got this." He waves a container marked "Uncrossing Powder," pausing momentarily for our approval. "You need luck, I got lodestone. You need courage, I give you 'High John the Conqueror Powder!' Washington gives a gummy grin. "Sure to fix you good." ("Courage," I learn later, is a root-cult euphemism for sexual potency.)

"Let me show you what I got las' week," Eagle says, producing a huge container of "Drawing Powder," designed to attract wealth. "Come from the Holy Land," he mutters, "I get all my stuff from overseas." (Contrarily, the label proclaims the magical substance a product of a Baltimore company.)

It is obvious that Washington regards McTeer as a powerful equal. The former sheriff plays on this adroitly, addressing the old man by his adopted root name and referring respectfully to his powers. It's almost as though they're working from a script as McTeer plays Eagle off against his most famous and successful predecessor, the late Dr. Buzzard.

"I ain't gonna fault you, doctor, but Dr. Buzzard did have powers. I was in court one time and he was there chewing the root on me and I could feel my skin getting tight and the back of my neck raise up like he was pulling my scalp."

When hired to "chew the root," a witchdoctor will sit in a courtroom during a trial literally (and visibly) chewing on a piece of root. This act is said to render evidence harmless, to influence the outcome of a trial.

Washington scowls during this recital of his predecessor's powers and then allows McTeer to steer him into what obviously has become a standard rejoinder. "Man, what I need with a buzzard, when I'm an eagle?"

Nonetheless, Dr. Buzzard was nationally known, eminently successful. It was not unusual to see cars from 10 or 15 states parked outside his house. Significantly, however, when root doctors get sick, they usually go to MD's and hospitals.

Most notorious of root doctors was Dr. Bug, who for $50 would guarantee anyone who did not want to be drafted into the service that he would fail the physical. Violating the usual root-doctor tenet, Bug gave his clients a potion to swallow.

He had a high percentage of success. In fact, so many young men with a particular type of heart condition were seen by physicians at Fort Jackson that they named the complaint the "hippity-hoppity heart syndrome."

Dr. Bug's downfall came when one of his clients, wanting to make no mistake about escaping the draft, took a double dose. He died. An autopsy showed the potion causing the heart irregularities was a mixture of oleander leaves (digitalis), rubbing alcohol, moth balls and lead.

Eventually root doctors become so obsessed with their own powers, suggests Ed McTeer, that they brainwash themselves into believing in their own omnipotence. "After they have practiced awhile and people come back and say, 'Man, you've saved my life' or 'All the burning has gone from my legs,' and so on, they get to believe it."

Suddenly, Washington gets up and rummages behind a battered dresser. It, too, is a clutter of jars, faded family portraits, framed newsclippings, an incense burner and a mysterious shoebox. The root man fishes out an ancient guitar and launches into a barely intelligible rendition of "Nearer My God to Thee."

Clearly, our interview is at an end, and we file out of the strange household as Dr. Eagle continues his spiritual recital. We are about to climb into the car when Ramsey Mellette pauses, wrinkling his brow.

"Maybe we should have taken a good-luck root from Dr. Eagle."

"Why?"

He can't restrain the grin. "Because you never know when another coincidence is going to happen."

27 / Insects in the Diet

MARSTON BATES

*Sit down, relax, and eat a grasshopper. Or perhaps your taste is di-
rected toward eating witchetty grubs—the larva of giant ghost moths.
No matter, both are very nutritious. Oh—it is the idea of eating these
things, not the nutritional value to which you object. In the following
article Marston Bates illustrates that what a given group of people eat is
highly selective, and that the diet does not approach the tremendous
variety of things considered edible by the whole of mankind. The selec-
tivity of what a group of people eat is based upon two major factors—
what is available and what is desirable. Bates's article is a prime example
of the well-known anthropological concept of "cultural relativism" as it
relates to the variety of man's food customs. Our stomach might reject a
handful of termites if eaten, but only because we do not believe it to be
the "proper" thing to eat. In this sense it is the mind that rejects the termites and not the stomach. So sit back and read in Bates's words why
we perhaps should include insects in our diet.*

Insects are the most abundant class of animals on land. No one knows
how many kinds there are because a large proportion of the inconspicuous
tropical species have never been catalogued, but it is commonly estimated
that there must be at least a million. And some of these, like houseflies
in the Near East or mosquitoes in Alaska, occur in incredible numbers.

A great many insects are vegetarian, living directly off plants; when
they in turn are eaten by other animals, the energy captured by the plants
from sunlight is made available to the whole animal complex. Thus one
can look at insects as the major "key-industry animals" of the land, to
use a phrase coined by the British ecologist Charles Elton. Many insects,
of course, prey on other insects or parasitize them; but all of these insects
together form a basic food supply for spiders, fresh-water fishes, frogs
and other amphibians, lizards and small snakes, and a wide variety of
insect-eating birds and mammals.

Most primates are insect eaters. The few that do not deliberately hunt insects, like the howler monkeys of tropical America, undoubtedly get many insects accidentally along with their vegetable food—very likely thus improving their diet. I have become most aware of monkey-insect relations since getting a pair of marmosets and a pair of squirrel monkeys (Saimiri), which I keep in my greenhouse. Every day they are given crickets, bought at a fish-bait place. It is always a marvel to watch them eating these insects—they are like greedy children with a supply of lollipops. I have never had the courage to see how many one monkey could eat—I am afraid it would make itself sick with a surfeit of crickets. And any fly that gets into the monkey compartment is a goner; the squirrel monkeys in particular are expert flycatchers. It is obvious that insects are very good food for a wide variety of animals. But they are taboo for people in Western civilization. Perhaps this will change.

American food habits are changing. The popularity of pizza is obvious enough proof, but there is better proof in the great diversity of things offered for sale in any supermarket, or in the recipes included in any cookbook now compared with one published a few years ago. The gourmet may feel that we still have a long way to go, but clearly we are moving.

In our household I am left in charge of one food department—things to eat with drinks. In the store where I do most of the buying there is a wonderful assortment of temptations: fish eggs of many kinds other than the authentic but expensive caviar; fish of many species, prepared in many different ways; a wide range of cheeses and sausages, of crispy fried things, of olives and nuts and minced clams and smoked oysters. Lately several kinds of insects have appeared on the shelves: canned ants and silkworm pupae and bees from Japan, maguey worms from Mexico, fried grasshoppers (the can doesn't say where they are from). I have tried them all out on cocktail guests. Mostly I must admit that they are not very good, but this is not so much the fault of the insects as of the method of preparation. The Mexican maguey worms are almost as good from the can as they are fresh; and it is an interesting experience to watch a Midwestern housewife gingerly getting up courage to try a worm on a piece of toast—and then acknowledging that it tasted good, and trying another.

It is difficult to understand our prejudice against eating insects. We are not against all invertebrates: we eat oysters, clams, snails, squid, octopus. Among the *Arthropoda*—the phylum to which insects belong—we eat lobsters, crabs and shrimp. True, not all of these are eaten by everyone, and some people will eat none of them. But they are rather generally accepted—in the United States snails, squid and octopus less than the other food mentioned.

It seems that we are reluctant to eat invertebrates that live on land, though it is puzzling why this should be so. Maybe the sea is remote enough from our everyday lives so that its inhabitants are unfamiliar as living creatures. In support of this we have the attitude of people in Florida toward eating land crabs. These crabs abound and they are, I know from experience, very tasty. But local people shudder when it is suggested, though the same people eat crabs from the sea readily enough. This attitude toward land crabs is a North American peculiarity. The Puerto Ricans prize their land crabs, and so do most tropical peoples. Our attitude toward snails also supports this land-sea theory; by and large, we have never really accepted these land-living mollusks in the way we have shellfish from the sea.

There is one striking exception to the Western refusal to eat insects— honey. To be sure, honey is not an insect, but it is an insect product— and a very intimate product at that, since the bees carry the nectar home in their crops to regurgitate it into the honeycomb.

Honey is an ancient human food. One of the famous paleolithic cave drawings clearly shows a man climbing down a cliff on a rope ladder to rob a nest of wild bees, a method of honey collecting still followed by the Vedda tribes of Ceylon. Bees, hives and honey are represented on the earliest Egyptian monuments, and the nectar and ambrosia of the Greek gods were both based on honey. The nectar of the gods was mead —a fermented mixture of honey and water which bee enthusiasts claim is the oldest of man's alcoholic drinks. Ambrosia, according to Robert Graves, was a fivefold mixture of oil, wine, honey, chopped cheese and meal. It doesn't sound very divine, but I haven't tried it.

In the Bible honey is coupled with locusts in several places. Honey is still on our dinner table, but the locusts are not, though they are eaten in many parts of the world, including the Near East. It is curious that we have acquired a negative attitude toward the eating of locusts and other grasshoppers. Perhaps it is because species of suitable size, taste and abundance are not available in Western Europe and eastern North America—fortunately for our farmers. Our grasshoppers are too small and too scattered to be easily collected as an important food item.

Even people of Orthodox Jewish faith in our culture are dubious about grasshoppers, though they are specifically permitted by the Jewish dietary laws. There is some confusion in the Bible about the number of insect legs—Leviticus 11:21 in the King James Version reads: "Yet these may ye eat of every flying creeping thing that goeth upon all four, which have legs above their feet, to leap withal upon the earth." It is quite clear that the intention is to sanction six-legged grasshoppers. But all other flying, creeping things are an abomination, as are all things in the water that have neither fins nor scales.

. . . .

But to get back to grasshoppers: there are several references among Greek historians and geographers to a people called the *Acridophagi*, or grasshopper eaters. These were small black people living in what is now Ethiopia. According to Diodorus of Sicily, they were short-lived because of the grasshopper diet, which caused all sorts of horrid things to breed in their flesh. Interestingly enough, there are actual cases in modern medical literature of grasshopper-eating Africans who became seriously ill because of intestinal obstruction from the indigestible legs and wings of locusts. This, however, is clearly a consequence of piggishness: the legs and wings are broken off by any civilized locust eater. A friend of mine, just back from Iraq, remarked upon the crunching sound made by squashing discarded locust legs as one walked across the room of a coffeehouse where people were having snacks with their drinks.

Wherever locusts and grasshoppers are common enough to make their collection worthwhile, they form a part of the diet of primitive peoples. They are especially important in many parts of Africa, and explorers of that continent have described a variety of ways in which they may be toasted, fried or boiled. Ground, dried and salted, they may be kept for months, making a food reserve. Grasshoppers were also an important element in the diet of some of the North American Indian tribes living in the Rocky Mountain area, where swarming species occurred.

Along with locusts and honey we might well consider the manna of the Bible as a possible insect product. Dr. F. S. Bodenheimer, professor of zoology at the Hebrew University in Jerusalem, wrote a book entitled *Insects as Human Food,* from which I have culled many facts. In this book he describes his efforts to identify the biblical manna. Some scholars have thought that it was a lichen, *Lecanora esculenta,* which grows on rocks in many parts of the Middle East, producing pea-sized fruiting bodies that are prized as sweet delicacies. These fruiting bodies are light enough to be blown about, so that they could conceivably form a manna rain. But it would be a unique event, and the Bible reports a regular appearance of the manna every morning. Furthermore, no one has ever found this lichen growing in the Sinai region.

There are, on the other hand, many reports from travelers in the Sinai region of a manna associated with the tamarisk thickets. This granular, sweet manna appears every year for a period of some weeks in June, though it varies greatly in abundance from year to year. It has generally been assumed to be a secretion of the tamarisk itself, but Dr. Bodenheimer, who visited Sinai to study the manna, found that it was the product of two species of scale insects living on the tamarisk shrubs. His argument that this insect is the source of the biblical manna is, for me, convincing.

Many kinds of insects that live by sucking the sap of plants produce sweet secretions. This is especially true of the aphids (plant lice) and scale insects. Ants have learned this and assiduously cultivate many species of aphids to get the sweets they produce.

The tamarisk manna is a rather special case of this general phenomenon. It corresponds in place with the biblical account: it is characteristic to this day of the parts of Sinai through which the Exodus passed. It corresponds also in season. The Israelites first discovered the manna on the fifteenth day of the second month after leaving Egypt, which Dr.

Bodenheimer calculates would be about the middle or end of Sivan—late May or early June. Both the Book of Exodus and the Book of Numbers state that the manna fell at night. The scale insects produce their sweet secretion constantly, but it is most apt to accumulate in quantity during the night, when ants are not carrying it off. This is reflected in our own word "honeydew" and in the "dew of heaven" of other languages.

Moses required the Israelites to eat the manna on gathering it and not to "leave of it till the morning." Exodus 16:20 states: "Notwithstanding they hearkened not unto Moses; but some of them left of it until the morning, and it bred worms, and stank; and Moses was wroth with them." Dr. Bodenheimer notes that the "worms" could easily enough be explained as ants, which are very fond of honeydew and would swarm over it in an open tent. The "stinking" would, in this case, be a later misinterpretation and addition.

Dr. Bodenheimer finds many cases of manna production and utilization in the Middle East, although not generally noticed by European travelers. *Man,* he says, is the common Arabic word both for the aphids and for their honeydew; a *man-es-simma,* or manna from the skies, is often mentioned in Persian and Arabic pharmacopoeias. "We find that manna production," he writes, "is essentially a biological phenomenon of dry deserts and mountain steppes. The liquid honeydew secretion . . . speedily solidifies there by rapid evaporation. From remote times the resulting sticky, and often hard or granular, masses have been collected under the name of manna."

The *man-es-simma* of modern Arabic countries comes mostly from the oak forests of Kurdistan, and Dr. Bodenheimer considers that there is not the slightest doubt but that it is the secretion of an aphid, although the species has not been identified. The Iraqi authorities estimate that something like 60,000 pounds of this manna are sold annually in the markets of Baghdad and other places in the country. It is made into confections, mixed with eggs, almonds, and various essences.

The peasants of Kurdistan, who collect the manna from the oak forests in the coldest hours of early morning, believe that it drops from the sky. The manna accumulation depends on favorable weather conditions—no rain and cool winds. The gummy secretion of the innumerable aphids then drops and sticks to the leaves, branches and soil. Manna-bearing branches are gathered and beaten until the manna drops off; the crystallized substance, mixed with leaf fragments and dirt, is then brought into market and sold to the confectioners. Dr. Bodenheimer had a chemical analysis of the manna made and found that it consisted mostly of a rare disaccharide sugar called trehalose. He reported that confections made out of this manna were "delightful."

The sweet secretions of aphids, scale insects and the like are occasionally collected in other parts of the world where species with suitable habits occur, but they are always a rare article of diet, a special delicacy.

After honey and locusts, ants and termites ("white ants") are probably the most common and important insect elements in human diets around the world. Termites and ants are quite different groups of insects, but it is useful to deal with them together because of their parallel habits. Both are social insects, sometimes forming huge colonies of hundreds of thousands of individuals. Both show "swarming" behavior in that, at certain times of year, the winged sexual forms of a particular species will appear in immense numbers, boiling out of all of the nests in the region at the same time—a ready and tempting food supply for bird, beast or man.

Termites are especially prominent in the diet of many of the peoples of tropical Africa. Travelers, from the time of the early European contacts, have commented on this food, so that there is a considerable literature describing the various ways of collecting and preparing the insects.

Many of the African termites (as well as those of other parts of the tropical world) form large mounds that make striking features of the landscape. These mounds are often staked out as the private property of individuals or groups, and they may be valuable enough to be the cause of fights. Various sorts of ingenious traps have been devised to catch the winged sexual forms when they swarm out of the nests at certain seasons. Generally it is these sexual forms that are eaten, but some tribes eat the workers and soldiers, which can be obtained by breaking into the termite mounds. The big, fat termite queens, which may be two inches or so long, are always considered a great delicacy. But they live in special chambers in the depths of the mound, where they carry on their unending function of laying an egg every few seconds, and they can only be obtained by destroying the colony.

The Europeans who have been able to bring themselves to try eating termites have generally reported them as pleasant, or at least unobjectionable. The Africans have a more positive application of the taste of termites. David Livingstone nowhere admits to eating them himself, but he does report on African opinion: "The Bayeiye chief Palani, visiting us while eating, I gave him a piece of bread and preserved apricots; and as he seemed to relish it much, I asked him if he had any food equal to that in his country. 'Ah,' he said, 'did you ever taste white ants?' As I never had, he replied, 'Well, if you had, you could never have desired to eat anything better.' "

Dr. Bodenheimer, with his usual thoroughness, has combed the literature for information on the nutritive value of insects. The results are rather meager, because Western dietitians tend to ignore insects in their nutrition studies. French and Belgian colonial agencies, however, have given some attention to the subject, and it is interesting that termites turn out to be among the richest of all foods in terms of calories, comparable with peanut oil. A Belgian analysis gave a value of 561 calories for 100 grams—several times the caloric value of local beef or fish. Apparently no study has been made of the vitamin content of termites; grasshoppers are rather rich in vitamins B_1 and B_2, and silkworm pupae in vitamin A.

Ordinary ants (as distinguished from white ants or termites) are also eaten in many parts of the world. The nests may be dug out for larvae, pupae and workers; but most commonly, as with termites, the winged sexual forms are eaten at the times when they swarm. In the small town in South America where I used to live, bags of the toasted sexual forms of the leaf-cutting ants were sold at the movie theater at the proper season. They had about the same quality and served the same function as popcorn. The Japanese now export canned fried ants, but these canned ants seem to me quite tasteless, lacking the crisp, toasted character that I remember for the South American species.

In the semiarid regions of the southwestern United States and Mexico, and in Australia, there are a number of species of honey ants. Among these ants, some of the workers convert themselves into living bottles, clinging to the roof of the nest cavity and taking honey from the active workers until their abdomens are completely distended. They thus form a system of food storage to tide the colony through adverse seasons. The Indians of America and the aborigines of Australia discovered this source of honey and utilized it as fully as they could.

The honey ants were especially important in the meager diet of the aboriginal Australians and were sometimes tribal totems. The Australian tribes, in fact, often had insect totems, which shows the importance of insects in their way of life. I have been especially intrigued by the "witchetty grub" people since I first came across them in the writings of Sir Baldwin Spencer, the great authority on aboriginal Australian customs. These insect-descended people, with their ceremonies to insure that their totem grubs will flourish and multiply, should have the sympathy of every entomologist.

Unfortunately no one is quite sure what animal the witchetty grub is—the field studies have been made by anthropologists rather than entomologists. Probably "witchetty" is a collective word for the larvae of several of the giant ghost moths that are as characteristic among the insects of Australia as are kangaroos among the mammals. Large, woodboring grubs are fancied in many parts of the world, even though they do not play as important a part in the human diet as they do in Australia. Generally they are occasional delicacies.

Among such delicacies in America is the famous maguey worm of the highlands of Mexico. This is the larva of a butterfly, *Aegiale hesperialis*, which bores into the maguey, or agave plant—the source of pulque, the national drink of Mexico. The same plant thus supplies the drink and the snack to eat with the drink, and the two have been combined by Mexicans since ancient times.

The maguey worms have been canned for the local market in Mexico for some time, and now some of the stores that specialize in fancy foods are importing them into the United States, as I remarked earlier. The canned worms are best if eaten hot; they have a pleasant, nutty flavor, which blends as well with a martini as it does with mescal, the potent drink that the Mexicans distill from fermented pulque. Maybe insects will get into our diet by way of this worm, at least for the cocktail hour.

So far, however, all efforts to persuade modern Europeans or Americans to eat insects have failed. There are, to be sure, traces of insect-eating in scattered places in Europe. Dr. Bodenheimer, combing the literature, has come up with a number of instances. It is said that the beggars of Spain and Portugal have the habit, widespread among primitive peoples and monkeys, of eating their lice. It is also said that peasants in parts of southern Russia to this day eat locusts, smoked or salted. The habit of eating larvae and adults of cockchafer beetles was probably once widespread in Europe, and there are reports of the custom surviving here and there.

Among Western peoples there are also accounts of occasional individuals addicted to insect- or spider-eating—usually reported circumspectly, as though one were dealing with a sort of sporadic and rare, but repulsive, food perversion. Gilbert White, in his classic *Natural History of Selborne,* tells of a village idiot who, from childhood on, loved to eat honeybees, bumblebees and wasps, skillfully avoiding being stung. Dr. Bodenheimer finds mention of a young Swede addicted to eating ants; a German who spread spiders on his bread instead of butter; and of a young French lady who, "when she walked in her grounds, never saw a spider which she did not catch and eat on the spot."

In 1885, an Englishman, V. M. Holt, published a small book, now extremely rare, entitled *Why Not Eat Insects,* with this motto: "The insects eat up every blessed green thing that do grow and us farmers starve. Well, eat them and grow fat!" Holt was fully aware of the anti-insect prejudice, but he pointed out that many people freely eat cheese mites as part of the cheese; why not eat cabbage worms as part of the cabbage? After a review of insect-eating in classical times and among primitive peoples, he gave a series of recipes which he had worked out and tested. A sample menu will give the idea:

Snail Soup

Fried Soles with Woodlouse Sauce

Curried Cockchafers

Fricassee of Chicken with Chrysalids

Boiled Neck of Mutton with Wireworm Sauce

Ducklings with Green Peas

Cauliflowers garnished with Caterpillars

Moths on Toast

The noninsect aspects of this menu, incidentally, nicely reflect the eating habits of the Victorians!

Entomologists, understandably, have sometimes experimented with different ways of cooking insects and reported on the results in entomological journals. During the First World War, L. O. Howard, the leading American entomologist, strongly advocated the use of insects as one way of relieving the food shortage. He and his friends tried various recipes and published their findings in the *Journal of Economic Entomology*. Among other things, a stew of May beetle grubs was said to "taste agreeably like lobster."

My father-in-law, David Fairchild, famous for his work in introducing new plants into this country and always willing to experiment with new and interesting food, was infected by Howard's enthusiasm. One of my wife's earliest memories is of the time when her father decided the family had better get over prejudice and start eating grasshoppers. He fried the grasshoppers in sugar, but even that did not help with the children. The experiment was not a success and it took great will power on my wife's part to try eating grasshoppers again. She still does not really like them. The moral, I suppose, is that it is all right to experiment with cocktail guests, but be careful with your children.

28 / Cannibalistic Revenge in Jalé Warfare

KLAUS-FRIEDRICK KOCH

The Jalé of New Guinea are cannibals. But, before you wrinkle your nose in repulsion, first look at the type of cannibalism practiced and why it is carried out. Westerners have done scant justice to the reasonableness of eating human flesh. This selection by Klaus-Friedrick Koch examines Jalé cannibalism in light of Jalé cultural values, and he notes that Jalé cannibalism is a way of taking revenge on an enemy in an act of war. Most forms of warfare are considered ways of resolving conflicts in the absence of effective means of political control. The Jalé practice near-continual warfare, and the act of eating a slain enemy is an aid to comfort relatives who have recently lost a kinsman in battle. Thus flesh-eating among the Jalé is regarded as an act of duty.

In October, 1968, two white missionaries on a long trek between two stations were killed in a remote valley in the Snow Mountains of western New Guinea, and their bodies were eaten. A few days later, warriors armed with bows and arrows gave a hostile reception to a group of armed police flown to the site by helicopter. These people, described by the newspapers as "savages living in a stone-age culture," belong to a large population of Papuans among whom I lived for nearly two years, from 1964 to 1966.

People living to the west, in the high valley of the Balim River, call them "Jalé," and this is the name that I use for them. When I read of the killing of the missionaries I was reminded of how I had first heard that the people whom I had selected for ethnographic study had anthropophagic (man-eating) predilections. After arriving at Sentani airport on the north coast, I began negotiations for transport to a mission airstrip located in the Jalémó, the country of the Jalé. "I hope the Jalé will give us permission to land," one pilot said to me. "Just a few weeks ago the airstrip was blocked because the Jalé needed the ground for a dance and a cannibalistic feast to celebrate a military victory."

Our cultural heritage predisposes many people to view the eating of human meat with extreme horror. No wonder then that the literature on the subject is permeated with grossly erroneous and prejudicial ideas about the practice. Few anthropologists have been able to study cannibalism because missions and colonial governments have generally succeeded in eradicating a custom considered to epitomize, more than any other, the alleged mental primitiveness and diabolical inspirations of people with simple technologies. However, the Jalé, completely isolated from foreign influences until 1961, still practice cannibalism as an institutionalized form of revenge in warfare, which is itself an integral aspect of their life.

The Jalé live in compact villages along several valleys north and south of the Snow Mountains in east-central West New Guinea. Until the first missionaries entered the Jalémó in 1961, the Jalé were ignorant of the "outside" world. Five years later, when I left the area, many Jalé villages still had never been contacted, and culture change among the people living close to a mission station was largely limited to the acceptance of a few steel tools and to an influx of seashells imported by the foreigners.

Two weeks after I had set up camp in the village of Pasikni, a yearlong truce with a neighboring village came to an end. Three days of fierce fighting ensued, during which the Pasikni warriors killed three enemies (among them a small boy), raided the defeated settlement, and drove its inhabitants into exile with friends and relatives in other villages of the region. At that time I understood little of the political realities of Jalé society, where neither formal government nor forensic institutions exist for the settlement of conflicts. Later, when I had learned their language, I began to comprehend the conditions that make military actions an inevitable consequence of the absence of an effective system of political control.

From an anthropological perspective any kind of war is generally a symptom of the absence, inadequacy, or breakdown of other procedures for resolving conflicts. This view is especially applicable to Jalé military operations, which aim neither at territorial gains and the conquest of resources nor at the suppression of one political or religious ideology and its forceful replacement by another. All armed conflicts in Jalémó occur as a result of bodily injury or killing suffered in retaliation for the infliction of a wrong. Violent redress may be exacted for adultery or theft or for a breach of obligation—usually a failure to make a compensatory payment of pigs.

Jalé warfare is structured by a complex network of kin relationships. The Jalé conceptually divide their society into two parts (moieties) whose members must marry someone from the opposite side. By a principle of patrilineal descent a person always belongs to the moiety of his father. Links between kin groups created by intervillage marriages— about half the wives in a village were born elsewhere—provide the structure of trade networks and alliance politics.

Most villages contain two or more residential compounds, or wards. One hut among the group of dwellings forming a ward is considerably bigger than all the others. This is the men's house, a special domicile for men and for boys old enough to have been initiated. Women and uninitiated boys live in the smaller huts, each of which usually houses the family of one man. The residents of a men's house constitute a unified political and ritual community, and it is this community, not the village as a whole, that is the principal war-making unit.

As in all societies, there are some individuals who have more influence over the affairs of their fellows than most. In Jalémó a man gains a position of authority (which never extends much beyond the immediate kin group) through his acquisition of an esoteric knowledge of performing rituals and through the clever management of his livestock to the benefit of his relatives, for every important event demands the exchange of pigs —to solemnify or legitimate the creation of a new status or to settle a conflict. Most disputes are over women, pigs, or gardens, and any one of them may generate enough political enmity to cause a war in which many people may lose their lives and homes.

In every Jalé war one person on either side, called the "man-at-the-root-of-the-arrow," is held responsible for the outbreak of hostilities. These people are the parties to the original dispute, which ultimately escalates into armed combat. Being a man-at-the-root-of-the-arrow carries the liability of providing compensation for all injuries and deaths suffered by supporters on the battlefield as well as by all others—including women and children—victimized in clandestine revenge raids. This liability acts as a built-in force favoring an early end of hostilities.

On rare occasions blood revenge has been prevented by delivery of wergild compensation, in the form of a pig to the kinsmen of a slain person. But only those people who, for one reason or another, cannot rally support for a revenge action and who shy away from solitary, surreptitious ambush attacks will accept such an offer if it is made at all. A negotiated peace settlement of this nature is most likely if the disputants are from the same village or if the whole settlement is at war with a common outside enemy.

When two villages are at war with each other, periods of daily combat are interrupted by short "cease-fires" during which the warriors attend to the more mundane task of garden work, but they are always prepared to counter a surprise attack launched by the enemy. After several weeks of discontinuous fighting, however, the threat of famine due to the prolonged neglect of proper cultivation induces the belligerents to maintain an informal and precarious truce. During this time small bands of kinsmen and members of the men's house of a victim whose death could not be avenged on the battlefield will venture clandestine expeditions into enemy territory, from which a successful raiding party may bring back a pig as well. It is a revenge action of this kind that often precipitates a resumption of open warfare.

Fighting on the battlefield follows a pattern of haphazardly coordinated individual engagements, which rely on the tactic of "shoot-and-run." This technique requires a warrior to advance as far as the terrain affords him cover, discharge an arrow or two, and then run back to escape from the reach of enemy shots. When one side has been forced to retreat to its village, the fighting turns into sniping from behind huts and fences. Women and children always leave the village if an invasion is imminent and take refuge with friends and relatives in other villages. As a last resort the men retreat into the men's house, which a taboo protects from being burned. When a battle reaches this stage, the victorious warriors often plunder and burn family huts. Following a catastrophe of this extent the defeated side usually elects to abandon their village, and the warfare ceases, but the hostilities linger on until a formal peace ceremony reconciles the principal parties. Arranging the ceremony, which features the ritual slaughter and consumption of a pig, may take years of informal negotiations between people who have relatives on both sides. Afterward, dances in both villages and pig exchanges on a large scale consolidate the termination of the conflict.

"People whose face is known must not be eaten," say the Jalé. Consequently, cannibalism is normally not tolerated in wars between neighboring villages, and the few incidents that did occur during the lifetime of the oldest Pasikni men are remembered as acts of tragic perversion. In wars between villages separated by a major topographic boundary such as a mountain ridge, however, cannibalistic revenge is an integral part of the conflict.

While territorially confined hostilities usually end within a few years, interregional wars may last for more than a generation. During this long period revenge parties from either side venture sporadic expeditions into hostile areas, keenly avoiding any confrontation in battle and seeking instead to surprise lone hunters or small groups of women working in distant gardens. The geography of interregional wars favors long-lasting military alliances that have a stability quite unlike the temporary and shifting allegiances that personal kin connections and trading partnerships create in local conflict.

If an enemy is killed during a foray into hostile territory, the raiders will make every effort to bring the body home. If tactical exigencies demand that the revenge party retreat without the victim, an attempt is made to retrieve at least a limb. The avengers always present the body to an allied kin group that has lost a member in the war. In return they receive pigs and are feted at a victory dance, during which the victim's body is steam-cooked in an earth oven dug near the village. Before the butchering begins, the head is specially treated by ritual experts: eyelids and lips are clamped with the wing bones of a bat to prevent the victim's ghost from seeing through these apertures. Thus blinded, it will be unable to guide a revenge expedition against its enemies.

After the head has been severed, it is wrapped in leaves. To insure more revenge killings in the future, some men shoot reed arrows into the head while it is dragged on the ground by a piece of vine. Then the head is unwrapped and swung through the fire to burn off the hair. This is accompanied by loud incantations meant to lure the victim's kinsmen into sharing his fate.

Following this ritual overture the butchers use stone adzes and bamboo knives to cut the body apart. The fleshy portions are removed from the skull, and in an established order of step-by-step incisions, the limbs are separated from the trunk, which is split open to allow removal of the gastronomically highly prized entrails. Some small, choice cuts, especially rib sections, are roasted over the fire, but the bulk of the meat is cooked with a variety of leafy vegetables.

Before and during the operation, people who are preparing the oven, tending the fire, or just standing around appraise the victim. A healthy, muscular body is praised with ravenous exclamations, but a lesser grade body is also applauded.

When the meat is done, the pit is opened and the "owners of the body," as the Jalé call the recipients of a slain enemy, distribute much of the food among the attending relatives of the person whose death the killing has avenged. It is also distributed to the allied kin groups of a person maimed or killed in the war. Eligible people from other villages who could not participate in the celebrations are later sent pieces reserved for them. If mood so moves the Jalé, they may place some of the victim's bones in a tree near the cooking site to tell travelers of their brave deed.

In the course of the dancing and singing, a poetically gifted man may introduce a new song. If the lyrics appeal to others, it becomes a standard piece in the repertoire. The songs commemorate fortunate and tragic events from past wars, and a typical verse goes like this:

> Ngingi, your mother
> bakes only tiny potatoes for you.
> Isel, your mother too
> bakes only the ends of potatoes for you.
> We shall bake big potatoes for you
> On the day of Kingkaen's return.

Ngingi and Isel are the names of two men from a hostile village, the home of a young woman named Kingkaen who was killed in an ambush attack in September, 1964. The lines make fun of the men who, because of Kingkaen's death, have to eat poor food prepared by the inept hands of senile women.

When the festival of revenge is over, the members of the men's house group of the owners of the body arrange for the ritual removal of the victim's ghost from their village. Rhythmically voicing efficacious formulas and whistling sounds, a ceremonial procession of men carries a special arrow into the forest, as far into enemy territory as is possible without risk. A small lump of pig's fat is affixed to the arrow by an expert in esoteric lore. (Pig's fat used for ritual purposes becomes a sacred substance that is applied in many different contexts.) The arrow is finally shot toward the enemy village. This, the Jalé believe, will make the ghost stay away from their own village, but as a further precaution they block the path with branches and plants over which spells are said.

Protective rites of this kind, and the vengeance ritual described above, are the only aspects of Jalé cannibalism that may be viewed as "religious." The actual consumption of human meat and organs does not constitute an act with intrinsic "supernatural" effects. Instead, as my Jalé friends repeatedly assured me, their reason for eating an enemy's body is that man tastes as good as pork, if not better. And they added that the bad enemies in the other valley had eaten some of their people.

These descriptions of Jalé rituals and beliefs do not sufficiently explain the practice of cannibalism. To do so would necessitate the compilation of all available information about this custom from every part of the world. On the basis of these data an extensive study would have to be made of the ecological and cultural variables found to be associated with institutionalized cannibalism. Perhaps it would then be possible to recognize specific ecological and sociological features that appear to be correlated with the consumption of human meat, but the task of interpreting the custom as a sociopsychological phenomenon would still remain.

It is obvious that the enigmatic nature of cannibalism has invited many writers to speculate about its origin and its biopsychic basis. Aristotle attributed anthropophagy among tribes around the Black Sea to their feral bestiality and morbid lust. In 1688 a treatise was published in Holland entitled *De natura et moribus anthropophagorum* ("On the Nature and Customs of Anthropophagi"), and some ethnographers writing in the nineteenth century still regarded the rejection of cannibalism as the "first step into civilization." Certainly, the consumption by man of a member of his own species is as much a problem for evolutionary bioanthropology as it is for ethnology and psychology. I have made an extensive survey of the various theories proposed by earnest scholars to elucidate the phenomenon, and I have found that, at best, a few hypotheses appear plausible for the interpretation of certain aspects of some cannibalistic practices.

In Jalémó the eating of a slain enemy, in addition to its dietary value, certainly indicates a symbolic expression of spite incorporated into an act of supreme vengeance. Violent retaliation, in turn, must be seen as a consequence of certain sociopsychological conditions that determine the degree of aggressive behavior expected and tolerated in their culture. Cross-cultural studies by anthropologists have supported theories that are applicable to Jalé society. An accepted model of personality development demonstrates that societies in which boys grow up in intimate association with their mothers, who dominate a household situation in which the boys' male elders, especially their fathers, do not take part, are characterized by a high level of physical violence. Sociological models developed from large-scale comparative research predict that in societies in which small kin groups operate as relatively independent political units, warfare within the society is a common means of resolving conflict.

Both models squarely apply to Jalé society. First, young boys, separated from the community of the men's house until their initiation, are socialized in a female environment. Second, the wards of a village are not integrated by a centralized system of headmanship, and no political cooperation exists between them until they are threatened by, or faced with, actual hostility from other villages. These are the critical variables that partially determine the bellicosity and violence I have observed.

No specific hypothesis can be given to explain the cannibalism that the Jalé incorporate in their vengeance. It is certain, however, that no understanding can be achieved by applying precepts of Western thought. In a missionary's travelogue published seventy years ago, the author, speaking of an African tribe, recounted:

> Once, when told by a European that the practice of eating human flesh was a most degraded habit, the cannibal answered, "Why degraded? You people eat sheep and cows and fowls, which are all animals of a far lower order, and we eat man, who is great and above all; it is you who are degraded!"

29 / The Chest-Pounding Duel

NAPOLEON A. CHAGNON

The Yąnomamö people of northern Brazil are called the "fierce people"; their life-style is enmeshed in the activities of violence. In Western societies violence is regarded as undesirable (although frequently endorsed and practiced); in these "civilized" societies, pride is taken in the ability to negotiate unsettled conflicts. The Yąnomamö, however, endorse the frequent use of violent actions, such as chest-pounding and side-slapping duels, as part of a system of controls that regulate conflict. At first glance these duels may appear to be in opposition to the way in which Western societies settle conflicts, but upon further analysis, the differences dissolve. As Chagnon points out, these duels and other activities (club fighting and spear fighting), bear marked similarities to a policy with which we are most familiar—brinksmanship.

When the dancing was over and darkness fell, the men began to chant again. The first pair of chanters had not completed their rhythmic presentation when the jungle around the village erupted with hoots and screams, causing all of the people in the village to jump from their hammocks and arm themselves. When the men had found their arrows and were prepared, they began yelling back at the unseen guests, rattling the shafts of their arrows together or against their bows and/or pounding the heads of axes against pieces of firewood or on the ground to make noise. The Boreta-teri and Mahekodo-teri had returned to accept the chest-pounding challenge and entered the village, each man brandishing his axe, club, or bow and arrows. They circled the village once, feinting attack on particular men among the hosts, then grouped at the center of the village clearing. The hosts surrounded them excitedly, dancing with their weapons poised to strike, then entering into the mass of bodies. Heated arguments about food theft and gluttony developed, and the hosts and guests threateningly waved their weapons in each other's faces. Within minutes the large group had bifurcated and the chest-pounding began. The Karohi-teri aided Kąobawä and his followers, whose joint numbers were even further swelled when the Lower Bisaasi-teri rushed to the village after hearing the commotion. There were about sixty adult men on each side in the fight, divided into two arenas, each comprised of hosts and guests. Two men, one from each side, would step into the center of the milling, belligerent crowd of weapon-wielding partisans, urged on by their comrades. One would step up, spread his legs apart, bare his chest, and hold his arms behind his back, daring the other to hit him. The opponent would size him up, adjust the man's chest or arms so as to give himself the greatest advantage when he struck, and then step back to deliver his close-fisted blow. The striker would painstakingly adjust his own distance from his victim by measuring his arm length to the man's chest, taking several dry runs before delivering his blow. He would then wind up like a baseball pitcher, but keeping both feet on the ground, and deliver a tremendous wallop with his fist to the man's left pectoral muscle, putting all of his weight into the blow. The victim's knees would often buckle and he would stagger around a few moments, shaking his head to clear the stars, but remain silent. The blow invariably raised a "frog" on the recipient's pectoral muscle where the striker's knuckles bit into his flesh. After each blow, the comrades of the deliverer would cheer and bounce up and down from the knees, waving and clacking their weapons over their heads. The victim's supporters, meanwhile, would urge their champion on frantically, insisting that he take another blow. If the delivery were made with sufficient force to knock the recipient to the ground, the man who delivered it would throw his arms above his head, roll his eyes back, and prance victoriously in a circle around his victim, growling and screaming, his feet almost a blur from his excited dance. The recipient would stand poised and take as many as four blows before demanding to hit his adversary. He would be permitted to strike his opponent as many times as the latter struck him, provided that the opponent could take it. If not, he would be forced to retire, much to the dismay of his comrades and the delirious joy of their opponents. No fighter could retire after delivering a blow. If he attempted to do so, his adversary would plunge into the crowd and roughly haul him back out, sometimes being aided by the man's own supporters. Only after having received his just dues could he retire. If he had delivered three blows, he had to receive three or else be proven a poor fighter. He could retire with less than three only if he were injured. Then, one of his comrades would replace him and demand to hit the victorious opponent. The injured man's two remaining blows would be canceled, and the man who delivered the victorious blow would have to receive more blows than he delivered. Thus, good fighters are at a disadvantage, since they receive disproportionately more punishment than they deliver. Their only reward is status: they earn the reputation of being fierce.

Some of the younger men in Kąobawä's group were reluctant to participate in the fighting because they were afraid of being injured. This put more strain on the others, who were forced to take extra turns in order to preserve the group's reputation. At one point Kąobawä's men, sore from the punishment they had taken and worried that they would ultimately lose the fight, wanted to escalate the contest to an axe dual. Kąobawä was vigorously opposed to this, as he knew it would lead to bloodshed. He therefore recruited the younger men into the fighting, as well as a few of the older ones who had done nothing but demand the others to step into the arena, thereby reducing the strain on those who wanted to escalate the level of violence. A few of the younger men retired after a single blow, privately admitting to me later that they pretended to be injured to avoid being forced to fight more. The fighting continued in this fashion for nearly three hours, tempers growing hotter and hotter. Kąobawä and the headman from the other group stood by with their weapons, attempting to keep the fighting innocuous, but not participating in it. Some of the fighters went through several turns of three or four blows each, their pectoral muscles swollen and red from the number of blows each had received. The fight had still not been decided, although Kąobawä's group seemed to be getting the worst of it. They then insisted on escalating the fighting to side slapping, partly because their chests were too sore to continue in that fashion, and partly because their opponents seemed to have an edge on them.

The side slapping duel is nearly identical in form to chest pounding, except that the blow is delivered with an open hand across the flanks of the opponent, between his rib-cage and pelvis bone. It is a little more severe than chest pounding because casualties are more frequent and tempers grow hotter more rapidly when a group's champion falls to the ground, gasping for wind, and faints. The side slapping only lasted fifteen minutes or so; one of the more influential men in Kąobawä's group was knocked unconscious, enraging the others. The fighting continued for just a few minutes after this, but during these few minutes the men were rapidly changing the points of their arrows to war tips: curare and lanceolate bamboo. The women and children began to cry, knowing that the situation was getting serious, and they grouped into the farthest corners of their houses near the exits. One by one the men withdrew, returned to their houses, and drew their bows. The visitors pulled back and formed a protective circle around their own women and children, also fitting arrows into their bows and drawing them. The village grew almost silent. The leaders of the respective groups stepped into the no man's land separating the two groups of armed men and began arguing violently, waving axes and clubs at each other. Suddenly, the spokesmen from the visiting group surged toward Kąobawä and his supporters, swinging their axes and clubs wildly at them, forcing them back to the line of men whose bowstrings were drawn taut. Kąobawä and his followers regained their footing and repelled their adversaries at this point, while the women and children from both groups began fleeing from the village, screaming and wailing. It looked as if they were about to release their arrows point-blank at Kąobawä's attackers, but when he and his aides turned them back, the crisis was over. The leaders of the visiting group rejoined the other men, some of whom had picked up glowing brands of firewood, and they backed out of the village, weapons still drawn, their way illuminated by those who were waving the brands.

Kaobawä's group took no further action in this affair and was not invited to feast at Mahekodo-teri. Later in the year, their relationships worsened because of a club fight in yet another village, and for a while both groups threatened to shoot each other on sight. A temporary rapprochement developed after the club fight, when a group of raiders from Kaobawä's group met a group of hunters from Mahekodo-teri while en route to attack the village of one of their enemies. The men from both villages traded with each other and departed on friendly terms, the raiders abandoning their raid and returning to their village lest they be later ambushed on the way home by the Mahekodo-teri. They are presently on trading terms with each other, but their relationship is still somewhat strained and potentially hostile.

In general, feasts are exciting for both the hosts and the guests and contribute to their mutual solidarity. Under normal circumstances, allies that customarily feast with each other do not fight. Nevertheless, even the best allies occasionally agree beforehand to terminate their feast with a chest-pounding duel, thereby demonstrating to each other that they are friends, but capable of maintaining their sovereignty and willing to fight if necessary. Kaobawä's group had a chest-pounding duel with one of its staunchest allies in 1966, as each had heard that the other was spreading rumors that it was cowardly. Of the six feasts I witnessed during the nineteen months I spent with the Yanomamö, two of them ended in fighting.

Any Yanomamö feast can potentially end in violence because of the nature of the attitudes the participants hold regarding canons of behavior and obligations to display ferocity.

Still, the feast and its attendant trade serve to reduce the possibility of neighbors fighting with each other at a more serious level of violence, and they contribute to intervillage solidarity and mutual interdependence.

From "The Impact of Money on an African Subsistence Economy," by Paul Bohannan, *The Journal of Economic History,* Vol. 19, No. 4, 1959, pp. 491–503. Copyright © 1959 by The Economic History Association. Reprinted by permission of the
publisher and the author.

30 / The Impact of Money on an African Subsistence Economy

PAUL BOHANNAN

*What do you do with a used brass rod? Well, if you are a Tiv of African
Nigeria you might have once used it as a means of payment. Traditionally,
the Tiv used brass rods as a medium of exchange in the acquisition of
cattle, slaves, magic charms, and other items; however, brass rods were
not used to obtain subsistence items (food). The Tiv distributed most of
their subsistence goods on the basis of either reciprocity and redistribution
or by barter. Paul Bohannan describes early Tiv economy and shows how
their three spheres of exchange—subsistence, prestige, and women marital
partners—were separated by the understanding that goods from one sphere
could not be used to obtain goods in another sphere. To do so would have
meant loss of prestige to one of the parties involved in the exchange. The
introduction later into the Tiv system of all-purpose Western money allowed for the equation of values in each of the three spheres. What happened to the old brass rods? Colonial administrators created an exchange
rate between rods and coinage; the rods were withdrawn and replaced by
currency. Bohannan considers the far-reaching changes in the Tiv cultural
system resulting from the introduction of money.*

It has often been claimed that money was to be found in much of the
African continent before the impact of the European world and the extension of trade made coinage general. When we examine these claims, however, they tend to evaporate or to emerge as tricks of definition. It is an
astounding fact that economists have, for decades, been assigning three or
four qualities to money when they discuss it with reference to our own
society or to those of the medieval and modern world, yet the moment they
have gone to ancient history or to the societies and economies studied by
anthropologists they have sought the "real" nature of money by allowing
only one of these defining characteristics to dominate their definitions.

All economists learned as students that money serves at least three purposes. It is a means of exchange, it is a mode of payment, it is a standard

of value. Depending on the vintage and persuasion of the author of the book one consults, one may find another money use—storage of wealth. In newer books, money is defined as merely the means of unitizing purchasing power, yet behind that definition still lie the standard, the payment, and the exchange uses of money,

It is interesting that on the fairly rare occasions that economists discuss primitive money at all—or at least when they discuss it with any empirical referrent—they have discarded one or more of the money uses in framing their definitions. Paul Einzig, to take one example for many, first makes a plea for "elastic definitions," and goes on to point out that different economists have utilized different criteria in their definitions; he then falls into the trap he has been exposing: he excoriates Menger for utilizing only the "medium of exchange" criterion and then himself omits it, utilizing only the standard and payment criteria, thus taking sides in an argument in which there was no real issue.

The answer to these difficulties should be apparent. If we take no more than the three major money uses—payment, standard and means of exchange—we will find that in many primitive societies as well as in some of the ancient empires, one object may serve one money use while quite another object serves another money use. In order to deal with this situation, and to avoid the trap of choosing one of these uses to define "real" money, Karl Polanyi and his associates have labeled as "general purpose money" any item which serves all three of these primary money uses, while an item which serves only one or two is "special purpose money." With this distinction in mind, we can see that special purpose money was very common in pre-contact Africa, but that general purpose money was rare.

This paper is a brief analysis of the impact of general purpose money and increase in trade in an African economy which had known only local trade and had used only special purpose money.

The Tiv are a people, still largely pagan, who live in the Benue Valley in central Nigeria, among whom I had the good fortune to live and work for well over two years. They are prosperous subsistence farmers and have a highly developed indigenous market in which they exchanged their produce and handicrafts, and through which they carried on local trade. The most distinctive feature about the economy of Tiv—and it is a feature they share with many, perhaps most, of the premonetary peoples—is what can be called a multi-centric economy. Briefly, a multi-centric economy is an economy in which a society's exchangeable goods fall into two or more mutually exclusive spheres, each marked by different institutionalization and different moral values. In some multi-centric economies these spheres remain distinct, though in most there are more or less institutionalized means of converting wealth from one into wealth in another.

Idigenously there were three spheres in the multi-centric economy of the Tiv. The first of these spheres is that associated with subsistence, which the Tiv call *yiagh*. The commodities in it include all locally produced foodstuffs: the staple yams and cereals, plus all the condiments, vegetable side-dishes and seasonings, as well as small livestock—chickens, goats and sheep. It also includes household utensils (mortar, grindstones, calabashes, baskets and pots), some tools (particularly those used in agriculture), and raw materials for producing any items in the category.

Within this sphere, goods are distributed either by gift giving or through marketing. Traditionally, there was no money of any sort in this sphere—all goods changed hands by barter. There was a highly developed market organization at which people exchanged their produce for their requirements, and in which today traders buy produce in cheap markets and transport it to sell in dearer markets. The morality of this sphere of the economy is the morality of the free and uncontrolled market.

The second sphere of the Tiv economy is one which is in no way associated with markets. The category of goods within this sphere is slaves, cattle, ritual "offices" purchased from the Jukun, that type of large white cloth known as *tugudu*, medicines and magic, and metal rods. One is still entitled to use the present tense in this case, for ideally the category still exists in spite of the fact that metal rods are today very rare, that slavery has been abolished, that European "offices" have replaced Jukun offices and cannot be bought, and that much European medicine has been accepted. Tiv still quote prices of slaves in cows and brass rods, and of cattle in brass rods and *tugudu* cloth. The price of magical rites, as it has been described in the literature, was in terms of *tugudu* cloth or brass rods (though payment might be made in other items); payment for Jukun titles was in cows and slaves, *tugudu* cloths and metal rods.

None of these goods ever entered the market as it was institutionalized in Tivland, even though it might be possible for an economist to find the principle of supply and demand at work in the exchanges which characterized it. The actual shifts of goods took place at ceremonies, at more or less ritualized wealth displays, and on occasions when "doctors" performed rites and prescribed medicines. Tiv refer to the items and the activities within this sphere by the word *shagba,* which can be roughly translated as prestige.

Within the prestige sphere was one item which took on all of the money uses and hence can be called a general-purpose currency, though it must be remembered that it was of only a *very limited range.* Brass rods were used as means of exchange *within the sphere;* they also served as a standard of value within it (though not the only one), and as a means of payment. However, this sphere of the economy was tightly sealed off from the subsistence goods and its market. After European contact, brass rods occasionally entered the market, but they did so only as means of payment, not as medium of exchange or as standard of valuation. Because of the complex institutionalization and morality, no one ever sold a slave for food; no one, save in the depths of extremity, ever paid brass rods for domestic goods.

The supreme and unique sphere of exchangeable values for the Tiv contains a single item: rights in human beings other than slaves, particularly rights in women. Even twenty-five years after official abolition of exchange marriage, it is the category of exchange in which Tiv are emotionally most entangled. All exchanges within this category are exchanges or rights in human beings, usually dependent women and children. Its values are expressed in terms of kinship and marriage.

Tiv marriage is an extremely complex subject. Again, economists might find supply and demand principles at work, but Tiv adamantly separate marriage and market. Before the coming of the Europeans all "real" marriages were exchange marriages. In its simplest form, an exchange marriage involves two men exchanging sisters. Actually, this simple form seldom or never occurred. In order for every man to have a ward (*ingol*) to exchange for a wife, small localized agnatic lineages formed ward-sharing groups ("those who eat one Ingol"—*mbaye ingol i mom*). There was an initial "exchange"—or at least, distribution—of wards among the men of this group, so that each man became the guardian (*tien*) of one or more wards. The guardian, then, saw to the marriage of his ward, exchanging her with outsiders for another woman (her "partner" or *ikyar*) who becomes the bride of the guardian or one of his close agnatic kinsmen, or—in some situations—becomes a ward in the ward-sharing group and is exchanged for yet another woman who becomes a wife.

Tiv are, however, extremely practical and sensible people, and they know that successful marriages cannot be made if women are not consulted and if they are not happy. Elopements occurred, and sometimes a woman in exchange was not forthcoming. Therefore, a debt existed from the ward-sharing group of the husband to that of the guardian.

These debts sometimes lagged two or even three generations behind actual exchanges. The simplest way of paying them off was for the eldest daughter of the marriage to return to the ward-sharing group of her mother, as ward, thus cancelling the debt.

Because of its many impracticalities, the system had to be buttressed in several ways in order to work: one way was a provision for "earnest" during the time of the lag, another was to recognize other types of marriage as binding to limited extents. These two elements are somewhat confused with one another, because of the fact that right up until the abolition of exchange marriage in 1927, the inclination was always to treat all non-exchange marriages as if they were "lags" in the completion of exchange marriages.

When lags in exchange occurred, they were usually filled with "earnests" of brass rods or, occasionally, it would seem, of cattle. The brass rods or cattle in such situations were *never* exchange equivalents (*she*) for the woman. The only "price" of one woman is another woman.

Although Tiv decline to grant it antiquity, another type of marriage occurred at the time Europeans first met them—it was called "accumulating a woman/wife" (*kem kwase*). It is difficult to tell today just exactly what it consisted in, because the terminology of this union has been adapted to describe the bridewealth marriage that was declared by an administrative fiat of 1927 to be the only legal form.

Kem marriage consisted in acquisition of sexual, domestic and economic rights in a woman—but not the rights to filiate her children to the social group of the husband. Put in another way, in exchange marriage, both rights *in genetricem* (rights to filiate a woman's children) and rights *in uxorem* (sexual, domestic and economic rights in a woman) automatically were acquired by husbands and their lineages. In *kem* marriage, only rights *in uxorem* were acquired. In order to affiliate the *kem* wife's children, additional payments had to be made to the woman's guardians. These payments were for the children, not for the rights *in genetricem* in their mother, which could be acquired only by exchange of equivalent rights in another woman. *Kem* payments were paid in brass rods. However, rights in women had no equivalent of "price" in brass rods or in any other item—save, of course, identical rights in another woman. *Kem* marriage was similar to but showed important differences from bridewealth marriage as it is known in South and East Africa. There rights in women and rights in cattle form a single economic sphere, and could be exchanged directly for one another. Among Tiv, however, conveyance of rights in women necessarily involved direct exchange of another woman. The Tiv custom that approached bridewealth was not an exchange of equivalents, but payment in a medium that was specifically not equivalent.

Thus, within the sphere of exchange marriage there was no item that fulfilled any of the uses of money; when second-best types of marriage were made, payment was in an item which was specifically not used as a standard of value.

That Tiv do conceptualize exchange articles as belonging to different categories, and that they rank the categories on a moral basis, and that most but not all exchanges are limited to one sphere, gives rise to the fact that two different kinds of exchanges may be recognized: exchange of items contained within a single category, and exchanges of items belonging to different categories. For Tiv, these two different types of exchange are marked by separate and distinct moral attitudes.

To maintain this distinction between the two types of exchanges which Tiv mark by different behavior and different values, I shall use separate words. I shall call those exchanges of items within a single category "conveyances" and those exchanges of items from one category to another "conversions." Roughly, conveyances are morally neutral; conversions have a strong moral quality in their rationalization.

Exchanges within a category—particularly that of subsistence, the only one intact today—excite no moral judgments. Exchanges between categories, however, do excite a moral reaction: the man who exchanges lower category goods for higher category goods does not brag about his market luck but about his "strong heart" and his success in life. The man who exchanges high category goods for lower rationalizes his action in terms of high-valued motivation (most often the needs of his kinsmen).

The two institutions most intimately connected with conveyance are markets and marriage. Conveyance in the prestige sphere seems (to the latter-day investigator, at least) to have been less highly institutionalized. It centered on slave dealing, on curing and on the acquisition of status.

Conversion is a much more complex matter. Conversion depends on the fact that some items of every sphere could, on certain occasions, be used in exchanges in which the return was *not* considered equivalent (*ishe*). Obviously, given the moral ranking of the spheres, such a situation leaves one party to the exchange in a good position, and the other in a bad one. Tiv says that it is "good" to trade food for brass rods, but that it is "bad" to trade brass rods for food, that it is good to trade your cows or brass rods for a wife, but very bad to trade your marriage ward for cows or brass rods.

Seen from the individual's point of view, it is profitable and possible to invest one's wealth if one converts it into a morally superior category: to convert subsistence wealth into prestige wealth and both into women is the aim of the economic endeavor of individual Tiv. To put it into economists' terms: conversion is the ultimate type of maximization.

We have already examined the marriage system by which a man could convert his brass rods to a wife: he could get a *kem* wife and *kem* her children as they were born. Her daughters, then, could be used as wards in his exchange marriages. It is the desire of every Tiv to "acquire a woman" (*ngoho kwase*) either as wife or ward in some way other than sharing in the ward-sharing group. A wife whom one acquires in any other way is not the concern of one's marriage–ward-sharing group because the woman or other property exchanged for her did not belong to the marriage-ward group. The daughters of such a wife are not divided among the members of a man's marriage-ward group, but only among his sons. Such a wife is not only indicative of a man's ability and success financially and personally, but rights in her are the only form of property which is not ethically subject to the demands of his kinsmen.

Conversion from the prestige sphere to the kinship sphere was, thus, fairly common; it consisted in all the forms of marriage save exchange marriage, usually in terms of brass rods.

Conversion from the subsistence sphere to the prestige sphere was also usually in terms of metal rods. They, on occasion, entered the market place as payment. If the owner of the brass rods required an unusually large amount of staples to give a feast, making too heavy a drain on his wives' food supplies, he might buy it with brass rods.

However, brass rods could not possibly have been a general currency. They were not divisible. One could not receive "change" from a brass rod. Moreover, a single rod was worth much more than the usual market purchases for any given day of most Tiv subsistence traders. Although it might be possible to buy chickens with brass rods, one would have to have bought a very large quantity of yams to equal one rod, and to buy an item like pepper with rods would be laughable.

Brass rods, thus, overlapped from the prestige to the subsistence sphere on some occasions, but only on special occasions and for large purchases.

Not only is conversion possible, but it is encouraged—it is, in fact, the behavior which proves a man's worth. Tiv are scornful of a man who is merely rich in subsistence goods (or, today, in money). If, having adequate subsistence, he does not seek prestige in accordance with the old counters, or if he does not strive for more wives, and hence more children, the fault must be personal inadequacy. They also note that they all try to keep a man from making conversions; jealous kinsmen of a rich man will bewitch him and his people by fetishes, in order to make him expend his wealth on sacrifices to repair the fetishes, thus maintaining economic equality. However, once a conversion has been made, demands of kinsmen are not effective—at least, they take a new form.

Therefore, the man who successfully converts his wealth into higher categories is successful—he has a "strong heart." He is both feared and respected.

In this entire process, metal rods hold a pivotal position, and it is not surprising that early administrators considered them money. Originally imported from Europe, they were used as "currency" in some part of southern Nigeria in the slave trade. They are dowels about a quarter of an inch in diameter and some three feet long; they can be made into jewelry, and were used as a source of metal for castings.

Whatever their use elsewhere, brass rods in Tivland had some but not all of the attributes of money. Within the prestige sphere, they were used as a standard of equivalence, and they were a medium of exchange; they were also a mode for storage of wealth, and were used as payment. In short, brass rods were a general purpose currency *within the prestige sphere*. However, outside of the prestige sphere—markets and marriage were the most active institutions of exchange outside it—brass rods fulfilled only one of these functions of money payment. We have examined in detail the reasons why equivalency could not exist between brass rods and rights in women, between brass rods and food.

We have, thus, in Tivland, a multi-centric economy of three spheres, and we have a sort of money which was a general purpose money within the limited range of the prestige sphere, and a special purpose money in the special transactions in which the other spheres overlapped it.

The next question is: what happened to this multi-centric economy and to the morality accompanying it when it felt the impact of the expanding European economy in the 19th and early 20th centuries, and when an all-purpose money of very much greater range was introduced?

The Western impact is not, of course, limited to economic institutions. Administrative organizations, missions and others have been as effective instruments of change as any other.

One of the most startling innovations of the British administration was a general peace. Before the arrival of the British, one did not venture far beyond the area of one's kinsmen or special friends. To do so was to court death or enslavement.

With government police systems and safety, road building was also begun. Moving about the country has been made both safe and comparatively easy. Peace and the new road network led to both increased trade and a greater number of markets.

Not only has the internal marketing system been perturbed by the introduction of alien institutions, but the economic institutions of the Tiv have in fact been put into touch with world economy. Northern Nigeria, like much of the rest of the colonial world, was originally taken over by trading companies with governing powers. The close linkage of government and trade was evident when taxation was introduced into Tivland. Tax was originally paid in produce, which was transported and sold through the Hausa traders, who were government contractors. A few years later, coinage was introduced; taxes were demanded in that medium. It became necessary for Tiv to go into trade or to make their own contract with foreign traders in order to get cash. The trading companies, which had had "canteens" on the Benue for some decades, were quick to cooperate with the government in introducing a "cash crop" which could be bought by the traders in return for cash to pay taxes, and incidentally to buy imported goods. The crop which proved best adapted for this purpose in Tivland was beniseed (*Sesamum indicum*), a crop Tiv already grew in small quantities. Acreage need only be increased and facilities for sale established.

There is still another way in which Tiv economy is linked, through the trading companies, to the economy of the outside world. Not only do the companies buy their cash crops, they also "stake" African traders with imported goods. There is, on the part both of the companies and the government, a desire to build up "native entrepreneurial classes." Imported cloth, enamelware and ironmongery are generally sold through network of dependent African traders. Thus, African traders are linked to the companies, and hence into international trade.

Probably no single factor has been so important, however, as the introduction of all-purpose money. Neither introduction of cash crops and taxes nor extended trading has affected the basic congruence between Tiv ideas and their institutionalization to the same extent as has money. With the introduction of money the indigenous ideas of maximization—that is, conversion of all forms of wealth into women and children—no longer leads to the result it once did.

General purpose money provides a common denominator among all the spheres, thus making the commodities within each expressible in terms of a single standard and hence immediately exchangeable. This new money is misunderstood by Tiv. They use it as a standard of value in the subsistence category, even when—as is often the case—the exchange is direct barter. They use it as a means of payment of bridewealth under the new system, but still refuse to admit that a woman has a "price" or can be valued in the same terms as food. At the same time, it has become something formerly lacking in all save the prestige sphere of Tiv economy—a means of exchange. Tiv have tried to categorize money with the other new imported goods and place them all in a fourth economic sphere, to be ranked morally below subsistence. They have, of course, not been successful in so doing.

What in fact happened was that general purpose money was introduced to Tivland, where formerly only special purpose money had been known.

It is in the nature of a general purpose money that it standardizes the exchangeability value of every item to a common scale. It is precisely this function which brass rods, a "limited-purpose money" in the old system, did not perform. As we have seen, brass rods were used as a standard in some situations of conveyance in the intermediate or "prestige" category. They were also used as a means of payment (but specifically not as standard) in some instances of conversion.

In this situation, the early Administrative officers interpreted brass rods as "money," by which they meant a general purpose money. It became a fairly easy process, in their view, to establish by fiat an exchange rate between brass rods and a new coinage, "withdraw" the rods, and hence "replace" one currency with another. The actual effect, as we have seen, was to introduce a general purpose currency in place of a limited purpose money. Today all conversions and most conveyances are made in terms of coinage. Yet Tiv constantly express their distrust of money. This fact, and another—that a single means of exchange has entered all the economic spheres—has broken down the major distinctions among the spheres. Money has created in Tivland a unicentric economy. Not only is the money a general purpose money, but it applies to the full range of exchangeable goods.

Thus, when semi-professional traders, using money, began trading in the foodstuffs marketed by women and formerly solely the province of women, the range of the market was very greatly increased and hence the price in Tiv markets is determined by supply and demand far distant from the local producer and consumer. Tiv react to this situation by saying that foreign traders "spoil" their markets. The overlap of marketing and men's long-distance trade in staples also results in truckload after truckload of foodstuffs exported from major Tiv markets every day they meet. Tiv say that food is less plentiful today than it was in the past, though more land is being farmed. Tiv elders deplore this situation and know what is happening, but they do not know just where to fix the blame. In attempts to do something about it, they sometimes announce that no women are to sell any food at all. But when their wives disobey them, men do not really feel that they were wrong to have done so. Tiv sometimes discriminate against non-Tiv traders in attempts to stop export of food. In their condemnation of the situation which is depriving them of their food faster than they are able to increase production, Tiv elders always curse money itself. It is money which, as the instrument for selling one's life subsistence, is responsible for the worsened situation—money and the Europeans who brought it.

Of even greater concern to Tiv is the influence money has had on marriage institutions. Today every woman's guardian, in accepting money as bridewealth, feels that he is converting down. Although attempts are made to spend money which is received in bridewealth to acquire brides for one's self and one's sons, it is in the nature of money, Tiv insist, that it is most difficult to accomplish. The good man still spends his bridewealth receipts for brides—but good men are not so numerous as would be desirable. Tiv deplore the fact that they are required to "sell" (*te*) their daughters and "buy" (*yam*) wives. There is no dignity in it since the possibility of making a bridewealth marriage into an exchange marriage has been removed.

With money, thus, the institutionalization of Tiv economy has become unicentric, even though Tiv still see it with multi-centric values. The single sphere takes many of its characteristics from the market, so that the new situation can be considered a spread of the market. But throughout these changes in institutionalization, the basic Tiv value of maximization—converting one's wealth into the highest category, women and children—has remained. And in this discrepancy between values and institutions, Tiv have come upon what is to them a paradox, for all that Westerners understand it and are familiar with it. Today it is easy to sell subsistence goods for money to buy prestige articles and women, thereby aggrandizing oneself at a rapid rate. The food so sold is exported, decreasing the amount of subsistence goods available for consumption. On the other hand, the number of women is limited. The result is that bridewealth gets higher: rights in women have entered the market, and since the supply is fixed, the price of women has become inflated.

The frame of reference given me by the organizer of this symposium asked for comments on the effects of increased monetization on trade, on the distribution of wealth and indebtedness. To sum up the situation in these terms, trade has vastly increased with the introduction of general purpose money but also with the other factors brought by a colonial form of government. At the same time, the market has expanded its range of applicability in the society. The Tiv are, indigenously, a people who valued egalitarian distribution of wealth to the extent that they believed they bewitched one another to whittle down the wealth of one man to the size of that of another. With money, the degree and extent of differentiation by wealth has greatly increased and will probably continue to increase. Finally, money has brought a new form of indebtedness—one which we know, only too well. In the indigenous system, debt took either the form of owing marriage wards and was hence congruent with the kinship system, or else took the form of decreased prestige. There was no debt in the sphere of subsistence because there was no credit there save among kinsmen and neighbors whose activities were aspects of family status, not acts of money-lenders. The introduction of general purpose money and the concomitant spread of the market has divorced debt from kinship and status and has created the notion of debt in the subsistence sphere divorced from the activities of kinsmen and neighbors.

In short, because of the spread of the market and the introduction of general purpose money, Tiv economy has become a part of the world economy. It has brought about profound changes in the institutionalization of Tiv society. Money is one of the shatteringly simplifying ideas of all time, and like any other new and compelling idea, it creates its own revolution. The monetary revolution, at least in this part of Africa, is the turn away from the multi-centric economy. Its course may be painful, but there is very little doubt about its outcome.

Part 6 / QUESTIONS AND PROBLEMS FOR DISCUSSION

1. Discuss the peyote ceremony in terms of the functions it seems to serve in the Winnebago culture. Can you see any similarities in the functions of the peyote ceremony and ceremonies conducted in your own church organization or other organizations to which you belong?
2. Does sorcery really work? If not, how do you explain the fact that so many victims of sorcery die soon after a curse or hex is put on them? Interview a few persons in your community in an attempt to determine if persons around you actually believe in sorcery or witchcraft.
3. List in a descending order of preference several potential food items that are not considered by your peers to be acceptable items to eat. Why did you list each item, and how would you justify your ranking in terms of being either high or low on your list?
4. Examine the chest-pounding duel as a means of social control, and discuss specific activities in your culture that operate in a similar capacity.
5. What do you believe are some of the reasons members of the Jalé and Yanomamö societies engage in conflict? Can you see any similarities in these reasons and reasons you might select from your own culture?

7 / MAN-STUDY PUT TO USE

Quite often a student will make the comment: "Anthropology is interesting, but of what use is it?" In recent years it has become popular to question the usefulness, or applicability, of certain disciplines, such as history, philosophy, and anthropology. Although I hold the personal conviction that the task of gathering and distributing knowledge among mankind is a valid end in itself, I also hold the position that knowledge gained from the discipline of anthropology can be used for the betterment of mankind. In this section attention is focused inward to examine how "man-study" is put to use. Anthropology has had far-reaching influence on thought during the last three or four decades. The essence of this influence can be traced to the fact that anthropology has helped us to realize that the reasons various peoples behave differently are essentially cultural rather than biological.

Since anthropologists have long stressed the need to analyze the entire range of human behavior, now referred to as the *holistic approach,* it is easy to understand that it is in the field of anthropology that most contributions had been made toward the understanding that different aspects of behavior are strongly interrelated. By this approach it realized that kin ties are just as real whether determined through biological or social bonds, that language affects how we think, that the distribution and consumption of economic goods is often reflected in the type of social organization present, and that the complexity of religious systems is affected by the amount of leisure time people have. It has been through such realizations that anthropology has traditionally been put to use in the area of human understanding.

Basically, there are two extreme views of how man-study should be put to use. One position includes those individuals who advocate action by assigning to anthropology the task of conducting specific activities in support of solving social problems. The other position holds the view that anthropology should maintain a more neutral or objective stand regarding social problems. The latter view supports the basic pillar upon which anthropology rests. That is, peoples and their cultures should be viewed in an objective, dispassionate position. There appears, then, to be a basic incompatibility between the roles of the anthropologist as a scientist and the anthropologist as an activist. It would be most difficult, if not impossible, to play both roles at once without sacrificing one for the other. Of course, not all anthropologists fall into these two categories. Indeed, most fall someplace in between.

These are crucial times for the discipline of anthropology. During the next decade or two we shall see in which direction applied anthropology is to go. Which do we betray—ethics or idealism? Perhaps a middle-of-the-road course will be followed. Whatever it turns out to be, let us hope that there is careful direction in the setting of the course and that applied anthropology does not become like a lost satellite in space, pulled and pushed by whatever forces happen to be there at the time.

31 / The Applications of Anthropology

ROGER M. KEESING
FELIX M. KEESING

"Don't just stand there! Do something!" This is the cry often heard in Western societies when a crisis erupts. The crisis in this instance is the steady growth of rapidly changing value systems and how to best resolve cultural conflicts. In the following pages the Keesings tell us a little of what has *been done, a little of what* should *be done, and a little of what* should not *be done in the area of applied anthropology. The reader should be particularly concerned with what the Keesings say on the current problems of minority groups, urban development, and poverty pockets. The authors have no sugar-coated answers, so do not bother to look for them. Look for their remarks on what the problem is. It is also suggested that the reader take careful note of the authors' comments on one of the most explosive issues in applied anthropology today: that anthropology is becoming a less Western-dominated field than in the past, and that Euro-American anthropologists should listen to the rapidly rising ranks of non-Western anthropologists. In the past we have leaned too heavily upon European experiences to solve non-Western problems. More will be said about this in the next selection.*

At times anthropologists have had great surges of optimism about what they could tell governments and colonial administrators, or do themselves, to bridge cultural boundaries and make change more smooth or less costly in human terms. At other times the enormity and complexity of the problems and the inadequacies of their knowledge and theories have raised grave doubts and discouragement. The truth of what can and might be accomplished through "applied anthropology" lies somewhere between these poles of optimism and pessimism.

The optimism is generated by the fact that an anthropologist who has lived in a local community, who knows its leaders, its language, its details of custom, can very often see what is going wrong and how it might be set right. Many changes, procedures, laws, or policies that seem sensible enough to the administrator, the missionary, or the doctor may lead to problems the anthropologist can foresee immediately. What would happen in the Trobriand Islands if a missionary converted the "chiefs" and prohibited plural marriages? What might happen in a society where bridewealth signifies a contract between corporate descent groups and defined rights over the children, if an administrator or missionary outlawed bridewealth payments as "degrading to women"? What might happen among a people who believe in the magical power of substances introduced into the body, or the possibility of sorcery using substances from the body, if a well-meaning doctor gives injections or takes blood samples? I vividly remember watching nervously (and wondering how to avert a massacre or at least be on the winning side) while a member of a visiting medical team took fingernail and hair clippings from Kwaio pagans in the Solomon Islands and put them in cellophane bags; six months earlier a medical missionary had been speared nearby.

Administering, converting, educating, or ministering to the health of a tribal or peasant people involves communication across cultural boundaries, in both directions. Misunderstandings run rampant on both sides, as messages in one cultural code are interpreted in terms of another. The anthropologist, specialist in the nature of cultural codes and conversant with each one, can often serve as "cultural interpreter" or anticipate what messages would be misread and why.

He also can often suggest creative syntheses between the cultural traditions of a people and the changed situations and demands of modern life. A constitution may be possible that recognizes and builds on the authority of traditional leaders rather than bypassing them. A business cooperative might be formed in which the pattern of rights and responsibilities is modeled on traditional corporate or work groups (such as the Trobriand sub-clan or gardening team). Schools might teach the traditions, arts, and skills of a people, instead of European history. . . . Such enterprises can help to foster the pride and cultural identity so crucial to a people as they undergo sweeping changes.

Why, then, the pessimism? Basically, because anthropologists are no better than other social scientists in predicting and anticipating human behavior, in all its manifold complexity. When communication takes place between peoples, we are prone to view this as *two cultures interacting.* But cultures do not interact; warm-blooded individual human beings do, with all their idiosyncrasies and unpredictability. An anthropologist might, for example, persuade the government to build a well in the village he studied —and seemingly have anticipated and guarded against cultural misunderstandings. Yet the project might be rejected because political rivalry between two local leaders leads one to condemn the well, or because someone put a curse on it during a quarrel with his wife. Such turns of events are no more predictable in a village setting than they are in a modern nation.

There is another and related problem. When an anthropologist pene-trates into another way of life, he does so in layers or stages. After several months of fieldwork, a researcher learns the formal rules and groupings that lie on the surface of a society and its culture. At this stage, he may feel a confidence and understanding that later evaporates into a feeling of ignorance as he penetrates to a deeper level. Such alternating stages of insight and impotence continue as he probes further. Those who have penetrated most deeply into another way of life are more often left with a feeling of how complex it is and how profound and unpredictable are the ramifications of any decision or event than they are with a feeling that all is known, that prediction is possible.

Yet too often attempts at applied anthropology have been made in the flush of superficial understanding. Particularly when administrators need answers, they are not likely to want to wait years. Too often the role of the anthropologist as consultant has taken him into an area just long enough for the formal outlines to come into focus, and not long enough for them to dissolve into a blur again. This premature feeling of confidence has also been fostered by the involvement of partially trained or in-experienced anthropologists. Saving the world by anthropology, as by any other means, looks easier to the idealistic neophyte than to the experienced and battle-scarred campaigner. The partial cultural understanding of Peace Corps volunteers may produce the same overoptimism about the scale of the problems and the effectiveness of the tools we command to solve them. Both sources of premature confidence have contributed to a disillusionment on the part of some governments and anthropologists as to what anthropology can contribute in guiding policy. In the United States administration of Micronesian islands, for instance, the possibilities of applied anthropology were "oversold" in the early stages, and a more sober reassessment has been necessary.

A final problem in applying anthropological knowledge to practical policy is that very often the choice is between a set of dismal alternatives. It is often not a question of which course of action will work best; but rather, which will work less badly than the others. A people whose old order is breaking down, yet who if they opt for Western ways will be condemned by geography and resources to a life of poverty and isolation, have no desirable alternatives. They are the victims of a world that has swept past them; they can neither fully join nor ignore it. In such situations, the satisfactions of applied anthropology are few and the successes are still failures.

The possibilities and difficulties of applying anthropological knowledge to particular problems are set out in a number of books, to which the interested reader might usefully turn: Leighton's *The Governing of Men;* Spicer's *Human Problems in Technological Change;* Mead's *Cultural Patterns and Technological Change;* Barnett's *Anthropology in Administration;* Arensberg and Niehoff's *Introducing Culture Change;* Foster's *Traditional*

Cultures and the Impact of Technological Change; and Goodenough's *Cooperation in Change.* Each of them discusses in detail particular cases and problems—and shows (with varying degrees of optimism and pessimism) what has and has not been possible. Spicer's book, for example, describes a series of efforts to introduce technological changes—some of which "worked" and some of which failed dismally. What an applied anthropology might contribute to the problems of our own society, as anthropologists increasingly focus on ourselves rather than remote tribesmen, can be glimpsed if we consider the situation of urban blacks in America.

Social scientists have studied in great detail the problems of black Americans and the roots of hostility and prejudice in both directions. They have looked at the economic plight, psychological state, and sociological condition of urban blacks. But as of the time of writing we understand far less clearly the *culture* of American ghettos. The image urban blacks have of themselves, their condition, and the white majority is rapidly changing and inadequately studied. We know a good deal about how the mother-centered family without a permanently attached father looks to sociologists on the outside; we know much less about how it looks from the inside.

Endless predictions have been made about what would or would not happen if earning power increased markedly in the ghetto, if training for new jobs and access to them were made possible. Yet it is far too often assumed that values and motives in the ghetto are the same as those in white suburbia. The benefits of eliminating exploitative white landlords are explored, but much too little is known by "experts" about the position of such figures in the symbolic system and political process of the ghetto. Black policemen might—for cultural reasons—cause more problems than they eliminate. And the Negro "leadership" visible to white planners and administrators may have little to do with the subtleties of political process within the ghetto community.

"Experts" on urban development and poverty have repeatedly created housing projects that were sterile and inhospitable; and welfare projects that caused alienation and eroded pride. Many of the problems reflect cultural differences: an architect who thinks the apartment he designs is much "nicer" than a tenement may be creating an environment that would turn a bustling and human community into a series of isolated cells. An act intended as friendly concern and humanitarian involvement may be interpreted as condescending charity or alien intrusion. The cultural and symbolic dimensions of black identity and aspirations are emerging as central but remain little understood.

If the anthropologist has a special contribution to make in the study of black or other American minorities, it is because he does not take for granted that his subjects share his code of meanings and premises. He is trained to expect what is different and distinctive—to discover the foundations on which he is to build, not assume them. He knows that ringing doorbells to administer questionnaires, and the "game" of answering them, are elements of white American culture. He is more likely to treat a single family, or a single tenement, or a single street corner as a microcosm of the whole—not to see how large a sample size he can build up to make his numbers valid. He would seek to penetrate a code from inside, not document it from outside.

Whether a white American anthropologist can gain rapport in such an enterprise raises another question. For there is in these days of increasing sensitivity on all cultural frontiers a strong element of condescension and possible insult in "being studied." Increasingly this feeling pervades the non-Western world as well as American minority groups. Having thrown out the "imperialists," a people emerging onto the world scene may be faced with hordes of visiting social scientists. The anthropologist can hardly be surprised if they come to view this as a new wave of imperialist exploitation and a threat to growing pride.

In the black revolution, there is a quite legitimate feeling that when white America sends its social scientists to the ghettos to "find out what is wrong with them," the same smug assumptions that helped Columbus (and not the Indians) discover America are at work again. What is "wrong" could not be in the hearts and minds of the nice respectable inhabitants of white suburbia: it must be in the ghettos. The anthropology of American suburbia, perhaps most wisely conducted by Trobriand Islanders or Tiv, has scarcely begun. But it is encouraging to note that at the University of Papua–New Guinea, as of 1970, there is a growing body of anthropological literature by Trobrianders and Dobuans concerning themselves and the anthropologists who studied them. With luck we may some day have a Trobriand anthropologist's diary of the rigors of fieldwork among the North American natives.

Anthropology will soon be a less provincial and Western-dominated field. Scholars from India, Japan, Indonesia, Africa, and Latin America are increasingly active. Until anthropology is more broadly represented by scholars from the non-Western world, anthropologists cannot shrug off too casually the doubts some of their colleagues have recently raised: that they too have been in the colonialist ranks, and that academic imperialism can be as insidious as other forms. We also badly need a broadening of perspective such scholars can give. Anthropology has had to rely far too heavily on stretching the premises, logics, and semantic categories of European experience to fit non-Western cultures. We urgently need some stretching of the assumptions and categories of other peoples to fit us and to fit the tribal peoples from whose cultures we have sought to learn about human diversity.

. . . .

Whatever the national origin and credentials of the scholars who bring knowledge of cultural differences to bear on practical problems, they must share in some measure both the optimism and pessimism with which we began. On the one hand, policy laid down in ignorance of cultural differences wreaks havoc needlessly. The decisions that guide communication between peoples could be made much more wisely than they are, if those who perceived how and why could make themselves heard. On the other hand, man is an enormously complicated creature whose modes of thought and action we only partly understand. What experts take to be wisdom may in fact be folly. And in the emerging world of the latter twentieth century, solutions to the central problems of reconciling cultural pluralism with world order still lie beyond the horizon of our vision.

If anthropologists cannot provide simple answers about where man is, and should be going, they can perhaps bring their knowledge of human diversity wisely to bear on a final and crucial problem. In these days of social turmoil, of individual and collective revolution against the patterns of the past, what is the responsibility of the individual toward the codes and conventions of his society? And what are the possibilities that collectively we can reshape them for the better?

Views of man advanced through the centuries by Western thinkers have elevated and lowered him, seen him as debased deity or transformed animal, as perfectible or damned. They have seen men's customary ways of life as expressing their loftiest aspirations or as imprisoning man's true nature, as bringing him to fulfillment or as imposed on him at great cost.

With increased consciousness of man as a microorganism on a tiny speck in the cosmos, with the power to destroy himself and leave that speck barren, these questions haunt us. There is an increasing reverence for man as individual and as species, and a corresponding challenge to those tribal loyalties and conventions that, as a precipitate of men's past, divide them.

Must men then conform? Must they live by standards of cumulated tribal experience they find arbitrary, evil, or absurd? Or can they search individually and collectively for loftier visions of the cosmos and of man, and seek panhuman standards of value, morality, justice, responsibility, and dignity?

As modern thinkers apparently must, the anthropologist has moments of crushing pessimism when man seems in a downward spiral—poisoning and polluting his environment, madly overpopulating his planet, crushing the highest aspirations of the human spirit, and visiting death and destruction in the name of petty principles. But he is also led by visions of what man could be, if he would. His views of human nature, of social life, of cultural order and possibility, fluctuate accordingly.

But somewhere in midswing the anthropologist can bring his evidence to bear on the questions of conformity, individualism, and human nature so central in the vision quests of our time. Let us begin with first principles.

The notion that culture is something external to an individual—and which he can reformulate, flout, or do without—is untenable. First of all, human life is basically a process of *communication*. Communication requires a shared code, hence a large measure of conformity between an individual and at least some of his fellows. Being a philosopher-hermit, like returning to a life of self-sufficiency in the woods, is an escape possible to a few because the many maintain a social framework within which it is possible; and collective escapes produce new conformities at the same time they free people, often superficially, from old ones. The picture of rules and conformity that popular writings present is modeled more on the regulations of a swimming pool (no running, no diving) or an army post than on the unconscious rules of a grammar. If the superficial levels of conformity can be manipulated and discarded, the deeper levels constrain and shape the behavior of the most imaginative nonconformist. Moreover, the most avidly proclaimed freedoms from the conventions of society almost always lead the "rugged individualist" to wear the uniform of his particular subculture. Very few people do any really imaginative innovating, like growing a beard on one side of the face and shaving on the other, or painting themselves blue with woad.

But there is another and important side to all this. If man can express his humanity only through culture, if he can communicate only by conforming, that does not mean cultures cannot be reorganized and changed or that Utopias are impossible. The Menomini evidence shows that new ways can be learned and internalized; and the evidence of millennial and other "revitalization" movements shows that world view and social conventions can be radically restructured.

The answers to the dilemma of man, if there are answers, must lie not in a retreat into tribalism (as in quests for a miniature Utopia in the wilderness), but in a transcendence of tribalism. Human values *are* in grave danger in a world of technology and mass society; but dropping out cannot solve problems on a planetary scale, and that is how they must be solved. The challenge, somehow, is to achieve for modern man what the massive intrusion of the West has forced on tribal man—a radical restructuring of world view and experience, and a new integration. Whether that is possible can well be doubted; the challenge is increasingly grave. For our vision of the future, we need not less conformity but conformity to new patterns, collective exploration of new visions. As Margaret Mead pointed out, even our views of Utopia are constricted and drab. Such visions must also be wise and informed. If they are not illuminated by sound understanding of man's biological, social, and cultural nature and the limits of human possibility, they could destroy man, not save him. Here we have no better source of wisdom than the diverse ways of life, the many variations on the theme of being human, that we have glimpsed in these pages.

From "Decolonializing Applied Social Sciences," by Rodolfo Stavenhagen, *Human Organization*, Vol. 30, No. 4, 1971, pp. 334–343. Reproduced by the permission of the Society for Applied Anthropology and the author.

32 / Decolonializing Applied Social Sciences

RODOLFO STAVENHAGEN

The following article by Stavenhagen zeroes in on one topic that the Keesings alluded to in the previous selection—the need for Western anthropologists to listen to anthropologists from non-Western societies. This controversial article is an abridgement of Stavenhagen's talk given to a 1971 applied anthropology audience that was reeling from an earlier discussion on whether or not anthropology is "alive." Some replies to this article praise Stavenhagen. Other replies state that he is politically naive and is a Marxist humanist. Stavenhagen spins the heads of traditional applied anthropologists! He states that social sciences must change from the established study of the "underdog" (the ruled) to a study of the "dominate elite" (the rulers) and the "system of domination itself." Also, Stavenhagen forcefully states that applied social scientists cannot put themselves in a neutral position regarding ideological and political issues. He is proposing a strongly activist anthropological position, and many anthropologists raise doubts about the results of the approaches he advocates. Right or wrong, Stavenhagen is making applied social scientists take a hard look at their field.

It lies perhaps in the destiny of the social sciences that they should not only reflect the dominant forms of social organization of their times, but also—as they have done ever since they grew out of the social and political thought of the Enlightenment—that they should become major vehicles for the expression of the radical countercurrents and critical conscience that these very forms of organization have brought forth. This dialectical relationship between the social sciences and society finds its way into the ambiguous and frequently conflictive roles that social scientists as individuals are called upon to play in modern society.

It has lately been found necessary in some quarters to decry anthropology in general, and its applied variety in particular, for its links to colonialism and imperialism. I believe this to be a healthy development, for the historical relation between colonialism and imperialism as world-wide systems of domination and exploitation on the one hand, and the use of social science in the management of empire, on the other, has up to recently been overlooked or ignored. It can no longer be neglected, and it has become clear to many of us that the methods, the theories, the various "schools of thought," the very objects of study and observation in anthropology and other social disciplines have been deeply colored by this historical relationship. . . .

Let me add right away that I am deeply convinced of the very important contributions that anthropology and the other social sciences have made to the advancement of knowledge, irrespective of their various relationships with colonialism and imperialism; and particularly to knowledge of and about the so-called underdeveloped countries. I am also one of those who recognize the deep strain of humanism, progressivism, liberalism and radicalism that has been imbedded in the development of anthropology, and even in some of its colonialistic varieties.

Thus it seems to me that it is equally mistaken to deny the evident historical relationships between colonialism and anthropology (or between imperialism and the so-called sociology of development)—a question that lies in the domain of the sociology of knowledge—as it is to simply treat these disciplines as handmaidens of colonialist or imperialist domination.

For it is precisely out of the science of society that the most powerful critiques of colonial systems, imperialist domination, totalitarian political structures and bourgeois class society have sprung. New generations of radical social scientists have arisen—mainly in the Third World—who question some of the basic assumptions upon which social science in the industrial countries seems to stand. Yet it must be recognized that these social scientists themselves are a product of the way social science in general has developed.

I think we may look at the issues involved from two angles: the uses or application of social scientific knowledge in general, and the professional practice of applied social science.

Like all knowledge, social scientific knowledge forms part of humanity's cultural heritage. It is there to be used or applied by those who can and know how to make use of it. While social scientists may be held partially responsible for the uses to which the knowledge they produce is put, they can do little to actually control the process if they remain within the established rules of the scientific game (research, publish, teach). It is rules of the game that must be changed.

I think the issue hinges on two important aspects: the nature and quality of the research, and the diffusion of the information to potential users. But these two aspects are intimately linked, and they condition each other.

Anthropological studies are commonly criticised for being concerned with small-scale, part societies and it is held that this approach does not enable them to see wider issues and relationships necessary for a meaningful understanding of reality. The radical critique demands a holistic approach in terms of global social units and total societies. It is, however, not sufficient to simply state that tribal or peasant peoples, or village communities, are integrated into wider wholes (a truth that has not escaped anthropologists from the beginning). The task for anthropology is to unravel the mechanisms which relate the traditional anthropological unit of study to the wider society, to discover the mutual relationships and interconnections; to analyze cleavages, conflicts and contradictions. This is a question not of ideology, as some would have it, but of research methodology and adequate theory.

In general, anthropology—by concentrating on the small-scale, the isolated, the traditional—has not handled the theoretical aspects involved in these links and relationships satisfactorily. Few anthropologists who have carried out field work among tribal or peasant peoples have had a theory—even a general theoretical orientation—to help them explain such linkages. Unlike sociologists and political scientists, anthropologists have not given much attention to the interpretation of the national societies of which the object of their study is a part. On the average, anthropologists have been rather naive concerning national social structures or world systems. (I do not mean studies of national cultures or national character, which are quite numerous.) In fact, anthropological studies in underdeveloped countries have been much too culture bound, in the two meanings of this term. On the one hand, despite disclaimers to the contrary in the name of cultural relativism, whenever problems of social change are considered, we find linear models based on the assumption that modernization or development will lead necessarily to some kind of social structure similar to the capitalist industrial, middle-class, consumer societies we are ourselves a part of. On the other hand, by stressing, and more often than not, by reifying culture as a concept, anthropology has been unable to handle the problems involved in the analysis of total social systems.

Theories about national societies (or world-wide systems, for that matter), are of course not true or false in any absolute sense; they are simply more or less relevant in attempting to explain adequately a set of observable facts and their interrelationships. None of the existing theories, as far as I can judge, are directly verifiable or testable (in the laboratory sense that some "scientific purists" would like to have it). They necessarily reflect the value orientations of those who use them, but in their capacity to explain particular sets of facts they will in the long run turn out to be more or less adequate. And this of course has to do with what, indeed, one wishes to explain.

I am always touched by the prefaces to published monographs on Latin America, in which the grateful author expresses his acknowledgment to Don Simpatico, Donna Gracias and the other helpful inhabitants of San Pedro or San Miguel (or whatever the name of the barrio or the village might be), but for whose collaboration and hospitality the study might never have been written. Yet how frequently do those communities and these helpful informants whose lives are so carefully laid bare by proficient researchers actually get to know the results of the research? Is any effort made to channel the scientific conclusions and research findings to them; to translate our professional jargon into everyday concepts which the people themselves can understand and from which they can learn something? And, most importantly, to which they can contribute precisely through such a dialogue? Would it not be recommendable that efforts be made by the sponsoring institutions, with direct participation of the researchers themselves, to ensure that research findings be freed from the bonds of the specialized journals, the university libraries or the limbo of government files? Can books about peasants be brought to the attention of, discussed with and used by peasant organizations? Can studies on urban migrants be made to help labor unions and neighborhood voluntary associations to better understand, and thus solve, their problems? Cannot studies on social movements, popular rebellions and revolutions be shorn of their scientific and scholarly paraphernalia and made available to the revolutionaries themselves?

. . . .

In French-speaking Black Africa intellectuals and students tend to grade visiting foreign social scientists (particularly Frenchmen) according to their degree of mental decolonization before they begin to judge their professional capacities. In these countries the identification between colonialism and ethnology is such that the very name and nature of the discipline is in disrepute and rejected by many Africans. . . .

Still, in most cases, scholars in academic communities (particularly when they go back to their own foreign countries) can do relatively little to control the uses or misuses (or simply the nonuse) of the fruits of their labour. We often hear it said amongst radicals that social scientific produce is really only of use to repressive governments, the exploiting classes or the self-seeking imperialists. Some younger radical social scientists now refuse to publish their work, or to carry out research at all, on these grounds. While it is certainly necessary at times to delay or refuse publication of research findings because of possible harm it may cause to the groups involved, those who stand on this as a matter of principle will simply radicalize themselves out of meaningful social scientific activity. The point here, it seems to me, is to save social science and to ensure its use for humanitarian, not destructive, ends—but not to abandon the field altogether.

As I said earlier, I believe a part of the problem is the diffusion to the desired publics of the product of research. Yet it is not only a question of information transmittal per se; for the nature and characteristics of this transmittal (if built into the research itself, through a creative dialogue between researcher and Object-Subject of research) will turn it into a process of mutual learning and will thus change the very nature of the scientific activity. . . .

Yet precisely one of the more criticable and increasingly criticized aspects of social science—at least as far as the Third World is concerned —is that it is mainly concerned with studying the oppressed—from the outside. It should have become abundantly clear in recent years that the causes of oppression, or exploitation, or deprivation (relative or absolute), or simply backwardness and traditionalism, are to be found in the functioning of total systems, in the nature of the relationships binding the oppressed and their oppressors (or, if these words shock the sensibilities of those who think they are too value-laden, we may say the deprived and the privileged), into a total system. We must thus try to channel to the former not only scientific knowledge about themselves, but also about how the system works. And this requires giving attention to the other pole of the relationship, and perhaps the most important pole: that of the dominant groups.

The truly comprehensive understanding of social forces in a process of social change requires more than an analysis of the so-called underprivileged social groups or of social movements against established systems of domination. It requires the study of the system of domination itself, and particularly of the mechanisms whereby the social groups at the top, that is, the elites, fit into the general structure; how they react to and participate in the process of change; how they operate to maintain, adapt or modify existing systems. It is here that I see a vast new field of inquiry opening up for the radical social scientist. Compared to studies of Indians, peasants, tribal peoples, urban poor, marginal migrants and so forth, the scientific study of elites and decision-making at the upper echelons of the social edifice is still very sketchy. One would think that because of his social origins, his university education and his general place within the social structure, the social scientist should be well placed to carry out such studies; yet up to now his scientific and mental equipment does not seem to have carried him into this direction. By concentrating his attention upon the "underdogs" in society, the social scientist has revealed precisely those tendencies which are most subject to the radical critique: the paternalistic or "colonial" approach to the study of society. More than any of the other social disciplines, anthropology has been bound by these limitations. And perhaps for this very reason it is incumbent upon anthropology to break with its own past and set out upon new paths.

How many studies do we have of political elites and their decision-making processes; of the functioning of bureaucracies; of entrepreneurs (not only as innovators or modernizers but as political and economic interest groups); of foreign business communities in underdeveloped countries; of corruption among labor leaders; of advertising and the manipulation of ideologies, opinions, attitudes, tastes and the innermost emotions; of the role of estate owners in the maintenance of traditional agrarian society; of regional and local *cacicazgos* or *coronelismo;* of the influence of foreign diplomatic missions on national politics; of ecclesiastical hierarchies; of military cliques; of the role of the mass media; of oppressive educational systems; or simply of the varied and multiple aspects of repression (physical, cultural, psychological, economic) that dominant groups use to maintain the status quo? When studying Indian communities, how often have we analyzed regional political systems? When studying peasant villages, how frequently have we given attention to the operation of national market systems? When describing the urban poor, what role do we attribute to real estate speculation and economic interest in the development of cities? When addressing ourselves to the rural migrant in the process of industrialization, how conscious are we of the role and function of the multinational corporation in determining levels of investment, technology and employment opportunities? When judging the effects of community development, health or nutrition programs at the local level, how much do we actually know of the bureaucratic and political processes involved? Admittedly, these are difficult areas for the field worker to get involved in. And by tradition we have chosen the path of least resistance. It is easier to walk into a peasant hut than into an executive office, besides, the peasant is not likely to ever read our field report.

Nevertheless, if social science is to avoid becoming irrelevant to the social change process as it is occurring in the underdeveloped countries, then we must face these new challenges, make use of our sociological imagination, become observers, perhaps even participant observers of those institutions and areas of activity which are of significance. This is not easy, and such a change of focus will encounter enormous—but I hope, not insurmountable—difficulties.

Social scientific knowledge has long since ceased to be merely an academic fixture. Like all scientific knowledge, it has become (and increasingly so) an element of power (economic, social, political). Hence the rapid proliferation of "think tanks," data banks, documentation centers, clearinghouses, etc. The academic researcher (particularly the younger one) is no longer able to select his research activity simply by following his intellectual whims. His choice is governed by available funding, university institutes specialising in this or that area, "scientific fashion" (which is perhaps as tyrannical in its own way as are women's fashions in theirs), and other institutional considerations. Under these circumstances the accumulation of knowledge follows predetermined patterns over which the individual researcher exercises relatively little control. In the face of this situation, he can take one of three alternatives:

1. He can simply continue producing information—like an assembly line worker produces spare parts—without regard to its ultimate use. But surely such scientific alienation stands in direct contradiction to the role of the intellectual in society as a humanist and a social critic.

2. Or he can produce knowledge suited to prevailing and established interpretations of society, accepting and using in his work the premises upon which are predicated the continuity and stability of existing social systems. I would include under this heading the majority of studies on, say, acculturation, social class mobility, modernization, socioeconomic correlates of individual attitudes and behaviour, community monographs, etc., within the framework of functionalism and behavioralism. While such research has contributed considerably to an accumulation of knowledge in general, it has had little influence on changing prevailing patterns of the uses to which such knowledge is put and on the distribution of productive knowledge among different social groups. I am here consciously drawing an analogy between the accumulation of capital and the accumulation of knowledge in a capitalist society, insofar as both processes are an expression of the prevailing mode of social and economic organization.

3. Thirdly, he can attempt to offer alternative explanations; explore new theoretical avenues; and exercise his intellectual critique of established or accepted "truths," and at the same time promote the redistribution of knowledge in the fashion suggested earlier. At this point, the accumulation of knowledge may become dangerous in the eyes of those who control the academic or political establishment, and our scientists will have diminishing access to research funds, his contract may not be renewed, he may be forced to leave the university; and in extreme cases he will be obliged to leave the country or may be imprisoned. In some Latin American countries (such as Brazil and Argentina) this process has been notorious in recent years—but I do not think that it is specific to the southern part of the hemisphere or to the Western hemisphere at all.

While the accumulation of knowledge is an element of power, it does not necessarily always serve to maintain existing power structures. On the contrary, it may—and must—become an instrument for change which, through the awakening and development of a creative critical conscience, enables the powerless, the oppressed, the downtrodden, the colonized, first to question, then to subvert and finally to modify existing systems.

. . . .

Next to the important questions of what kind of research, for whose benefit, and the role of the social scientist as teacher, we also have the issue of the direct involvement of social scientists in the application of their knowledge.

Applied social science is generally held to mean the practice of a quali-fied social scientist in the interests of an objective not directly determined by himself, but by another group or agency, with direct consequences for the management of human affairs.

The moment a social scientist either sells his labor to the highest bidder on the professional market or puts his knowledge at the service of a gov-ernment, a bureaucracy, a political party, a labor union, an international organization or a revolutionary movement, then he can hardly claim to be simply a neutral observer. He becomes directly involved in the value systems and ideologies of the groups or organizations he works with, for, or against. When an industrial sociologist adopts the ideology of manage-ment or an applied anthropologist helps to improve colonial administra-tion or to incorporate Indians into national societies in Latin America, then a number of ethical or ideological questions must be faced squarely. The social scientist must become aware that he has made a choice and it is only in terms of the conscious recognition of the implications of this choice that he can exercise his applied scientific activity. The importance of such considerations in the exercise of applied social science is para-mount: the fact that they have been ignored or neglected by applied social scientists (many of whom have considered themselves to be amoral technicians) has led applied social scientists into the quandary in which they find themselves at present.

I believe the time is past when innocent social scientists, happy with newly discovered knowledge about human beings, could engage in a little harmless "human engineering," in the belief that all's to the good and without questioning the deeper implications of their action. I am personally of the opinion that the difference between social scientists who wittingly contribute to counterinsurgency programs in Southeast Asia or Camelot-style projects in Latin America and elsewhere, and the doctors who experimented on human guinea pigs in Nazi concentration camps is one of degree and not of kind. The end result is genocide. Yet these are, admittedly, extreme cases, where the moral issues involved are fairly clear and the world scientific community has had ample opportunity to make its feelings known on them.

Not all cases of applied social science are equally clear-cut. Let us briefly analyze only two kinds of situations of particular relevance to underdeveloped countries, that of applied social science in the context of international aid, and within the context of national development.

In the second half of the twentieth century international technical aid has become something akin to what Christian missionary activity among heathens used to be earlier. The same apostolic zeal, the same moral justi-fication, the same naiveté about economic and political realities, the same basic subservience to and lack of critical appraisal of the international system of domination itself. Social scientists who work on various kinds of development programs within the international framework (either bilateral aid projects or those connected with international organizations) have not, until recently, challenged the basic assumptions upon which such aid has been based, many of which constitute theoretical misconceptions still widely held in social scientific circles concerning the nature of underdevelopment, the characteristics of the development process, and the interrelationships between the developed part and the underdeveloped part of the world. Nevertheless, this very experience over the last twenty or so years has demonstrated (to those who wish to see) the hollowness of many of these assumptions and the fruitlessness of many of these programs. The Andean Programme that was widely publicized by several South American governments and international agencies some fifteen years ago (and in which a number of sociologists and anthropologists sharpened their professional teeth), has been quietly laid to rest; fundamental or basic education coupled with community development has undergone agonizing reappraisals in various United Nations agencies; among Peace Corpsmen the Committee of Returned Volunteers has proceeded to demystify the whole operation. Other cases could be mentioned. The social scientists involved in these programs have been the first to recognize their limitations. This has been one of their positive results: they have contributed to the development of the radical critique that I have proposed earlier.

Though there has not been much publicity about this, the professional staffs of experts and technicians in a number of international agencies have lately expressed grave doubts and serious criticism about the operations they are involved in, and about the basic orientations that seem to guide the actions of these organizations. While some of this criticism simply proposes greater efficiency in existing programs, much of it is addressed to the implicit (and sometimes explicit) assumptions regarding the development process. Many social scientists thus employed have of course become simply cogs in the international bureaucratic machines that they serve; others however are engaged in a painstaking process of rethinking and reshaping the basic concepts of multilateral international technical assistance.

It is of course true that the basic tenets upon which rests the international capitalist system are not being questioned by these organizations—thus FAO is not only committed to raise agricultural productivity in the world, but hopes to do so by strengthening the medium-sized market oriented entrepreneur; the ILO, through its tripartite vision of the world, sees private employers and salaried workers as a permanent fixture of the social scene; UNIDO does not challenge the role of private enterprise in industrial development; and of course the international development banks see their own role as complementary to that of the giant multinational corporations. Yet even within this overall framework, and despite the fact that in terms of the Third World's development needs international technical aid is simply a drop in the bucket, it is clear that social scientists have contributed something important. In Latin America, for example, the UN's Economic Commission, ECLA, has been decisive over the last two decades in shaping what might be called a Latin American consciousness about social and economic underdevelopment and the area's foreign dependence. Whatever the present status of the policies recommended by ECLA might be, it is undeniable that even those who reject them today have been deeply influenced by the social and economic currents of thought generated by the activities of this organization.

Of course, international aid programs are a far cry from social revolution, and if taken in isolation their efforts will be minute; but then the role of the applied social scientist, as I see it, is to act to the best of his ability in terms of his personal ethical commitments, within the institutional framework that he has chosen as his field of action.

For example, social scientists working within a project of international technical assistance for agrarian reform would play a completely different role today in, say, Chile than in a similarly-named program set up by the present regime in Brazil, or even by the military government of Peru (which is committed to carrying out a drastic agrarian reform). The key variable here is the kind of reform that national governments are willing to undertake, and not the philosophy of the international agency.

International organizations are not monoliths, but rather, like all bureaucracies, monsters with many heads. A certain amount of flexibility is inherent in their nature, and there is leeway within their structures for the committed social scientist. Somewhat more, I would say, than in military establishments or intelligence agencies.

Much more complex, and much more important to my mind, is the situation of the applied social scientist working within his own country in the Third World. He usually finds himself in the maelstrom of conflicting professional, political and ethical crosscurrents.

First of all, he is motivated by a profound and sincere desire to change things for the better for his country's population with whom he identifies completely. This motivation probably led him to choose the social sciences as a profession in the first place.

Secondly, he is eager to exercise his profession to the best of his ability, confronted, as he often is, with limited occupational opportunities in the academic field and in his profession in general.

Thirdly, he is conscious—with so many of his fellow students or professionals—of the causes and nature of his country's underdevelopment and of the functioning of imperialism or neocolonialism as it directly affects his own country's chances for development.

But very often it is only a visceral consciousness; he feels it but does not understand it intellectually. This leads at times to exacerbated nationalism and chauvinism: the "we know it all; you've got nothing to teach us" attitude towards foreigners. Yet nationalism has become a powerful force and national ethics is an important ingredient in the makeup of Latin social scientists.

Fourthly, he becomes conscious of the nature of his own country's class and power structures, and of the conflicting interests of the ruling groups (landowners, bureaucracy, dependent bourgeoisie, etc.) and the oppressed masses (Indians, peasants, urban marginals, working class).

Moreover, his country's government (whatever its specific political color) is committed to social and economic development as a national goal and has established any number of agencies the declared purpose of which is to bring about such development (national planning offices, regional development authorities, community action programs, preventive medical and public health services, and many others).

Our social scientist with applied inclinations is peeved because many of the responsible positions in these programs are occupied, as he sees it, by illiterate politicians, narrow-minded doctors, socially ignorant architects and other kinds of uncivilized, technocratic vermin. He knows that all the mistakes and failures that such programs have incurred are due to an inexcusable ignorance of social realities and that a social scientist, well armed with the latest research designs, nondirective open-ended focused interview schedules, multivariate statistical analysis and a couple of good operational hypotheses, will soon be able to show 'em. Within this framework, a kindly patron (university professor, friend in the government, or well-connected mother's brother) will surely come up with a not highly paid but challenging proposal: here's your chance to show what you can do.

Alas, our well-meaning, ambitious social scientist soon becomes enmeshed in bureaucratic red tape, administrative paper-pushing, political in-fighting and general lack of receptivity to his world-shaking ideas. Furthermore, he is never actually given any *power,* and there is nothing as irritating to a social scientist in an underdeveloped country as *not having any power.* So either he accepts defeat and lets social science slowly slip away from him, or he stands and fights the system, with mixed results.

You will notice that I am only half joking when I draw this stereotyped picture. In truth, the dilemma of the applied social scientist, particularly of the radical type, is difficult. The urge to "do something," to contribute to social change at whatever level in countries as needy as these, is great. And small and large changes are in fact taking place everywhere; many of them, particularly in Latin America, seem at first glance to be truly revolutionary when seen within the framework of traditional social structures, especially in the rural areas.

. . . .

A particularly relevant issue in Latin America at the present time is *indigenismo,* a term which denotes the various government programs directed at the incorporation of backward Indian populations into the mainstream of national life. Recently such programs have come under heavy attack by radical social scientists, particularly in Mexico and in Peru. The basic goal of *indigenismo* cannot of course be quarreled with: to improve the living standards of the Indian populations. It is the ideological premises upon which *indigenismo* is based which are being questioned. And these have to do with the prevailing conceptions about what constitutes the so-called Indian problem and about the nature of the process of national development. Indian societies in Latin America have been traditionally viewed by anthropologists in terms of a number of cultural criteria which set them off from the so-called national culture. Changes undergone by these societies have been handled as a process of acculturation. Regional systems in which Indians and non-Indians interact have been termed caste systems. The guiding hypothesis for *indigenistas* has been that an accelerated process of directed acculturation or culture change will help break down this caste system, raise the Indian communities to the level of the surrounding environment and integrate Indians as fully fledged members of the national society. The nature of the national society itself was rarely analyzed. The mechanisms whereby the dominant classes of this national society (and before it, the colonial society) had in fact already integrated the Indians in a system of oppression and exploitation ever since the Conquest, but particularly since the expansion of capitalist production in agriculture, were referred to as historical background but were not considered relevant to the present situation. By refusing to recognize the essential characteristics of the national society to which they belonged (not to mention the nature of the State as an expression of the national class system), the *indigenistas* squarely placed the onus of backwardness on the Indian communities themselves; on their culture, on their value systems and, ironically, on their supposed isolation. (Elsewhere I have criticised this conception and proposed an alternative interpretation.)

Is it the role of applied anthropologists in *indigenismo* to hasten the disappearance of Indian cultures? To impose on them the middle-class urban values of a competitive, destructive, bourgeois society? To sanction, through official policy, the accelerated proletarianization or marginalization of Indian populations? To strengthen, through their action, other newer and perhaps more pitiless forms of economic exploitation? These are some of the questions that a newer generation of *indigenistas* is asking itself. Of course these processes are occurring by themselves, and official *indigenistas* will hold that they are in fact combating them through enlightened paternalism, technical assistance, education programs and the like. Critics, however, are doubtful, and would like to see a new kind of *indigenismo* as a powerful dynamic force which will serve not only bureaucratic palliatives to agonizing cultures and downtrodden peasants, but which will counter ethnocide as it is currently being practiced in Latin America and which will serve as a rallying point for the revolutionary transformation not only of the Indian communities but of the national societies themselves.

We may see by this example that the role of the applied social scientist in national development cannot be neutral; he cannot remain true to the ethical principles of his science and at the same time refuse to take a stand on the wider ideological and ethical issues of the societal processes in which he is involved as a practitioner. And as the case of the *indigenismo* shows, it is not a question of science versus politics, but of one kind of science-in-politics versus another.

Certainly no amount of applied social science, whether romantic, official, bureaucratic or radical, can alter by itself the social forces that are at work. But the committed social scientist has an obligation to raise the issues, to ask the embarrassing questions, to carry the critique through to its conclusions, to create new models in place of the ones he is obliged to discard. And if he can, to take the necessary action.

33 / The Plight of the Old Order Amish

JOE WITTMER

*In these pages Wittmer carries a plea to anthropologists and other social
scientists who assume the ethical responsibilities of social engineering.
Applied social scientists who play crucial roles in the determination of
governmental policies in relation to religion and ethical minorities are
being made more aware of the plight of the Old Order Amish. The Amish
are conservative religious peoples living in rural America who want to
pursue their traditional life-style but feel threatened by the turbulent
society around them. Wittmer, a former Amishman, describes the Amish
issue with both inside and outside views. Wittmer asks that we do not
hasten the disappearance of the Amish way of life; do not impose on the
Amish the middle-class values of a competitive society; do not force the
Amish to migrate to other countries to continue to enjoy religious freedom.
The reader should keep in mind the previous article by Stavenhagen, to
judge how Wittmer's plea is compatible with what Stavenhagen believes
the applied social scientist should do.*

The Old Order Amish came to America in the 17th century, at the in-
vitation of William Penn, to escape the persecution they suffered in Europe
because of their anti-Baptist views. The refusal of the Amish, who now
number over 50,000, to be assimilated into the American "melting pot"
has made them subject to much hostility and harassment. Many Amish feel
that their simple, pious life is threatened by the turbulent society surrounding them and are emigrating to Central and South America.

The mainstream society's emphasis on high-powered cars, computers,
and contraceptive devices is conspicuously absent from the horse-and-
buggy Amish world. The Amish live by the scriptural admonitions to
"Come out from among them, and be ye separate," and "Be ye a peculiar
people." In their isolated communities, they attempt to stay apart from
the secular influences of the outside world. All Amishmen are oriented
toward one goal, eternal life. Their traditions—industry, careful steward-

ship, the sweat of the brow, the wearing of beards by married men, German as a first language, drab home-sewn clothing, their methods of raising children—are seen as ways of attaining that goal. Everything they do has religious significance; religion is a seven-day-a-week affair.

The Amish prefer the traditional and old; anything new is considered of the devil. It is practically impossible for them to maintain these values in modern America. Some examples of the difficulties they face are the following:

1. The Old Order Amish have always maintained that their children do not need a high-school education. They believe that excessive contact with modern education will spoil the Amish youth for farm life. They are opposed to the modern curriculum of the new consolidated schools and feel that in these schools their children will be overexposed to the "world." Amish parents contend that, according to the Bible, their children belong to them, and thus are not to be educated by the state nor for the benefit of the state. Since the Amish do not believe in education beyond the eighth grade, they also maintain that the teachers of their children should have only eighth-grade educations. Amish parochial school systems have run afoul of the law in every state where they have been attempted. Literally hundreds of documented cases could be cited in which Amish fathers and mothers have gone to jail for refusing to send their children to the "contaminating" local schools. Amish emigrants usually cite the school problem as a basic reason for their leaving the country.

2. A law recently passed in one Midwestern state required that a large, triangular, bright-orange emblem be affixed to the back of all slow-moving vehicles. The Amish viewed this three-cornered emblem as a hex symbol, "the mark of the beast" described in the Bible, and refused to affix it to the back of their buggies. The color of the emblem was also offensive to the "plain" people. When the authorities refused to compromise on neutral-colored reflection tape, several Amish farmers went to jail for 20 days for following their religious scruples. (The Amish always refuse to pay their fines, as this would imply guilt in the "eyes of the Lord.") At least three Amish families emigrated from the state before the governor declared a moratorium on the emblem.

3. The roads through the Amish communities, made of dirt and gravel, are continually being replaced by local road departments with hard-surfaced ones. An Amishman's buggy horse can withstand being driven as long as ten to twelve years on the dirt-gravel roads, but will do well to maintain his legs for twelve months on a hard-surfaced road. Of course, the new roads also draw more and faster automobiles along with camera-toting tourists. The Amish are opposed to any graven images, and thus their religious scruples prohibit their being photographed.

4. An Amishman feels close to God when tilling the soil, and farming is the sanctioned occupation. Until recently, Amish farmers have been able

to buy farms from retiring non-Amish neighbors, often lending one another money at 2 or 3% in order to help the young Amish farmer obtain land. Non-Amish farmers in the community resent this. Perhaps for this reason, many public auctions of farm lands are now being held on Sunday, eliminating the Sabbath-abiding Amishman from the bidding. Because of the scarcity of land, many Amishmen have recently taken jobs in factories sanctioned by the church. Since the Amish religion does not permit a member to join the union, these jobs are usually short-lived.

5. An Amishman's income is supplemented by selling his farm products to local city markets. One of the largest economic supplements is the selling of fluid milk. However, new laws and new demands on the part of milk inspectors, in the absence of electricity, have made it almost impossible for the Amish to continue to sell milk to the local dairies. Also, the Amish refuse to allow their milk to be picked up on Sunday, and many dairies want the Amish farmer's milk seven days a week or not at all.

6. The Amish come under continual harassment as they drive along the road in their open buggies. The tossing of firecrackers and stones is a common occurrence. Recently an Amishman was killed in Indiana when struck by a piece of asphalt thrown from a passing car. Also, since it is known that an Amishman pays his bills in cash, Amishmen are often robbed at home or on the road.

7. The Amish do not believe in any kind of military participation, including noncombatant activities, and their young men leave the community to serve for two years in mental hospitals, regular hospitals, or other forms of civilian activity. These 18-year-old Amish youths, raised so carefully within the confines of the Amish home and community, often suffer from insecurity as they enter the strange working world of the hospitals and find themselves forced to defend their beliefs. Nervous breakdowns, ulcers, and so forth are often the result.

The Amish consider themselves "defenseless Christians" and will not employ any form of protection, including litigation. A committee known as The National Committee For Amish Religious Freedom was founded in 1967 to intervene for the Amish in court cases and other types of encounter. At first, the Amish were reluctant to permit the committee's intervention, and they have not as yet permitted any jury trials (not wanting the responsibility for sending to Hell the twelve people who would have to judge them). As of this writing, the committee has yet to win a court case on behalf of the Amish. A case involving school attendance is currently being taken to the Supreme Court. This court refused, by a vote of four to three, to hear a similar case in 1967.

The Amish are a tenacious people and are intent on maintaining their way of life. Several Central and South American countries, eager to have the Amish farmers help bring their bush country under cultivation, have guaranteed them complete religious freedom, freedom from any type of military participation, freedom with regard to educating their youth. Entire Amish communities have moved to these countries. It is sobering to realize that a peace-loving sect finds it necessary to emigrate from *America* to seek freedom from religious persecution.

To me, as one who left the Old Order Amish at age 16 and whose family remains Amish, their tradition represents a heritage that it would be foolish to destroy, and their forced emigration is an outrage. As a former Amishman and a member of the above-mentioned committee, I wish to bring the plight of the Amish to the attention of the world community of anthropologists and others in the hope that Amish culture can be preserved.

Part 7 / QUESTIONS AND PROBLEMS FOR DISCUSSION

1. Establish arguments for and against the following statement. "Scientists have no social responsibility."
2. Why is the field of anthropology concerned with such activities as economic development, technical assistance, and public health programs?
3. Review recent news magazines and select three or four areas in which knowledge gained from anthropology can be effectively applied. Why did you select these areas?
4. "Anthropologists in today's world have the important task of being active in initiating cultural change." Discuss this statement.
5. Formulate a few questions you would be sure to have answered before you would attempt to introduce a new program (farming technique, health plan, etc.) into an alien cultural tradition.

8/ ANTHROPOLOGISTS ARE HUMAN, TOO

It is a self-evident truth to state that anthropologists are human, but how often do students really visualize the anthropologist in the field as a human being as well as a scientist? Selections included here are intended to aid students to better understand anthropology and anthropologists from a point of view generally absent in introductory courses. The following selections add the dimensions of observation, personal experiences, and personal reactions of anthropologists who work in the field. Not only does the field anthropologist learn about human behavior and different cultural settings, but he also learns in a special way that he is a human being.

Fieldwork in anthropology is a stimulating and delightfully human experience in itself. To be sure, it is difficult work, requiring much preparation and time, but the rewards far outweigh the hardships. However difficult the hardships, the anthropologist in the field becomes a part of the world of the people with whom he is working, and close friendships often develop. Although the fieldworker is only a temporary part of these social networks and leaves after his research has been completed, he undergoes a variety of social experiences, which become a vital part of his character. Workers in the field attempt to be objective about their observations and records, yet to be completely dispassionate about human beings would itself be a nearly inhuman achievement. Anthropologists are human, too, and when we understand this we begin to realize that the use of human feelings and perceptions adds a new dimension to the scientific study of human life. The following selections allow the reader to observe the anthropologist in the field.

34 / Being a Palauan

HOMER G. BARNETT

This selection is from the diary of Homer Barnett, written in 1948 when he was engaged in ethnographic fieldwork in the Palau Islands of the South Pacific. Since this selection is from a personal journal rather than a formal monograph, it is of particular value in noting events and activities, both large and small, that make up the day-to-day life of a working anthropologist. The journal illustrates how Barnett related to the community in which he lived, the personal friendships he nourished, and the humor and the tragedy that he encountered while living with the Palauans. The reader should try to picture himself in Barnett's position so to better understand the difficulties of being both objective and subjective, of being both on the outside and inside of the Palauan way of life. Here, then, you will find a slice of life of the Palauan people and of an anthropologist in the field.

August 23 We were taken from Koror to Ngarard by two Navy vessels. We landed somewhat upriver at a house in the hamlet of Ngbuked. Our interpreter, Charlie Simmons, told us to remain in the boat until the chief of Ngbuked was summoned. When he arrived we shook hands and, after some conversation between him and Charlie, we went ashore. The young men who were to carry our heavy gear were fishing, so it was decided that the chief, Charlie, Al, and I should go on to Ulimang and send men for our equipment later. We ascended a low central crest along a wide, cleared pathway through Ngbuked, the chief of the village in the lead. Houses, some of them of the old-type construction, were irregularly spaced off the pathway that over most of its length through the hamlet was paved with stones. On the top of the rise was a men's clubhouse, in about the center of the hamlet. At one end there was a siren. Charlie sounded it three times —the call for an assembly of the people of Ulimang, of which Charlie is a chief.

After about twenty-five minutes we arrived at Ulimang, on the east coast. A middle-aged man came to meet us. We sat on a high bench on the edge of the school grounds while he sat on the ground in front of us. After a short talk we proceeded to the schoolhouse where we were to stay until other arrangements could be made. On the way to Ulimang a few women in doorways spoke to the two chiefs as we passed, but I was impressed by the apparent lack of curiosity about us. Even the children seemed indifferent. Heads were not hanging out of doorways; none apparently appeared from cover. People did not follow or congregate around us. There were several children playing on the broad sandy schoolyard, but they remained where they were, and only came near some time after we had stopped and two more chiefs from nearby villages arrived to greet us.

For the rest of the afternoon, until about 4:30, we sat with the chiefs while they chatted. In the meantime, school boys and girls were sent to get such pieces of our equipment as they could carry. By 5:00 I was getting rather hungry, and was undecided as to what to do. Finally Charlie explained that the first chief of the district, whom we had met in Koror, had sent a message saying that we were to arrive on the following day, and that the people had intended getting a feast ready for us then. As it was, food was being prepared but it would be late in coming. It did arrive after dark, brought by two women on trays carried on their heads. The school teacher had lighted a lamp on our table in the schoolroom building. He helped set the food before us. We ate alone while the Palauans sat outside talking. After we had eaten we joined them. Charlie asked whether we wanted food brought to us each day, or whether we wanted a girl or a boy assigned to help us prepare our food. I explained that we would do our own cooking and most of our other domestic chores.

Before eating we went to see a house nearby. It was being built by a young man, Kai by name, for his own use, but it was offered to us. It was quite suitable and I was pleased at our good luck, but I tried to make it plain to Charlie that we did not want to take it at the inconvenience of the owner. I was assured that he had enough room in another house just back of the one that we would occupy, which did not convince me, and I was determined to compensate him in some way.

August 24 The canned foods that we have brought with us are mostly the so-called C rations issued by the military government for its personnel. They are, I trust, nutritious, but they are nonetheless tasteless. I have realized over the past month in passing through Guam and Koror that one of my personal needs is for American-style fresh vegetables—carrots and cabbage exempted. I could add fresh beef, but that is out of reason, because here there is only fish, which I must learn to like. I think I will start a vegetable garden. If it succeeds that would amaze no one more than myself.

August 27 No progress has been made toward getting settled in our house. Monday afternoon Charlie told us we could move in yesterday.

We got packed in the morning, but no one came for our baggage, and since we are regarded as chiefs it would be beneath their expectations of us to transport our own effects. This attitude has its advantages but it belongs to another situation. If the people continue to regard us as sahibs the social distance thereby created will deny us the participation that is essential to our purposes. I am referred to and addressed as "Doctor," which may set up still another barrier. This stems from the auspices of the military government, from which I want to disassociate myself as much as possible. Charlie told me earlier that the Ulimang people were notified in advance by the officials in Koror that a "Doctor Somebody" would be coming to live in their village.

Yesterday I gave a package of mints to the oldest girl among about twenty children playing on the schoolground. The rest displayed no eagerness or curiosity about it, even the smallest of them, aged three to five years. The girl to whom I gave the mints walked around with them for awhile and all the children continued to play as they had done before. Finally, after fifteen or twenty minutes they all sat in the shade and the girl proceeded to divide the candy among them, the others sitting in a ring about her. I gave the same girl a package of mints today under the same conditions, and the same thing happened. The children, all of whom seem to be residents of this village, play most of the day on the schoolgrounds. They pay no attention to us, and remain at the opposite corner from us. This is presumably their normal habit. However, I am beginning to suspect that they, as well as the adults of this village, have been told to ignore us, or at least not to bother us.

. . . .

December 18   Just in the past few days I have noticed a change in the attitude of the people toward us. Or at least I think I do. Mingling as we have with them so regularly, they take us more for granted. They are less self-conscious, and there is no interruption in the proceedings, whatever they might be, when we arrive. No special attention is given to us. They are not so camera shy as they were in the beginning either—at least the men are not. The kids congregate around us as before but less out of curiosity than in friendliness.

December 19   The men from four of the villages of the district gathered at the Alap clubhouse to repair damages caused by the storm. All of them sewed nipa leaf patching, sitting in the shade on the platform in front of the clubhouse. Murphy sewed some too, which pleased the others. We came home at noon, and Al went back to work with the men and stayed until 4:30. He and I are invited to a completion feast tomorrow.

December 24   The blustery weather continued through the morning. I made a tour of the villages to check on activities, but was soon discouraged by the rain. I asked Kai if anything had been planned to celebrate

Christmas and he said no, that a person had to go either to Koror or to Ngerchelong where there were to be services. Al and I have heard rumors, however, that native dances will be held here, either tomorrow or on New Year's. The Protestants are planning to go to Ngerchelong, and one of them asked me to accompany them. I refused, thinking that maybe something more interesting was going to be held here and that they were again trying to lure me away so I could not witness it. It now appears that I was wrong, but it is too late to switch, because I invited Kai to dinner tomorrow.

December 25 Kai appeared early, all dressed up, with his hair oiled and plastered down. He had promised to make noodles, which he had learned to do from the Japanese. He also wanted to watch our biscuit-making and other preparations. Instead, Rdor, his brother-in-law from across the path, brought noodles and stayed to watch and to help. Kai and I killed and plucked a chicken; Rdor cleaned it. The four of us had a gay time while dinner was being prepared—Al doing all the cooking. We were ready to eat by 3:00. Still I had seen nothing of Kai's wife, Emei, so I asked about her. She had gone to her taro field. It still did not occur to me that she was not to eat with us. It took a minute for me to grasp this—which I should have known, for Emei would not eat with Kai and me when I went to his house about 8:00 P.M. last Saturday before the family had eaten and was invited to stay for a meal. Emei and the children went in the other room and ate there. Families do not eat together when a guest is present, I know; but I thought that with this family it would be different.

December 27 It was a beautiful moonlit night and I could not go to sleep. I thought I heard singing in the distance. I fell asleep and awakened at 3:00 A.M. and again thought I heard music so I got up and walked along the beach. The tide was out, and the moon was high. It was just right for a dance and I believe that one was going but I could not locate it.

December 29 In the afternoon, beginning at 2:00, Al and I attended a district court session. Two of the village chiefs served as judges. There were four cases: A young man recently returned from Guam had beaten on a high-ranking man's door late at night; another man was charged with something that was not clear to me—and I am not certain it was clear to him either; three young school teachers were severely reprimanded for being drunk and showing off; and another man wanted to divorce his wife. This last case developed into a discussion between all concerned, and it was only secondarily a court case. It took a long time to argue that one through. Court was not over until 5:30.

.   .   .   .

March 10 This morning I passed the home of Saig, whose wife had a baby on February 6. She was sitting in the doorway with nothing on but her pants, and was not at all embarrassed when I asked her how the baby was. She is the first woman who has not tried hastily to cover her upper body when Al or I appear. She was just as casual the other time I stopped to see the baby, though then she was partly covered with a ragged dress. Most women are embarrassed even to nurse children in my presence. Emei has several times hastily taken her breast from her baby when I have unexpectedly appeared. A few women on the Koror boat have gone ahead with their nursing in a half-concealed way when I have been near them in the cabin.

March 13   Emei told me this morning that Risa, an elderly woman of about sixty, came to her home last night and waited for me so she could tell me about old Palauan birth customs. Emei had asked her to do this. A little later I met Risa on the path in front of our house and we set a time for me to go to her house tonight. She talked freely and easily. She, like many others, knows about Kubary (a German ethnologist) and praises his knowledge of Palauan language and customs. She knows a few German words herself she said, and then proceeded to sing *The Kaiser Is a Good Man*—to the tune of *God Save the King*.

March 16   About 7:00 this evening Risa came to see me and whispered that a young woman living nearby had given birth, but that the placenta had failed to appear. She had been sent by the chiefs to see if I could help. I put two aspirin tablets in my pocket and followed her to a small house in one room of which the sick woman lay with several older women sitting close by. The other room was crowded with men. The sick woman had a headache and a slight fever, so I offered the tablets saying that there was nothing else that I could do. Some of those present were obviously skeptical. I found it almost impossible to explain to them that although I am a "doctor" I really am not.

March 19   The women's work group cleared the trails to the cemetery and around the clubhouse. I approached them with my movie camera and asked if I could take pictures of them at work. I was agreeably surprised, for they were quite willing, only showing embarrassment about stooping over with their backsides to the camera. Risa was especially helpful, and even made an old-fashioned hat of banana leaves, such as women used to wear in the fields, and put it on for my benefit. Many of the women sang as they worked. I was with them for an hour or more, after which I came back to the clubhouse and talked with three old women for awhile. They too were very friendly. One of them asked if I could get some dye for her graying hair. She explained that the Japanese women dyed their hair and that the Palauan women copy them.

March 22   I scarcely got out of my chair today from 8:30 in the morning until 2:00 this afternoon. While I was still writing notes after breakfast, Tura dropped in. He wanted a pair of spectacles. Last week I gave a pair to Rdor. (I brought fifteen pairs, having bought them at Woolworth's before I left.) The word that I have them spread rapidly. Several of the people really need glasses and this is the only way they can get them. I pumped Tura for an hour, and when his brother arrived I began on him. Soon another man showed up. I steered the talk to religion and Tura told some myths and described shamanistic practices. He shied away from contemporary religious beliefs. When this seemed to end in an impasse we turned to family histories and to kinship terminology.

March 26 About 9:00 A.M. I took Risa a package of cigarettes in return for a fish she brought me last night. She told me a child had died earlier in the morning in Alap. This was sudden news to me, so I got busy and asked the child's relatives if I could attend the funeral. All said that it would be O.K. I went to Alap with several of them around 10:00, and spent the rest of the day watching the funeral rites. Later I questioned Emei and Risa about what I had seen and about the relationships of the child to the people who were present.

From the preface of "Archaeological Survey of Northern Georgia," by Robert Wauchope, *American Antiquity*, Vol. 31, No. 5, Pt. 2, 1966. Reproduced by permission of the Society for American Archaeology and the author.

35 / Reminiscences

ROBERT WAUCHOPE

The experiences of an ethnographer in the South Pacific are in some ways similar, and in some ways dissimilar, to the experiences of an archeologist in the southeastern United States. Wauchope's reminiscences as an archeologist in Georgia from 1938 to 1940 are filled with personal experiences ranging from humorous events to frustrating activities. This selection is of particular value since it is one of only a few written accounts of fieldwork with the WPA projects during the 1930s. This era of American archeology was one of intensive work in rural America, using local and mostly inexperienced crew members. Wauchope vividly recalls the hardships of fieldwork: intensive heat, freezing weather, and rough terrain. He also recalls the hospitality and kinship of the people of that time and place. Here is a peek into the life of an archeologist at work.

For over twenty years I have remembered my 1938–40 stay in Georgia as one of the most interesting, certainly one of the busiest, and in many respects one of the happiest experiences of my life. I remember above all the wonderfully hospitable people who gave me their cooperation, help, and friendship in so many ways. . . .

The rural inhabitants of northern Georgia were among the most hospitable people, in their own way, I have ever met. Many a freezing night I warmed body and soul at their cabin fireplaces and listened to some of the finest folk music and tallest tales I have ever heard; for me, a stranger and flatlander, to be invited into their homes meant more to me than one who does not know these people can imagine. For when you approach a mountain house for the first time, in north Georgia, the man on the front porch is likely to disappear quickly, the womenfolk hide, and the hounds begin to bay. Once they become your friends, however, their concern for you can become downright embarrassing. I frequently unloaded my pickup truck in Athens or Atlanta after a winter drive down from the hills, and found, perched on top of piles of pottery bags, in plain sight of anyone who wanted to see, a half-gallon fruit jar of highly illegal, home-grown corn whiskey which some anonymous benefactor had felt I would need during the long cold ride home.

The famed "water boy" of WPA projects was a mere figurehead in north Georgia winter field work. Each man kept his own jug behind some nearby tree or bush, and about every half-hour, all day long during the bitter months on the windswept bottomlands, each workman would disappear for a moment, emerge wiping his mouth with the back of his hand, warm himself at the fire, and then, refueled so to speak, go back to his digging. I learned how to roll a Ford through the worst mudholes, taught by experts: the men who loaded their own old Model A's with moonshine and outran the sheriff across the lonely red clay roads almost every night of the week—less for profit, I always thought, than for sport.

It was often the independent small farmer who was quickest to give us permission to dig on his land. Many larger operators and absentee landowners were equally generous and interested in our work, but a few were suspicious, afraid, or simply uncooperative, and one or two deliberately tried to hold us up for money long after our excavations had begun. Although we were protected by written permits, nevertheless we were determined to leave only good will behind us everywhere, and more than once we filled our trenches and moved out rather than give the farmer any excuse for complaint. The infuriating belief we met everywhere was that we were really digging for gold. I do not know how many times crafty individuals tried to trick us into "reading" petroglyphs for them, on the pretense that they could read most of it but wanted us to fill in a few passages! Here is a typical entry in my log, for January 18, 1939:

A man from Ball Ground walked all the way out to the dig to tell me about some Indian signs on the other side of the river. He said that he would take me to see them if we could slip off without anyone seeing us. I explained that we are not hunting gold and if we went anywhere it would have to be openly. We drove across the river and after devious wanderings parked the car. We walked a mile through the woods down the river. My guide looked back across his shoulder repeatedly and talked in a hushed voice. The petroglyphs turned out to be grooves caused by weathering and by roots growing along the surface of some big boulders. He then wanted to take me to another spot to see Indian signs on trees and rocks showing where gold was buried: the rocks we had just looked at "pointed to them." Declined.

On February 13, 1939, my diary records the following, which was about par for the course that winter:

To begin with, we found the 1½-ton truck absolutely dead. We transferred to the station wagon and drove to Mr. H.'s house for the permit which he had signed, but nobody was at home. We returned to Ball Ground and Mr. B. swore that he had personally seen the permit signed, so we took a chance and drove to work without it. On arriving at the Settingdown Creek site, which we thought was Mr. H.'s property, we were told that it belonged to Mr. F. in Ball Ground and that Mr. H.'s site was farther upriver, so we walked back to the road, climbed in the station wagon, and before going fifty yards we stalled in a terrible mudhole. Dug out with shovels and immediately bogged down again fifty feet farther on and had to repeat the performance. Then we parked the vehicle and walked two miles down into the river valley carrying all our tools and equipment. We finally found the site but it was almost noon before we got dirt moving. Neither Myers nor I had brought lunch with us, for we had intended to return to Ball Ground, so we worked all day long without a bite to eat. During most of the afternoon we had to listen to an old man who tagged about telling us how much gold the Indians had buried and how unlikely we were to find it at this particular place. In desperation to get away from him, Myers and I walked out in the middle of a big field and dug a very small hole with a trowel, and out of a possible two hundred acres our little six-inch hole hit a skeleton only a foot below the surface. We decided life was not too black after all.

Three days later, February 16, 1939:

The road to the site we found yesterday was very bad after two days of rain so we took the 1½-ton truck; it is unwieldy and skids, but it has the power to pull out of almost anything. Nine miles out of Canton, after turning into the field road that goes down into the bottoms, we had a puncture, and then found that our spare tire was also flat and we had no pump. So we unloaded all the tools and surveying instruments and walked the remaining mile and a half to work. Started an exploratory trench and several test pits; found two burials. Mr. W. came to see the work and carried me back to Canton with the spare tire; I bought some patching, repaired the tire, and then Mr. W. took me back as far as our stranded truck. Returned to Ball Ground at night and worked until after midnight on another WPA unit cost analysis. We found to our great alarm that the average cost per unit for our project had risen two ten-thousandths of a dollar! To bed, dead.

And now to show that troubles could mount on all fronts, I quote the next two entries two days later. Here is February 18:

After work I drove to Atlanta and met with the Atlanta members of the Executive Committee of the Society for Georgia Archaeology at the home of Mr. X. He gave a fine short report on the work of the survey and then the committee spent the rest of the evening giving me hell for not keeping more publicity in the papers, and for not calling on or writing to each of them regularly to keep them in touch with the work. Mr. Z. of the Associated Press was there and put in the word that if I would only give him an article he would see that it went out over AP. They all kept referring to such trifling omissions in my work that I felt too disgusted to reply.

About two months ago while working at Sandtown, I took an Associated Press feature writer, at his own request, to the excavation and spent the entire day explaining everything to him and pointing out items of human interest that I thought he'd like to work into his story. Instead of using anything that I showed him or anything that he actually saw, he wrote me two days later asking me to furnish him with data supporting the following heading which he had decided on for his story: "First Gunmen or Gangsters in America were the Roving Hill or Mountain Indian Tribes Who Preyed on the More Peaceful Indian Tribes Habitating Swamps." [This is a direct quote.]

And then the next day's entry, Sunday, February 9:

The Executive Committee of the Society and a great many guests, which it had invited, came up to Cherokee County to inspect our work. First I showed them our maps and field records, in which they displayed little interest. Then we spent several hours at the excavation at Ball Ground, and they were enthusiastic. Since the weather had been clear for several days I took them to our dig at the other site, for the road to it is the best around here. After leaving the highway, I had them park their cars and transfer to our vehicles so their own cars would not be scratched or muddy. Before going very far, about half the crowd decided they would not go any further and we had to take them back. The others went down into the valley with me and I showed them what we had done; they were wonderful sports all the way in and out. I brought my group out safe and sound, but the group in Mr. W.'s car stalled in the mud twice. I think that those who accompanied us all the way now realize some of the difficulties we contend with in the field. Mrs. Y. of the Executive Committee was appointed to write up the excavation for the paper. [She never did, but twelve days later Mr. X. telephoned from Atlanta to complain about the continued lack of publicity.]

Personnel problems with WPA labor were constant, for along with the deserving cases there was always assigned to us the usual quota of alcoholics and bums. For several weeks our regular practice every morning before driving off to work in Fulton County was to lock our "timekeeper" in his rented room to let him sleep off the previous night's binge. By evening when we returned, he had almost invariably left by a window and was well on his way with another spree. Our principal "engineer" disappeared so often and for such long periods we finally asked that he be transferred; he retaliated by bringing charges against us in Atlanta, where the foreman and I had to appear at a formal hearing to defend ourselves against accusations of having forced our workmen to cross a river repeatedly in an unsafe, overloaded boat, and of requiring the men to work in trenches deeper than regulations permitted. Then the new engineer assigned to us ran up fifty-two dollars in unpaid rent and food bills before we got rid of him.

. . . .

One more letter, which I shall not quote in its entirety because it goes on much longer than the manuscript quoted above, begins:

May 24, 1940
Santa Cruz, Calif.

Dear Professor:

Enclosed is a picture which I hope I may be able to persuade you, with the help of the description attached, is a really genuine, honest-to-goodness likeness of a young lady who lived during the latter part of the Ice Age, about 20,000 years ago. I should know because I have drawn it myself from the young lady in person, and she was my wife!

However it is really quite simple. I happen to possess very strong dreams intuitions. I have seen many of our hairy ancestors in my dreams, of various types, and some, like the enclosed, clearly enough that I can draw them. Nearly everyone has the falling dreams that come down to us from the long ages that our forbears found refuge from their enemies on the cliffs (they never lived in trees) and often fell off; but it appears that I dream of many other scenes and incidents as well.

I believe that my dream pictures should be accorded a proper place in our human family album because they came to me while I was studying the scientific revelations of the Bible. . . .

In spite of the malcontents, the gold hunters, the grifters, the mystics, and the cranks, I look back on my stay in Georgia as rich in friendships. Lest I have given too black a picture, let me cite a few instances that stand out brightly in my memory. Late one afternoon in April 1939, near dusk, I was reconnoitering the rolling terrain along Mountain Creek in DeKalb County. I had picked up a few artifacts at one place, when a farmer about fifty years old came out and talked to me and invited me to his house, where I sat on the floor (he had no chairs) and talked with him about this and that for almost two hours. Just before I left, to my astonishment he went to the back of his house and brought out a box of a great many very beautiful flint and chert projectile points and told me to take my pick of them for the University. I gingerly picked out three or four, but he impatiently selected about three dozen of the best specimens and insisted that I take them. He said that he had declined to give them to a great many private collectors, but as he had been financially unable to go to college himself, and he was afraid that his children would not be able to go either, he would like to give these relics to the University if in a small way he would be contributing something to education.

In a small village up in Gordon County the following summer, when I looked up a property owner to ask permission to dig on his land, I was told at the front door that he was dying. I murmured abject apologies and was leaving hastily when a weak voice called from an adjoining room and demanded to see me. The old man insisted that I explain what I was doing there, then he had me lean over close to him, and mustered his failing strength to whisper detailed instructions as to which part of his farm we could dig, which land we could walk on, and what we were to do with the earth and rocks removed. He asked me to promise to stick to these directions, and then he gave me permission to work also in a cave on the property. He told his wife, and sent word to some of the tenant's boys to guide us to the cave and show us around the farm. The next morning he was dead, and a few days later his widow called us and gave us the written permission he had promised.

Twenty years afterward, when my wife and two children and I stopped to ask questions of a young farmer in Forsyth County, he left his tractor, got out the pickup truck, and spent the rest of the day driving us around the farm to spots where he had found arrowheads and pottery, then urged us to stay for supper. Georgia hospitality, I was glad to see, had not diminished with the younger generation.

. . . .

Another thing that I should like to mention here is the astonishing change that the Georgia landscape underwent in the twenty years from 1938 to 1958. This was brought most forcibly to my attention during the two summers that my wife, my daughter, and my son and I tried to re-visit certain sites to get new surface collections to supplement those we already had or to replace some that had been lost. Even though I had the most detailed directions and had visited these sites myself, in most cases we had great difficulty in finding them again; more often we failed entirely.

The first rule of site survey is to record one's sites in purely geographic terms and locate them on a detailed topographic map, so that they can be found again regardless of what man does to the landscape. This we had of course done, but everyone knows that in vast rural areas one also needs considerable help from directions based on landmarks of a more transitory nature. I had expected that in twenty years a few old things might have changed, a footpath here or a fence there, perhaps a new highway cutting across my old familiar roads. But I was unprepared for the wholesale changes that had taken place; archaeologically speaking, we were lost most of the time.

The old roads were almost all gone, or so improved as to be unrecognizable. New bridges spanned the rivers and creeks, with new approaches from different routes. But most confusing of all, small streams had dried up—simply disappeared—and what were once vast acreages in corn or cotton had been abandoned to jungles of giant weeds, towering 10 feet high and interlaced with almost impenetrable branches and spiny vines, or their once deeply plowed surfaces now hard-packed green meadow. Presumably this was "soil bank" land, under government contract no longer cultivated. As long as these lands remain uncultivated, the Indian sites on them will be as unrecognizable as those today covered by the huge artificial lakes. Thus our survey of the 'thirties served another purpose: it located sites that might never again have been discovered. A good example is the rich Lithonia site (Da-1) on the once cultivated summit of a hill high over Yellow River in DeKalb County. When Mr. W. Julian Thomas took me to this site in 1938, the hill slopes were seamed with gulleys, exposing scores of quartz crystals and Early to Middle Woodland potsherds. In the middle of the plowed red clay at the top of the hill was a distinct area of black earth that could be seen as one approached the summit. On top, in this plowed earth, were thousands of potsherds, hammer stones, chipped stone implements, quartz crystals, and projectile points. I have seldom been more impressed with a site, and I remembered (or thought I remembered) almost every detail of its appearance and the surrounding topography. I took minutely detailed notes on how to reach it. In 1958, when I took my wife and children to this place to show them what a really rich surface collection could be, the surrounding roads had so changed that first of all I had difficulty locating even the group of hills, then I climbed three of these before deciding, with considerable doubt, which ones I had visited twenty years before. The slopes were overgrown in tall pine, and by the sheerest chance I found a quartz crystal on a footpath that led up through the woods to an old lumber mill. That was our only clue that we were on the right track. When we reached what I calculated must be the site of the ancient village, half the area was in pine, the other half was meadow. Not a potsherd was in sight; I broke off a heavy dead branch and gouged a hole into a slight terrace in the meadow slopes, and in a matter of seconds the sherds began to appear, but after several hours of hunting and scratching in this fashion we got a few handfuls of artifacts rather than the bagfuls I had come prepared to carry away. If this rich and apparently pure Woodland site is ever excavated—and it should be—it will be due to the fact, I am sure, that our survey once recorded its location, unless, as seems unlikely, it should some day be cultivated again.

Or take the Thomas Site (Fo-4) on the Chattahoochee River west of Suwanee in Forsyth County. When Mr. Thomas showed me this site in 1938 I wanted to start digging it then and there. River floods year after year had exposed masses of potsherds, burned clay floors, refuse pits, and restorable vessels. In mind's eye I can picture it exactly as it looked then. In 1958 I wanted to show this beauty to my long-suffering family, who by now must have become disenchanted with Georgia archaeology; this site, I knew, would cure that. We drove out of Suwanee, Georgia, on a street I remembered clearly and, on the basis of my old notes, turned left at a fork. We followed this road 0.4 mile past a house on the right side and at the next fork turned right; we were soon (to my considerable surprise and pleasure) crossing a bridge over the river, just as my old field notes said we would. We drove part way up the hill on the west side of the Chattahoochee, parked, and I walked confidently upstream to look for the mound. Everything was as it should have been; true, the bridge was new and the road wider, and what had once been cornfields was now part meadow, part scrubby woods, but I had come to expect such changes. Half a day later, having walked the river banks for miles, clambered up and down the deeply eroded sand bluffs along the water's edge, and fought our way through jungles of vines, poison ivy, willow, and underbrush, and paced the hot meadow hundreds of yards back and forth in near 100° temperature, we gave up. We found one small sandy mound, holes in which yielded, if I remember correctly, three miserable potsherds. Luckily we had left a jug of cool water and a bottle of martinis in the car.

Fall and early winter is the season for archaeology in northern Georgia and the Piedmont south. Crops are harvested, the ground is not yet frozen, mornings, the weather is likely to be bright, and clay roads are still not hazardous. Labor is more available; everyone is not fretting over making a good crop. Last summer's cotton fields, now dark brown but still flecked here and there with white, sweep in slow curves along the contours of the rolling terrain, and one can walk through them briskly, scanning several rows on each side, while the projectile points and potsherds lie on little pedestals of earth as if on display. Skimpy, shoulder-high, buff-colored stubble corn has replaced the tall green stalks under which, in summer, you could walk for hours without seeing the outside world. The endless miles of grazing land, brown and yellow, are dotted black or brown with herds of beef cattle, and partitioned by easel-shaped groves of brown and red oaks, bright gums, and green pines. The air is brisk; one tends to overestimate his capacity to walk to the next horizon, but the once deeply plowed fields are now firm underfoot, easy to traverse, and one need not fear the rattlesnakes. There are few threats. The great ropes of poison ivy on steep river banks are deceivingly stripped of their telltale leaves and seem to be innocent roots placed there for your climbing convenience. One must beware of eating rabbits that were trapped or shot wild in the riverbottoms. What appear to be firm banks along the little swamps that bar your way from one slope to another may actually be hip-deep soft mud, and if you miss your footing and stumble in the ice-cold streams you must build a fire against what you had just before considered a delightfully bracing wind.

Unfortunately, archaeological schedules do not always follow the appropriate seasons and latitudes. We worked in all environments and in all climates. We lived in a drafty log cabin on the banks of the ice-covered Nacoochee River during the subzero blizzard of 1939, sleeping nights in our long underwear under mountains of quilts, and mornings, by lamp light, washing in ice water. We sacked down on the freezing bottomlands of the Chattahoochee with our boots almost smoking in our campfire, and subsisted for months on a steady diet of sausage, pork, chittlins, sweet potatoes, and collard greens from the nearest farmhouse. We sweltered in 110° summer scorchers as far south as Blakely, and even up in Bartow County we would spend our summer lunch hour lying naked in the closest cooling stream, seeking some respite from the merciless sun. It seemed that winters we were always scraping ice from our windshields in the frigid mountains, and summers we were forever slogging through the steaming swamps of the lower Savannah. But from Atlanta to the sea, from No Business Creek to Shake Rag, from Between and Social Circle to Box Ankle and Settingdown Creek, Georgia was for me a wonderful experience that I shall always cherish with deep affection.

36 / Women as Fieldworkers

NORMA DIAMOND

The distinction between male and female is a common feature of all societies; the nature of the distinction, of course, varies from society to society. Here Norma Diamond describes the attitude people had toward her while she was doing fieldwork in a predominantly male-oriented society located in Taiwan, Republic of China, between 1960 and 1962. Sex as a factor in doing field research is made clear when Norma Diamond discusses her sex role in her relationship with men and women and the young and old.

Some problems arise when the fieldworker is a woman trying to do research in a culture that is strongly male-oriented and male-dominated. China is such a society, one in which sons are strongly preferred over daughters, and in which women have traditionally held low status. There is a common Chinese saying that in childhood a girl follows her father, in adulthood her husband, and in old age her sons. With such an attitude toward women, one might reasonably expect considerable reserve, resistance, or open hostility toward a woman researcher. Her very presence in the community makes her a deviate from the feminine role, a personification of the fears of the more traditionally minded males, and, for better or worse, the model of what happens when women receive education and jobs, and gain independence from their families.

To be sure, the position of women in Taiwan has changed considerably over the past half century. By the late 1940s it was quite acceptable for girls to attend primary school and by the late 1950s only a few failed to complete the six-year course of study. In K'un Shen there were even some girls who went on to enroll in the middle schools (the equivalent of American junior and senior high school). Villagers were also aware of the presence of girl students in the provincial colleges. In fact, most of the village school teachers were women. A number of unmarried village girls worked in shops and factories in Taiwan, though they continued to live at home and to remit most of their earnings to their parents. Usually, these earnings went toward their dowries. Also, because of economic pressures, most of the village women hired themselves out to do some form of wage work at home or around the village. Even so, women did not enjoy economic or political equality and traditional ideals for feminine behavior were still strongly encouraged.

In my case it proved difficult to separate the problems created by sex role from those rising from my age. Taiwan is also beginning to face the problems of the "generation gap." Within Taiwanese society, there is an increasing demand for more independence and involvement in decision-making by the young people, male *and* female. Major differences in values and attitudes have begun to develop between the generations. Still, ideally, people under forty are not expected to have much to say, nor are they given the chance to say it publicly. And I was usually considered to be less than forty, though estimates of my age varied widely, from sixteen to sixty depending on the criteria used.

As a self-confessed student, I was an example of modern youth. Technically, I should not have been a youth. Already in my midtwenties but still a student I was something of an anachronism. By normal Taiwanese standards, I should have been married five or six years before and had several children. Yet as a student, albeit an overly advanced one, I could not really be an adult, and I was obviously not a child or teenager.

Thus, on two counts I presented problems for definition and acceptance. Being a young woman closed off from me certain kinds of information and experiences. I could never, for example, be a sit-in participant at everyday informal gatherings where community matters were being discussed, gossip exchanged, and commentary made on events at large. Such gatherings, which usually took place in the evenings, were simply not attended by women. They stayed close to home after dark. The only possible compromise was to send my male field assistant to sit around the village shops in the evenings and act as my eyes and ears. No doubt people were aware that he relayed to me some parts of the conversations, but that did not seem to matter. People also passed on information and gossip to their wives when they came home, censoring out the dirty jokes or things that they did not regard as women's concerns.

Similarly, the need to conform to some of the minimum requirements of the female role prevented me from forming ties with males of my generation level. This could easily have been interpreted as having sexual overtones. Interviews with males between roughly twenty and forty years of age I left to my assistant much of the time. However, I could talk freely with children, teenage boys, or elder men without causing raised eyebrows.

Still, there were occasions when my status as a *nu-shih* ("female scholar") or "student of Taiwanese culture" proved strong enough to override my sex-ascribed activities. Certainly I would not have been welcome at the equivalent of bull-sessions, gambling parties, and similar male activities. But I was accepted into some situations where females could not normally be present. When one of the young village men got married, for example, his uncle insisted that I take part in a visit to his new in-laws. Customarily, the day after the bride is brought to her new home, the groom and his wife, friends, and male kinsmen pay a visit to the bride's house, there to be treated to a feast and formally introduced to her kinsmen. Female relatives of the groom do not attend, nor do female friends of the family. However, with the uncle's backing I became an acceptable member of the party. On another occasion, I was invited to join the local temple committee in an all-night meeting at which rituals for the well being of the village were carried out. Again, women do not participate in this ceremony, nor do ordinary members of the village community. The ritual is performed by a closed group of hired priests and elected members of the temple committee.

In both instances, there were leading members of the community who thought it important that I be present if I were to understand local ways of doing things. My sex role then became neuter. In similar fashion, my role as outsider-observer overrode my sex role in gathering certain other kinds of information. What I learned about the fishing industry had to be learned from men. The details of raft building, use of fishing gear, casts, fishing lore, and so on are not women's knowledge, but the men were patient in explaining to me the workings of the fishing industry and its problems. The same attitude helped me in collecting material on religious beliefs and practices. With backing from members of the temple committee I was even given access to more esoteric materials such as the texts of chants used in religious ceremonies, which is not at all women's business.

Thus, while being female hampered me in some social relationships and restricted participation in some groupings, it was not a serious barrier in dealing with village men as a group or in learning about the male side of the culture. One explanation of this may be the high esteem in which scholarship is held in China, although I would not lean too heavily on that as a reason since in the village itself education beyond the sixth grade was not a goal, even for most boys. Besides, I was not operating as the villagers conceived a scholar should. The things I was interested in did not fall within the framework of traditional scholarship. Indeed, I was consciously evincing a respect and curiosity about a way of life that most traditionally oriented Chinese scholars would "put down." While I was still doing language work in Taipei, I showed up for a tutoring session carrying a monograph on a peasant village by a well-known Chinese sociologist. My tutor glanced through it and in great puzzlement asked me why *anyone* would bother to write a book about some unheard of and obviously unimportant village. It was much easier to convince my villagers that peasant life was important, and it was perhaps this, more than my scholarliness per se that enabled them to drop the normal standards for female behavior and topics of conversation. Besides, the men recognized how important their part of the culture was; in their eyes it was certainly more important than the kinds of things women could talk about. It would give a misleading picture of Taiwanese ways if these things went unmentioned just because the investigator was a woman.

Unfortunately, being a woman did not automatically open the doors to close friendships, confidences, and outpourings of information from village women. Those most receptive to me as a person fell into the same age groupings as my male informants. I was accepted most easily by the unmarried girls and by older women. Admittedly, older women whose children had already grown up and whose daughters had left home to be married had more leisure time and a need to talk. They were flattered at being asked for information and opinions and at being listened to seriously. Despite the fact that respect and care for the elderly is one of the values held in Taiwanese culture, the later years can be lonely and unsatisfying. Sons are busy with outside concerns and invest more of their emotions in their wives and children. Daughters-in-law often have neither the time nor the inclination to devote much attention to older women of the household. The anthropologist as sympathetic stranger becomes for them a sounding board for the value of traditional ways and the injustices and difficulties of present day existence.

For the young unmarried women, I represented something else—an extreme model of freedom and independence. Not that they would want to go half way around the world alone, to live in a strange village, but my doings made their own demands seem like reasonable compromises between traditional ways and the Taiwanese view of modern ways. However, the young married women seemed uncomfortable in my presence, despite their politeness and cordiality when talking with me. I was in their generation, but not of it. Some may have feared that too close an association with me would create dissension at home. Others may have felt that they were still too young to speak with any authority and that I should be instructed by the older men and women. Certainly they were more comfortable when interviewed by my female assistant alone, particularly when talking of such things as marriage and child-rearing Perhaps they feared that I had set ideas on such things and would be critical of their opinions because of my foreign origins and "book learning," and they did not have the wisdom of years' experience to give them confidence.

Part 8 / QUESTIONS AND PROBLEMS FOR DISCUSSION

1. After having read Barnett's selection on "Being a Palauan," discuss why you think a personal journal or diary, in addition to more formal

notes, would be of importance to an anthropologist when he returns home to write up the life-style of a given group of people.

2. What are some questions about fieldwork you would want answered before you would attempt to go out on your own field project? List these questions in order of their importance to you, and discuss why you ordered them as you did.

3. Why is the matter of personal relationships so important in doing fieldwork? Use examples from the three previous articles to illustrate your reply.

4. Compile a list of problems that might arise in fieldwork as a result of the fieldworker's age, sex, race, or any other biological factor.

5. This section is entitled "Anthropologists Are Human, Too." Discuss as fully as you are able what is meant by this statement.

9/ I AM MAN: WHAT WILL BECOME OF ME?

Suppose that you are about to make an important decision, such as whether or not to marry, buy a house, buy a new car, or change jobs. Before making a decision you probably would reflect upon how this would affect the future of you as an individual. Most people have a concern about the future; but in this final selection of *A Slice of Life* let us turn to a broader concern—the future of mankind. Of course, if you are a true follower of the Islamic faith you will think this section ridiculous, since the Moslem believes that only God knows the future and that it is presumptuous to talk about it. However, if you are not a Moslem, you may have a sense of curiosity about man's future. This concern is reflected in numerous articles appearing in newspapers and magazines. Such articles deal primarily with the problems of air and water pollution, urban expansion, and population control. However, problems aired in the following selections raise such questions as: Is man going to continue? If so, in what form? Is civilization going to continue? If so, in what form? Eventually, it may be assumed, man will disappear; but before this happens (a few million years) many changes, both biological and cultural, will have taken place, just as they have in the past. We have seen how man has changed in biological and cultural ways since the days of the crude chopping-tool industry of Olduvai Gorge in Africa, to the agricultural era and the development of civilization, to the industrial age, and now to the nuclear era. All these changes have been impressive, but they will seem to have occurred at a slow pace when considering the rapid change of the future. How will man be able to cope with such an accelerative rate in cultural growth? Although it is impossible to predict in terms of specifics how man will deal with the future, some generalizations can be formulated. We must keep in mind that man is an animal but that he is a human animal. He has an edge on survival. He is the only animal that understands something about himself and his place in his environment. He can govern his activities. However, the fact that he can govern is no guarantee that he will use his expertise to direct his future to the most desirable end. We can look back in time and see how principles of biological and cultural evolution have resulted in the present state of man. Man can learn from the past or he can ignore it. But to ignore it puts man in a perilous position. The following articles by John Pfeiffer, Gerald Feinberg, and Jean Hiernaux provide a glimpse of the possibilities for the future of mankind.

37 / The Future of Man, an Ex-Hunter, in a World That Has No Place for Hunters

JOHN PFEIFFER

Generally, man experiences anxiety when he faces situations over which he has no control. We do not have effective control over the future. Are we then in a state of anxiety about the future? The response of many persons to this question is a resounding "yes." But what if we could control the future or at least could solve problems over which we now believe we have little or no control? In this selection John Pfeiffer explores the future of man by exploring such questions as: Are there species outside our solar system that confront problems like man's? Do computers speed the pace of evolution? Can the computer be used to increase the effectiveness of human adaptation? Pfeiffer does not ring out the popular cry that man cannot cope with the future. Instead, Pfeiffer appears to believe that man can control the course of change. And illusions often become reality.

The problem of the future is whether there will be a future fit for human beings to live in. The question arises now after more than twenty million years of evolution in the hominid line, after the transformation of a clever ape into a creature with unprecedented and increasing powers to create and to destroy. The crisis man faces is the first of its kind on earth, the first involving the entire species. As the only remaining members of the family of man, we may or may not survive. The issue will almost certainly be decided within the next hundred years.

There will be a future if man can avoid nuclear warfare for that long. If he is sufficiently impressed by the sheer horror and impracticality of the "ultimate solution," he will probably survive to create and surmount other crises, and human evolution will probably continue for millions of years on earth and other planets. If he does not avoid nuclear warfare, he can expect extinction and not the swift and sudden "big bang" sort. Such an ending would amount to mercy killing, and we dare not count on that. It would probably be a slow process, the fading of a species that had lost will and purpose and the capacity for caring.

One's notions about what will actually take place must in the last analysis rest on a personal, essentially an aesthetic, basis. No precedent exists for the human situation, that is, no known precedent. Looking at the problem from a wider point of view, however, there is good reason to suspect that man is not the first species to find itself facing a similar crisis. The Milky Way is one of many islands or galaxies in the universe, a concentration of some hundred billion stars, and practically every one of them is a solar system complete with central sun and set of planets.

It would be a miracle if life had arisen only on the planet earth, if evolution were not taking place in billions of solar systems. There is good reason to believe that the universe contains planets in various stages of development—planets forever barren because conditions there are not right for life of any sort, planets so young (say, half a billion to a billion years old) that life has not yet appeared, planets with species just starting to make nuclear weapons and nuclear power plants. On slightly more advanced planets, species have recently formed stable world governments and are well on the way toward creating life in the laboratory, tapping unlimited sources of thermonuclear energy, establishing permanent settlements on other planets, communicating with creatures in other solar systems, and accomplishing other feats that man may yet accomplish. Planets also exist which have had their all-out nuclear wars and have passed out of the community of civilized worlds.

There are a great many possible universes and this universe of evolution everywhere, survival of the fittest on a cosmic scale, may not be the real one. But it is a probable universe, sufficiently probable so that those convinced of the complete uniqueness of what is going on here must bear the burden of the argument. The notion that the human species will be among the survivors may turn out to be unduly optimistic. In that case, our consolation will have to be that others probably survived before us and will survive after us.

Assuming that man does not succeed in bringing about his own destruction, he will certainly be involved in changes more radical than any which have occurred in times past. And of all inventions the one that hints most strongly at the spirit of things to come is the large-scale electronic computer. This machine has the feel of the future about it, marking an area where evolutionary forces are active and change seems to be particularly intense. It represents a taking-off point, a new direction in the human journey, and its effects promise to be as far-reaching and unpredictable as those of fire.

As a matter of fact, it is the fire story all over again, the sort of story that opens uneventfully, almost in a humdrum manner—and then, slowly at first and later at an accelerating pace, takes on the aspect of a major evolutionary adventure. The first electronic computer was not intended to blaze any trails, and was not regarded as a bold experiment. A development of World War II, it was designed primarily to do something that that had been done ever since the invention of guns, to prepare ballistic tables indicating the trajectories of shells for different elevations, wind directions and so on. Under peacetime conditions such tables had generally been produced by groups of mathematicians working at hand-operated desk calculators, but the war brought a serious shortage of mathematicians and the only alternative was to turn to automatic methods.

Today the computer has become far more than a device for the solution of routine problems. It permits investigators in all fields to deal with problems which would not even have been considered or conceived of in pre-computer times, because they would have taken centuries to solve. It permits the doing of things that could never have been done, and thus helps promote basic changes in the nature of research and planning. A new man–machine relationship is in the process of being formed, a relationship amounting to a kind of organic union. Computers are strong where we are weak, and weak where we are strong.

The hunting–gathering life did not foster an ability to do arithmetic efficiently. Man is sloppy and inaccurate when it comes to working with large numbers and cannot even carry out a moderately difficult series of calculations without making a dozen or more errors. A large electronic computer, on the other hand, may operate for a month and perform billions of calculations before a defective part results in an error. Furthermore, man works slowly. It would take a mathematician two years to do what a computer does in a minute or so, or a millennium to do what a computer does in an eight-hour day. On the other hand, no machine can yet think creatively in the sense of dealing with novelty, recognizing and discovering and exploring new problems.

The symbiosis between man and computer takes on a special significance from an evolutionary perspective. The computer serves as an accessory to the brain, a thinking aid built specifically to carry out operations which the brain cannot carry out by itself, logical as well as arithmetical operations. Man is inclined to view the world in terms of chains of events, to see things as cause-and-effect sequences, a phenomenon reflected in written sentences. Sentences, as formal items each starting with a capital letter and ending with a period, are symbols or models of a "linear" approach.

This tendency is another example of living partly in the past. The world of modern man is by no means linear, but the world of his prehistoric ancestors was. Most tasks were one-man, one-material tasks like making scrapers, which involved four broad activities in a fixed order: finding a flattish flint nodule, trimming the edges, striking off flakes, and retouching the flakes. Setting a blade in a handle or a spear point in a shaft was somewhat more elaborate, involving more materials and more activities. But any hunter could readily carry out the entire task on his own.

Today's tasks reflect enormously more complicated lives. They require hundreds of materials, thousands of men and activities, hundreds of thousands of parts to be assembled. Furthermore, the essential relationships are not straightforward sequences where one activity leads to another in a simple way; there are lattices and networks and nests of intricately related activities. Activities A and B and C and D may be carried out simultaneously, activity E cannot be started until A and C are completed, F depends on the completion of B and D, G depends on F and A, and so on. Producing a new-model automobile or airplane, a space vehicle or a housing development may require tens of thousands of interdependent activities all of which must be coordinated in flow charts and master plans.

Such problems, problems featuring the interaction of a great many variables, are a sign of the times. They may be found everywhere, not only in factories and on production lines but also in projects involving urban renewal, medical care, crime control and the administration of justice, economic opportunity, and education. The brain alone cannot handle them, but the combination of brain and computer can. The computer, programmed or instructed to apply special mathematical techniques to the analysis of complex systems, enables things to be seen whole. It happens that so far these techniques have been used widely to deal with business and military projects, and not so widely to deal with matters of public welfare. More attention seems to have been devoted to the mathematics of competition and warfare than to the mathematics of cooperative endeavors.

Computers have been developed to serve man, and their duties have been amply publicized. The most impressive are general-purpose machines which do anything they are "told" to do. At any time any one of them may be calculating payrolls or insurance premiums or the orbit of an artificial satellite, checking income-tax returns, simulating a flood or the evolution of a star, predicting election returns, or playing a fair game of chess—depending on the set of instructions, the program, which investigators have prepared for it.

But the computer has already exceeded its role as servant. Upon occasion it may function as an electronic goad, a helpful and necessary and at the same time an upsetting thing which often seems to acquire an impetus of its own. It is not capable of creative thinking. But it forces people to think creatively, perhaps more creatively and precisely than they would if computers did not exist.

The history of the Japan Broadcasting Corporation provides one of the best examples of this effect. The corporation "let a computer into the house" a number of years ago, and the net effect has been a widespread reorganization. The first computer served as an aid to program planners, helping them to schedule shows and allocate studio space well ahead of time. Later communications were speeded up when it was hooked to half a dozen terminals, including television-type screens on which schedules were displayed for immediate information or revisions. Success along these lines created a demand for still more ambitious plans to coordinate the activities of some 5,000 directors, engineers, and technicians concerned with producing shows—and these plans, in turn, demanded a special control center and other basic changes.

The company now has an entire system of computers, including some 200 terminals, and handles more than 1,800 programs on two television and three radio networks. The system is involved in everything from scheduling programs months in advance to putting programs on the air automatically a fraction of a second before broadcasting time. Among other things, this is the way to cut down on paper work and endless conferences and red tape of all sorts. The use of visual displays has eliminated more than 90 percent of the 1,800 daily telephone calls and meetings and the 5,000 daily memoranda and reports formerly required to run the business.

This, the first company-wide computer system of its kind, provides a model for research and development in many areas. Organizations in the United States, the Soviet Union and other countries are at work on similar systems to handle their own routines, and it is only a matter of time until larger organizations, including entire industries and government agencies, will proceed along the same course. Computers will bring about radical structural and management changes at these levels as they have already done at the company level in Japan.

They will also bring about a widespread amplification of intelligence. A man at a computer terminal is in effect many times more intelligent than a man without a computer at his service. In colleges freshmen sitting at terminals located in classrooms, laboratories and dormitories are already solving easily problems far too difficult for seniors to solve in the days before computers, and the same increase in brain power will continue throughout life. The computer, one of the latest and most remarkable products of human evolution, permits individuals and groups to cope with new complexities of their own making. It is thus actively speeding the process of evolution.

Finally, and this could turn out to be the most significant effect of all, the computer may be used to increase the effectiveness of human adaptation. The brain evolved in times of great physical danger and little social change, but must now cope with times of little physical danger and great social change. Once it was appropriate that ideas and ways of doing things should endure for millennia. But the pace of contemporary developments suggests that the ability to unlearn swiftly is becoming at least as important as the ability to learn swiftly.

In such a context computers may serve as powerful weapons against the persistence of habit, the tendency of people to stay the same as the world changes. Electronic memories are erasable. They can be wiped clean at the flick of a switch and prepared for a fresh start. Computers do not become more and more biased as they age, a distinct advantage in solving new problems.

So all things, even man's most ingenious "thinking" machines, seem to be pushing him along, emphasizing the pace and the prevalence of change, the need to reorganize himself in transit as it were, on the run. He has yet to develop artificial environments as appropriate for contemporary populations as natural wilderness environments were for prehistoric hunters and gatherers. But that is his job, and a renewed search for such environments is under way. It is characterized by increasing efforts to understand people in groups, grownups as well as children, and to base the design of living and working places on observations of what they do and prefer.

A number of studies indicate the existence of biases that seem to hold for people in many cultures. For example, Dutch investigators find that visitors to parks and other public recreation areas tend to concentrate in transition zones where two different kinds of terrain merge, along seacoasts and the banks of rivers and the edges of forests. At the same time they naturally seek out locations providing some cover at their backs, a cliffside or a sand dune or a dense growth of trees, and in front of them expanses of open space.

This tendency is made up of many things. There is a feeling for freedom and privacy, a preference for shady spots, and a strong attraction to panoramas and unobstructed views of distant horizons. One thinks immediately of forest-dwelling hominids or prehominids venturing into the plains and ready to dash back into the trees—and later of bands of early hunters living in shelters and caves high on rocky ledges, relatively safe from predators and with a wide view of valleys and grazing animals. Such places offered beauty and security in a world where men were few and bands rarely came across one another.

From "Survival? Yes. But in What Form?" by Gerald Feinberg, *Bulletin of the Atomic Scientists*, Vol. 58, No. 5, 1971, pp. 27–30. Reprinted by permission of Science and Public Affairs, the *Bulletin of the Atomic Scientists*. Copyright © 1971 by the Educational Foundation for Nuclear Science.

38 / Survival? Yes. But in What Form?

GERALD FEINBERG

Trying to "put it all together" is a formidable task no matter what the problem. In an attempt to tie together the outlook for man, Gerald Feinberg tells us that trying to predict the future is the wrong approach. Instead, efforts should be made to determine man's future in terms of what we, as human beings, consider to be desirable in terms of the biological and psychological functioning of man. Long-term goals should be drawn out, based not on the decisions of scientists but upon the consensus of the people of the world. This appears to be a utopian outlook in the view of man's survival, but Feinberg's views have merit and should not be dismissed out of hand. Man obtains the most desirable reality by striving for the most desirable ideal.

There has been no end of statements recently to the effect that we are going to hell in a handbasket. I feel, however, that this mood has gone farther than the facts warrant, and that such pessimism is not justified either by our present condition or its rate of change. Partly as a corrective to this mood, I will indicate some affirmative possibilities, and how we may deal with them.

In my view, the question is not of survival, but of survival in what form. We are now in a period in which our social institutions are being strenuously questioned, and in which we soon may be able to alter the most fundamental biological and psychological aspects of human life. It may well be that a continuation of the life that mankind has had in the past and has at present is neither possible nor desirable, compared to some of the alternatives that we could construct for ourselves.

I would even extend that notion to the effect of man on his environment. The preservation of the environment in its present form may not be consistent with other things we wish to do, such as to universalize the high living standards of the Western World. However, that is not necessarily a bad thing. The earthly environment was not created for man's benefit, but rather is the result of the random operation of physio-chemical processes. While certain aspects of the environment are desirable for human purposes, there is no reason to believe that the environment we now have or one that existed before human intervention is the best possible one. Indeed, human history records a series of man-made changes in the environment which have for the most part been for the better. A comparison of the present environment on Manhattan Island, for instance, with that of 500 years ago, or even 100 years ago, suggests very strongly that it is now a much better place to live, air pollution and all. Were any of us set down in the Manhattan environment of 1500 A.D. we would likely find our lives nasty, brutish and short, as did most of those who were in that situation. Of course, we should not allow thoughtless action to produce random changes in the environment. But neither should we, by identifying the natural with the desirable and by abjuring all environmental change, ignore the possibility of improving human life.

We should consider not just the survival of what we have, but rather what kind of world humanity might be able to create for itself if we set our collective minds to it. In this context it is important to realize that most of what we have been able to do through science until now, in the way of improving our common lot, has been to change the external world, that is, the world outside of each individual human being. However, there is reason to believe that this will not remain the case for very much longer. Coming developments in fields such as applied biology and psychology, which one can already begin to foresee from advances in pure science, may allow us to make radical changes in the biological and psychological functioning of man. Since the society we now have is in some approximate conformity with the present biological and psychological state of man, one would hope that if that state changes drastically, then the institutions of our societies will change as well.

For example, some gerontologists have speculated that it might be possible to slow down substantially the rate at which we age. At present, we age at such a rate that in about 70 years or so most of us will die. The reason for this 70-year period is not well understood; but some scientists working in the field believe that if we can understand the cause of the aging process, we might be able to do something to change it, so that we would age more slowly. If, for example, we could arrange it that after reaching adulthood we aged at one-tenth the rate that we do now, then our life expectancy would become several hundred years instead of 70 years. If that occurs, then many of our present social institutions would become inappropriate. If a person is going to live for several hundred years in the prime of life, it doesn't make sense to force him to retire at age 65. On the other hand, new possibilities such as multiple careers for an individual would probably lead to distinctive new life patterns.

It is not difficult to imagine a long list of technological developments that could produce far-reaching changes in our way of life, but I do not believe that trying passively to predict the future is the proper approach. If our lives may soon be changed by technology into something very different from what they now are, we can try to guide those changes along lines that we choose. The alternative, which is what has generally happened in the past, is to allow technological change to happen randomly and to affect our lives by chance developments.

Being a firm believer in the necessity and sufficiency of reason, I think that we should make the effort to choose which technological developments we want to implement, and to plan what the effects of these developments will be on our lives. Of course, even if we try to do this, there is no guarantee that things will come out the way we want. Some technological developments are sure to be unforeseen, and even those we expect will have unexpected twists. Yet it seems reasonable to suppose that there is a greater chance of things coming out as we want if we do make some plans than if we let things happen by chance. As I disbelieve in a divine providence that looks after human interests, I see no reason to expect that the results of chance developments will be beneficial to humanity.

Efforts to do long-range planning have not been very successful in the past, even in the few instances where societies have tried them. It seems to me that this lack of success has stemmed from a lack of the proper intellectual tools for dealing with the kind of situation involved in long-range planning. Most of our successful intellectual tools are those that have been developed in the natural sciences, particularly physics and astronomy. These tools are rather good for dealing with situations which in a certain sense are simple. By simple, I mean that there is a single dominant factor in the system, so that one can get a fairly accurate idea of the behavior of the system by taking just the dominant factor into account. An example of this procedure was the application of Newton's laws of motion to the solar system. This application was successfully carried through because in the solar system, the dominant effect is the gravitational attraction of the sun, and all of the other effects, such as the attraction of one planet by another, are much smaller, and can be neglected as a first approximation. If we happened to live in a planetary system with three stars instead of one, then even Newton would have had trouble figuring out the consequences of his laws, because in such a system there would be no obviously dominant factor.

I suspect that one of the major contributions that science will make to society in the future is the development of intellectual methods for dealing with nonsimple systems. This development might originate from problems arising in pure science, such as the one indicated above, where a physical system has many interacting components. Scientists have not been very successful in dealing with such problems where they arise within science. It is interesting that even in elementary particle physics, where one might expect to deal with simple systems in their purest form, it now seems that we really are faced with complex systems having many interacting components. While some efforts have already been made to develop methods for treating complex systems in various parts of science, these have not as yet been very successful. But eventually, if science is to follow its goal of understanding all phenomena, we shall have to develop the methods to treat such problems.

Another area that might lead to the development of such methods, which is related to long-range planning, is prognostication, or predicting the future. Of course, people have always been interested in predicting the future, and astrologers and fortunetellers have been hired by governments and others to do so for several millennia, rather unsuccessfully. Today we take a somewhat more rational approach, but it remains to be seen how much more successful present efforts at prognostication will be. Predicting the future rationally certainly requires dealing with complex systems because extrapolating even a short way forward means dealing with all kinds of interacting factors, and it is hard to know which are the dominant ones, if any. So I think that predicting the future is unlikely to be really successful until we have methods for treating complex systems. (The science fiction writers have been most successful at predicting the future, especially of technology. Perhaps organizations that are interested in such forecasts might study their methods, or might even do well to hire science fiction writers to make the predictions.)

In my view, however, the whole idea of prediction is the wrong approach to the future, because when you think of predicting the future, you are implicitly making the assumption that the future is more or less fixed, that it will come about independently of what we do in the intervening period. I believe that this is not, and should not be, an accurate assumption. I think rather that the future, particularly the more distant future, is going to be an outgrowth of decisions yet to be made. Therefore, instead of trying to predict the future, in the fashion of astrologers or entrail readers, we should try to determine the future, in the sense of trying to make things come out in the way we want them to. In other words, prognostication should not follow the astrological model of guessing what is going to happen. Rather, the approach should be hypothetical, asking such questions as: What will happen if we take this action now and this other action in five years? What kind of world would come about in 25 or 50 years as a result of these actions? We should then make comparisons as to desirability with other hypothetical worlds that would emerge from different sets of actions. After doing this, in many cases we should get some idea about which of these actions we really want to take. Presumably we would then take these actions, and hope that our predictions of their consequences are accurate enough so that the future that comes about is the one we wanted. Of course, there are limits to how accurately such analyses can be made; here, again, new methods for thinking about complex systems are urgently needed to improve accuracy.

Critical Question

In describing this process of hypothetical predicting, I glossed over at least one really critical question. This question, which brings me to the problem of what society can do for itself, is: What is it that we want to happen? If we think of possible futures as roads going off in many different directions, then the model of hypothetical prediction that I described can be thought of as making an accurate road map of what lies ahead along each of the different directions we might take. In order to know where you are going, it is essential to have an accurate road map. However, to plan a successful trip you need something else, which may be even more essential: You must know where you want to go. In determining the future, the obvious question is where we, the human race, would like to go.

This question is something that I believe that the human race must answer for itself. In particular, what the human race must do for itself is to establish ethical principles to guide the implementation of the spectacular technological developments that may come from scientific advances. These ethical principles, it seems to me, should, to a large extent, be based on what humanity sees as desirable long-range goals for itself. If we are to consider possible changes in society as fundamental as those I have alluded to, which could influence our future in such a comprehensive way, then our decisions should not be based on what we want to happen tomorrow, or next year. Rather, we should base them on what we wish to happen over 20 years, 50 years, and into the indefinite future.

It has been argued that it is the job of scientists to make decisions on matters like this. For example, if a group of scientists develop techniques for extending the human life span, then some people say that those scientists should take it upon themselves to decide what is to be done with their work. I think that this would be a very unwise principle to follow.

This argument involves a substantial misunderstanding of the nature of ethical principles. There is no good reason for this misunderstanding because it has been recognized by sensible philosophers since the time of David Hume what ethical statements are and what they are not. Ethical statements are not statements of objective fact, as are the statements of science, nor are they derivable from such statements of fact. Neither are ethical statements analytically true, as are the statements of mathematical theorems. Rather, ethical statements are expressions of people's individual feelings. This being the case, it is quite arbitrary to say that scientists should make the decisions about what is to be done with their discoveries. Of course, a scientist has every right to choose whether to tell people of a discovery he has made. But if he chooses to do so, he retains no proprietary interest in the discovery which entitles him to decide how others should use it. Scientists are no more "expert" in matters of ethics than anyone else, and to leave decisions on what are essentially matters of feeling to them, or to any other special group, is to give up the responsibility that really belongs to all members of society.

Also, it should be said that if decisions on what kind of world we want are made the exclusive concern of any elite group, then the special interests of that group are likely to play an important role in coloring the decisions that are made. For example, scientists as a group feel very strongly that the growth of human knowledge is a very important thing. If decisions are left to scientists, then the particular criterion of advancing human knowledge is sure to play an essential part in these decisions. Being a scientist, I believe that it is good to advance human knowledge. But I realize that others who are not scientists may have other principles which they feel should be more central in decisionmaking than the growth of knowledge. For that reason, I do not think that we can expect generally acceptable decisions to come from any special group. And in a situation where the future of mankind is being shaped, it is essential that decisions be generally accepted.

Consensus on Goals

How then can we set up ethical principles for decisions? My contention is that we should try to find a consensus among the people of the world as to what kind of long-range goals we want. Why do I think that any such consensus is possible, since nothing of this kind has been achieved up until now? Here I would argue that human beings are all biologically quite similar to one another. Furthermore, substantial aspects of our upbringing are also similar. For example, we each go through a period of early dependency when we cannot fend for ourselves, and must rely on adults for our sustenance. Both common heredity and common upbringing suggest that there should be goals that human beings can agree would be good for all of us. Of course, it is highly unlikely we can agree on everything, but it seems plausible that if we make the effort to find common principles to agree on, that we will indeed find such principles.

It also seems to me that it would be worth making the effort because of the possible benefits of reaching such agreement. One such benefit is that if there were some agreement among the people of the world as to what we want some aspects of our common future to be, then this might go a long way to mitigate the remaining disagreements among the people of the world, which now loom so large. In other words, it would help to make us recognize that human life is not a zero sum game, which is unfortunately the model that is often taken. By recognizing specific areas of agreement, we would abandon the notion that any development that is good for one group of people is necessarily bad for some other group at war (hot or cold) with the first group. The recognition of cases where something would be good for everyone could have the substantial psychological effect of making the areas of disagreement seem less important than they appear now. In this way, agreement on long-range goals could play a critical role in insuring the physical survival of the human race, which is a sine qua non for us if we are to have any kind of future.

If we can reach agreement on long-range goals, and if we develop intellectual tools for accurately calculating the results of our actions, then there are few limits to what we as a species can accomplish. There is nothing either in the laws of nature or in the incidentals of our environment that will prevent us from achieving our mutual heart's desire. This, again, is an outlook not lately in vogue. Popular accounts of the views of some of those involved in the environmental movement paint a much more restricted picture of what the human race can and cannot accomplish. I think that these views are based on a severely limited knowledge and imagination relative to the possibilities available to us. My own view is that what we now are and now have is only a very pale shadow of what we could be and could have if we set our minds to it. We have only to find out what we want, and then work together towards making it real. Let us not delay too long in doing so.

39 / The Future of *Homo Sapiens*

JEAN HIERNAUX

Of course, there is no answer to the tantalizing question "What will man be like?" but Jean Hiernaux attempts to answer the question of how man will probably change. Clearly, Hiernaux's message is that we should be concerned more with euthenics (improving social–cultural conditions) than with eugenics (genetic engineering). However, there is little question that genetic engineering will be a factor in man's future. Reluctance on the part of many people to endorse a eugenics program is the fear, unfounded or not, that social–political tragedies could result. The reader should keep in mind that eugenics and euthenics are not in opposition but in fact complement one another.

It takes considerable presumption to foretell the future, yet it is a task that the research worker cannot evade, although he may admit that his forecasts are based on incomplete knowledge and on hypotheses which are colored by his own personality.

Man is the product of the evolution of animate matter; and his future can be foretold only by projecting into the future evolutionary trends which are perceptible today. Throughout the natural history of life on our planet, we may trace a series of forms, rising from the simplest to the most complex—from giant molecules, not yet completely differentiated from inert matter, to mammals.

The main stages in this evolution reveal an increasing degree of freedom from close dependence on the environment. For example, by acquiring the ability to maintain the body temperature irrespective of the temperature of external environment, which scientists call "horiothermy," the higher forms of animate matter have entered regions in which previously they could not live.

As life became increasingly complex, the structure and role of the brain grew larger. The maximum development of the brain and the maximum freedom from the power of the external environment were to be achieved by man; and, having acquired that freedom, he gained increasing control over the forces of nature, which he harnessed to suit his needs.

Man is unquestionably the spearhead of evolution, but he does not follow its course in the same way as did those forms which lived before him; at least, it may be said that an evolutionary mechanism not previously in operation came into being with man. Before his coming, evolution was genetic in character; it consisted in changing the qualities inherited by the various species—in other words, changing the stock of genes borne by them. It had nothing to do with the will or with consciousness.

With the coming of man and, no doubt, as a necessary condition for his emergence, an entirely different evolutionary mechanism came into being and developed—the transmission from one individual to another and from one generation to the next of knowledge, inventions, and ways of life which are not inherited, and which can be perpetuated only through constant effort.

This is a less stable form of evolution, but it enables man to advance along the path of freedom and to gain control over his environment much more rapidly than he can through genetic evolution. This is probably the reason why, after a period of interaction between the two evolutionary mechanisms (lasting from the emergence of man, some two million years ago, until his appearance in his present form as *Homo sapiens* about 50,000 years ago), evolution towards a higher state now takes place essentially in the sphere of acquired ability, which we may call the cultural sphere.

There is no perceptible difference between the anatomical development of the skull of fossilized *Homo sapiens* and our skull, but man's control over the forces of nature has grown tremendously, and knowledge and techniques are progressing with ever-increasing speed; cultural evolution has taken the place of genetic evolution.

If this explanation of the lack of change in the brain over tens of thousands of years is correct, we must not expect man in the future to have an enormous head; the brain he has now is large enough for him, and in any case he is already extending its range by means of electronic computers.

It is true that, judging by the bone-structure, *Homo sapiens* usually had coarser features in the stone age than today (as have the modern representatives of that cultural stage, the Australian aborigines). A certain refining of the bony projections has accompanied cultural evolution. Yet it is not to be expected that this trend will continue until the head is markedly different; the ridges of the brow may vanish, but the frontal bone cannot. There is also a tendency for the teeth to become smaller, and even for the third molar to be missing. Here again, there is no reason to think that this situation will ultimately produce a toothless human being. In any case, these processes are extremely slow compared with cultural evolution.

A process still in operation today in the genetic sphere and there is no sign that it is nearing its end, is the modification of the inherited traits of populations so as to secure from the genetic point of view, the best possible adaptation to a changing environment. Our adaptation to our environment, too, is increasingly cultural in character (take, for instance, our clothing, heating and air-conditioning), and advances in medicine are helping to lessen the importance of natural selection; but we are constantly creating new environments (such as that of the great metropolises) which give rise to fresh biological problems. It will be a long time no doubt, before cultural measures make genetic adaptation to local conditions unnecessary, and so put an end to it.

All that has been said so far concerns the spontaneous biological evolution of man. Now, man has acquired knowledge and technical ability which enable him to influence his inherited traits. The branch of science which deals with this process is eugenics. It is based on the theory that, for each inherited characteristic in which men differ from each other (such as the A, B and O blood groups, in which individuals are divided into four groups), there is a determining factor (a gene) which is the best of its kind, and which is found in all parts of the world.

Natural selection will tend to eliminate all alternatives except the best. If a new gene appears, as a result of mutations, either it will be better than the existing genes, and will supersede them, or else it will be weaker, and will be eliminated.

The aim of eugenics is to assist what is good in nature, by discouraging deleterious genes (through preventing individuals possessing them from reproducing) and by encouraging the best gene (for instance by advocating artificial insemination by semen which bears that gene). The tendency is, therefore, for eugenics to produce a human race composed of genetically identical individuals.

In many cases (when it is recessive), the elimination of a deleterious gene, even by total eugenics (the complete prevention of reproduction by those who bear it), requires many generations. Apart from this practical aspect there is a serious argument against the general application of eugenics: recent research has revealed that in very many cases natural selection does not move towards a state of uniformity through the elimination of all genes except one, but rather towards a state of balance between the frequencies of different genes.

Mankind has always exhibited considerable diversity in respect of many hereditary traits, which is a good thing. This is not only because the vitality of each population depends upon such diversity (or polymorphism), but because a gene may be beneficial in certain environmental conditions and harmful in others. We know of genes, for instance, a certain frequency of which is beneficial in malarial regions, but which are by no means desirable in other regions.

Men have settled in all parts of the globe; they live in widely differing natural environments which they are constantly modifying in ways that are not always predictable. This being so, the genetic idea is to maintain diversity—the opposite of the aim of eugenics. Eugenics is unjustifiable except insofar as it can eradicate very serious hereditary diseases, of which there are few; if an apparently unfavorable trait occurs frequently in a population, it is very likely to be desirable in some respect at present unknown to us. If a gene is really undesirable in all respects, natural selection will keep its frequency very low.

This criticism applies to positive eugenics, the object of which is to increase the number of "good" genes, as well as to negative eugenics, which aims to eradicate the "bad" ones; underlying both is the same ideal —uniformity. We have no reason to hope that a Superman will be produced in the eugenists' test tubes; any highly gifted beings they might produce would not constitute a biologically viable human race.

We should do better to devote our energies to providing populations and individuals with living conditions in which their inherited potentialities can best be realized, rather than manipulating genes; and that is not eugenics, but what has been called euthenics.

There are hundreds of millions of human beings who, through hunger or disease, are prevented from realizing their physical potentialities as they would have done under better conditions. Differences between the intellectual achievements of the various human populations appear to be due entirely to the fact that their food, health and educational conditions are different. Euthenics opens up much broader and safer avenues for the betterment of mankind than does eugenics.

The processes in operation today—especially selection, which has the effect of differentiating populations by genetic adaptation to their living conditions, and cross-breeding which produces greater homogeneity, while at the same time putting a premium on polymorphism—can, of themselves, produce the state which appears to meet the biological needs of our race, that is, unity in diversity. Individual adaptations are never very marked, and they are much less characteristic of man than his genetic capacity for general adaptation to varied conditions.

It would seem, therefore, that man is not destined to undergo any striking biological transformation through either spontaneous or induced evolution. He is, however, undergoing an ever more rapid cultural evolution; it took him hundreds of thousands of years—the palaeolithic era— to bring his stone-cutting technique to a moderately high standard, but only a few thousand years to advance from the stone age to the atomic age. It is in the sphere of cultural achievements than man can undergo a profound evolution which, though different in kind from genetic evolution, as we have seen, is moving in the same direction, and is the specifically human form of evolution.

This kind of evolution has become self-conscious; it is dependent upon man's desire to advance and on the effectiveness of the measures he adopts to do so. It requires of men a sustained effort to improve, both as individuals and as a society. It does not appear to be necessarily inevitable; our present state of knowledge, indeed, provides mankind with the means of total self-destruction.

Are we then justified in predicting that the cultural evolution will continue to progress? We may be somewhat prejudiced on the side of optimism, but not without reason. Under pressure of the forces of selection, the genetic evolution has gone on, passing through numerous phases, for over a thousand million years; and in every case the more complex, more highly developed form has supplanted the lower form when they have been present together and in a competitive situation.

True mammals, for example, have supplanted marsupials in all parts of the world except Australia, where they have been but recently introduced. We may reasonably expect that by a similar mechanism a more highly-developed cultural form, when brought into contact with a less highly-developed one, will supersede it. Examples of this may be found in our past. One case is the extremely rapid expansion of the neolithic revolution, i.e., the invention of agriculture and cattle-breeding.

Biological evolutionary forces (using the word "biological" in the narrow sense) altered inherited traits; but cultural evolutionary forces preserve whatever is felt to be an incentive towards mankind's advancement. These include the desire for knowledge, which leads to scientific progress, and the desire of individuals and human societies to draw closer together, which impels us to love our neighbor, to feel ourselves involved in whatever affects mankind as a whole, and to strive for greater social justice.

It is true that, as in the case of genetic evolution, these forces produce nothing more than trends, and do not exclude the possibility of periods of retrogression and partial failure; but, if we look at history from a sufficiently high vantage-point, it seems reasonable to think that they will succeed.

Where can this sort of evolution take mankind? In some fields, it is moving very quickly; knowledge is advancing with great rapidity; and, amidst storm and stress, men are seeking for new forms of social morality consonant with their increasing awareness of their unity and of the interdependence of the elements of which the race is composed.

When we observe the rate of our progress we may wonder whether animate matter inhabiting the earth is not about to undergo, in man, one of those changes of state which dialectical thinking entitles us to visualize. It would seem that, in biology as in physics, slight but accumulated quantitative changes may somewhat suddenly lead to qualitatively new states (consider, for example, the changes undergone by a block of ice which is heated gradually).

Thus, the increasing complexity of inert matter gave rise to life, which had new properties, but within which chemical particles retain their ordinary characteristics; it is the interaction and organization of these particles which is characteristic of life. The increasing complexity of animate matter led to the emergence of man, a qualitatively new creature in certain ways, as in his capacity for abstract thinking, but whose cells possess the same general biological properties as the amoeba.

If we try to apply this principle still further, we shall see that the next critical threshold will bring us to a state in which men differing but little from present-day men will, by virtue of their desire to draw closer together and the intensity and nature of their interaction, constitute a qualitatively new stage of animate matter.

So, if we see the matter aright, we are advancing towards a Superman-kind, and not towards Supermen. We may be unable at our stage in evolution to gain a complete picture of this future state, but already we know the paths that lead to it. It may sometimes be difficult to abandon an untroubled immobility but if we are to accept our responsibilities as human beings and respond to the forces of progress, we must move forward along these paths—the ways that lead to knowledge and amity.

Part 9 / QUESTIONS AND PROBLEMS FOR DISCUSSION

1. Consider the social, political, and moral problems involved in organizing a national eugenics program in this country. Would you favor such a program? Why or why not?
2. What do you consider to be the most critical problem man will face in the future? How can the knowledge gained from the study of man be used effectively to solve that problem?
3. It is often stated that rapid technological changes in the future will result in slowing down or even stabilizing man's biological evolution. Discuss this idea in terms of what you know about the principles of biological and cultural evolution.